Ken Rosewall

TWENTY YEARS AT THE TOP

TWENTY YEARS

by Peter Rowley

Ken Rosewall

AT THE TOP

with Ken Rosewall

CASSELL
LONDON

CASSELL & COMPANY LIMITED
35 Red Lion Square, London WC1R 4SG
and at Sydney, Auckland, Toronto, Johannesburg,
an affiliate of
Macmillan Publishing Co., Inc.,
New York.

First published in Great Britain 1976

ISBN 0 304 29735 6

Typesetting by Malvern Typesetting Services
Printed in Great Britain by
Fletcher & Son Ltd, Norwich

For Terez

Acknowledgments

I am grateful to the following people and organizations for assistance in the preparation of this book. Firstly, I thank with special gratitude Nona Balakian, who arranged for me to use the New York *Times* morgue; Joe DeMartino of Feron's, who loaned me all of their tennis books; and Pret Hadley of the U.S.L.T.A., where I spent many hours working in the library.

Secondly, I am appreciative to these individuals and companies for loaning me films and/or projecting them: A. Barrable and R. G. Cammiade of Coutts and Co.; Robert Wussler, Richard Jencks and Eugene Peterson, all of CBS; Vic Edwards; Tim Fowler of *Newsweek;* Elaine D. Hess of Seamco; Robert Kaufman of Bristol-Myers Co.; George Pharr of WCT; Joe Walsh of International Sports Productions; Peter Whitchurch; and Slim Wilkinson of BBC-TV.

Thirdly, I thank these persons for the interviews they granted or other acts of assistance: Arthur Ashe, Freddie Botur, Marjorie Botur, Gurney Breckenfeld, Michael J. Burns, Colin Dibley, Dudley Doust, Steve Flink, Edward V. Hickey, Lew Hoad, Arnaldo Lacagnina, Gardnar Mulloy, Ivan Obolensky, Tom Okker, Raul Ramirez, Marty Riessen, Tony Roche, Robert Rosewall, Vic Seixas, Ilse Smith, Mark Stern and Roscoe Tanner.

Finally, I am indebted to Ken and Wilma Rosewall for their kindness and hospitality; Ken's business manager, James E. Hambuechen, and his assistant, Maureen O'Keefe; Edward T. Chase for a brilliant suggestion; my agent A. L. Hart for his patience, integrity and enthusiasm; and Terez, my wife, for her constant support and warm, constructive advice.

Contents

*Illustrations may be found
following page 148*

Romero's bull-fighting gave real emotion, because he kept the absolute purity of line in his movements and always quietly and calmly let the horns pass him close each time.
—ERNEST HEMINGWAY, The Sun Also Rises

1

The Beginning of a Star

Robert Rosewall, 'Bob,' who is Ken's father, is a round-faced little man with a stocky build. He was—like his son—immaculately, if less expensively, attired, wearing a dark suit with tie clip and cuff links. His hair is white, combed straight back over a ruddy-brown face. It was hot, and during the morning he took off his coat. His shirt sleeves were secured with wire rings to prevent the cuffs from slipping too far down. He speaks more than his son, with a broader Australian accent, but has something of the same precision of movement and thought.

'Ken's mother,' he said, 'died in 1966. After his mother died, I gave Ken all of his trophies that we had, as I thought it was better to make a break with the past. She looked more like Ken than me. She was slim with dark hair, though many of Ken's mannerisms are the same as mine. She was an ordinary tennis player, but she played with him occasionally. And she always had him turned out immaculately in his tennis clothes. She was always thrilled at his wins.

'He played with a shortened racket when he was about three, using two hands for forehand and backhand. When he was five, I had to make a decision whether he should change to one hand. Except for John Bromwich, all the top players used one hand.'

'Didn't the Australian star, Vivian McGrath, also use a two-handed backhand in the thirties?' I asked.

'Yes . . . that's right,' replied Robert Rosewall. 'I sawed off a racket handle within a few inches of the head so Ken could grip it with only one hand. I tossed it on the carpet. He threw left-handed, but he picked it up with his right hand, and he played this way for several years. I had about a dozen tennis books from all over the world. From books I taught him Fred Perry's forehand and Don Budge's backhand. The volley, overhead and lob he developed naturally. We would get up at four and five in the morning. We would spend weeks hitting only one stroke at a time. I would drop a handkerchief on the ground, and he would hit to it. I didn't worry much about the serve, as he had a natural overhead, and tennis in those days emphasized ground strokes.

'At the age of nine I entered him in a tournament, and he lost to the boy who won it. At eleven he entered the Metropolitan Hardcourts Championship for under fourteen and won it, beating a boy over six feet tall who was nearly fourteen. In my heart I thought I had a champion, but I never told him that.

'I'd put lumps of loaf sugar in his pocket and tell him to eat one every third game.' Father and son agreed that Ken's body naturally perspired little. 'I taught him footwork, the right forward on the backhand, left on the forehand—that's very important—but he invented himself these very fast little steps for getting into position.

'When he first went on tour with Harry Hopman, I told him, "If Mr. Hopman tells you to change this or that stroke, listen, but afterwards you only do what you feel is right."

'When I see him play, and I see a particular stroke—a forehand, perhaps, or a backhand—it reminds me of years earlier when we worked on it.'

Ken, Bob and I toured the Rockdale, Pensonhurst and Hurstville (where Ken was born on November 2, 1934) municipalities, all adjoining suburbs of Sydney, where the family lived in a series of tacky little houses, often with the grocery store in front or below the living quarters. Outside on the street was the constant noise of traffic. The district was red-brick dwellings with red tile roofs, and wore that look of lower middle-class aggression, brassiness and a sense of hopelessness. One house, where he lived from eleven to fifteen, prettier than the others as it was in a quiet street with lawns, away from the usual traffic and neon signs, had the usual grocery store in front, 'mixed business' as Bob described it.

Ken said, 'It was a grocery store.'

Almost the only time Rosewall showed any irritability with me was when his father was present.

Here Ken practised his volley against a white wall with an advertisement painted in black letters on it, and on another side of the home practised his ground strokes, after his father dug out a slope to make a flat earthen area for the ball to bounce on. A few houses away—and this was a key to the culture that produced Ken—was another, similar dwelling, with a tennis court behind. Frequently, I learned, such homes had tennis courts which the owners rented out for small sums.* This was where the father and son played every day. There we met the housewife in her dressing-gown under the bright summer sun with her fifteen-year-old son who played competitive tennis at a district level. The boy could have been a young Rosewall except that his sloppy appearance and note of discouragement about tennis difficulties indicated he would not be. The court was a sandy loam, rough, with the pebbles coming through, though 'it was in better shape twenty-five years ago,' Ken said, 'but the wire netting hasn't changed.' 'It didn't have much room in the backcourt,' said Ken, smiling. 'My father once ran into that wooden pole'—it was ten feet high and a solid two-by-four—'and broke it in two.' 'I ran for everything,' said his father. 'I was a good club player. I hit the ball hard, but when Ken was fourteen I told him he was too good for me, and I joined the tennis club in the Illawarra district which had the best players so that he could play. When he was eleven I could give him a good game, but we never played games, just worked for weeks on one stroke or another.'

While continuing to drive his father and me in his new car around the area where he had grown up, Ken said, 'That was the office of my old dentist. He wasn't much of a dentist.'

We visited a tennis club nearby, where the men were tough

---

* Like almost all other Australian boys whose families had low-to-middle incomes, Ken played virtually exclusively on clay, a hard sandy-coloured substance which in Australia is called a hard court. Most young Australian stars would only start playing on grass when they were invited to the more expensive clubs for tournaments and exhibitions. Thus, contrary to the belief of non-Australians that Aussies were bred on grass, most of them learned the game on clay.

and the sun shone brightly on groups of players in flashy
multicoloured outfits. Several old-timers came up to the
Rosewalls, including the affable president and a bitter oldster
who said to Ken, 'You don't remember me. I still play tennis,
but I don't get a bob for it.'

While Ken was making a phone call, his father said to me,
'Ken will never say he thinks he can beat someone in a match
even though he is a better player, though in his heart he feels
he can. Ken's career is a dream fulfilled for me.'

This club was where Fred Perry, the great English star of
the 1930's, three times a winner at Wimbledon and twice at
Forest Hills, had played an exhibition. This small dusty club
was where two famous American amateurs had demanded a
set of golf clubs for playing, which they sold to the
manufacturer the next day. This was where, later, Bobby
Riggs losing to Jack Kramer on their tour, seeing the sandy
clay, had said to Kramer, 'I'll bet you two hundred dollars on
the match.' Kramer had said, 'Okay.' Riggs had won.

When we drove to the railroad station, Bob got out. Retired,
Bob now lives by a golf course in the Blue Mountains area with
his second wife, whom he married a few years ago—'a very nice
woman.' He asked his son and family for Christmas, but Ken
seemed sort of reluctant to commit himself, and instantly the
father's face fell. He patted his son on the shoulder several
times. I said, 'I congratulate you on producing such a
great . . .' The father's face lit up, and he went off.

Ken said afterwards, 'My father loves the game, and he
follows everything I do, but he can be overly critical.' Several
times he had criticized to me his father's recent purchase,
against his advice, of a Leyland car, the manufacture of which
was discontinued. A little later he said jokingly, 'Hey, I never
told my father of my new Holden [an Australian GM car
similar to a Vauxhall]. Maybe he believed me when I said it
was a loan from a friend.' When we got back to the Rosewall
house, he said, 'I enjoyed going around the old places with my
father.' I wondered later if the slightly strained atmosphere
between them was caused by Ken's realization that they had
worked to fulfil a dream, and now Ken's career was waning.
Ken said, 'You wonder if a career is waning. At forty years of
age I wonder if I'm still in a position to play top-class tennis.

Maybe in future years, with so many more players in the game now, there'll be those as old as me who will be better. You have to be realistic. My career is waning because it's physically and mentally impossible for me to play as much as I know I should in competing with so many younger players. Youthful tennis training has to be good and stays with you for the rest of your life—the same as if you learn good manners.' And yet one could not help but be moved by the great accomplishment the two of them had wrought and the enormous pleasure they had given to millions of tennis lovers over the years.

Who is the greatest tennis player of all time? Who is currently the best player? The answer or answers to these two questions interest tennis lovers all over the world. But another intention of this book is to show that the subject of it, completely separate from his sporting brilliance, has a character which is relevant to the lives of all of us, a personality whose behaviour on and off the court is an example to all of us.

This book about a tennis player attempts to fulfil these needs. It supplies an answer to the identity of such a sports star, but not a definite one, for as Gertrude Stein and Alice B. Toklas said, 'What is the answer?' and 'What is the question?' It offers an example of life, an inspiration, and a drama that parallels—as the theatre does daily living—everyone's normal activity.

Ken Rosewall is the subject of this book. Who is Ken Rosewall? An Australian and a tennis star. Why should he be burdened with the twin responsibilities of being what I hope to show is the finest tennis player who ever existed and an example to the rest of us?

Rosewall was the youngest winner of the French Championship in 1953 at the age of eighteen and the oldest in 1968 at thirty-three. Half of this twin record still stands. Bjorn Borg, at eighteen a few months younger than Rosewall, won the French Open in 1974 but failed to win another Big Four title at the same age. Rosewall was the youngest to win the Australian Championship at age eighteen in 1953 and the oldest in 1972 at age thirty-seven. So Rosewall was, and still is, the most phenomenal teenager to burst upon the tennis scene.

Curiously, Rosewall has never been regarded as one of the top five players in the history of the game. And until a few years ago he was never even considered among the top ten. However, within the last few years some tennis enthusiasts and experts are beginning to list him among the 'ten greatest.' Why has this strange omission existed? There appear to be two reasons. One is the superficiality of most of the tennis press. The other is Rosewall's well-known reluctance to advertise himself, a modesty which is appealing but so extreme that it has helped to deny him the recognition he deserves. The attraction of such self-diminishment in a sports star today should be self-evident when Rosewall's name is compared to the roster of recent and current superathletes proclaiming their sexual prowess and sports brilliance, demanding ever-larger sums of money and setting themselves up as noisy paragons of self-glorification.

What a pleasure it is to meet Ken Rosewall, an athlete and superstar who is still married to the same woman after nineteen years, whose children do not currently have to go to psychiatrists, who—unlike certain other highly publicized sporting idols—is *not* known for his amorous hijinks, drinking, betting, loud advocacy of political causes, exhibitionism and fighting, who *is* a nice, quiet, hard-working family man. In this day and age, a sports hero whose only public curse is 'golly Moses' is almost too good to be true.

One of the objectives of this book is to search for the truth in answer to the basic question that fascinates all tennis buffs, as similar questions intrigue followers of other sports: Who really was the supreme tennis star? Rosewall has cooperated fully in its preparation. It is to be hoped that, for its part, the media will grant him the accolade he merits, rectifying its error over the years in underestimating his worth.

The best way to judge an athlete's performance is to study the record books. This is the objective approach. The subjective method, though of value for argumentation, is hopelessly individualistic. Surprising as it may seem, Rosewall has won more major championships than any other tennis star in the history of the game dating back to its inception in the last century.

As far as I know, no one has ever compiled the number of major-tournament wins by the leading players. The important tournaments include the Australian, French, Wimbledon and

Forest Hills. In the 1970's the finals of World Championship Tennis, always held in Dallas, and the winner of the Grand Prix-Masters should be added. This adds up to six so far.

Then we confront a serious problem in tennis statistics—the division of the game from the 1930's to the late 1960's into professional and amateur groups. The pros, of course, were not allowed to play in the amateur events, but only a tiny few were of world class in the thirties, from Karel Kozeluh, always a pro, to the two touring headliners. It might be suggested that the old head-to-head tours of the two top players is a statistical solution. The selection of the two stars depended on the choice of the promoter. Secondly, Laver played only once in the old two-man head-to-head tour (Laver v. Rosewall, 1963, which Rosewall won), and Rosewall only participated once (Rosewall v. Gonzales, 1957, which Gonzales won) before he reached his peak, and not long before the head-to-head system was phased out, except for the 1963 tour, which incidentally also included Laver v. Hoad, Laver losing (Rosewall also beat Hoad). Thirdly, Gonzales argued bitterly for years that Kramer excluded him after Kramer decisively beat Gonzales in their head-to-head tour, though to be fair to Kramer, the economics of the tour required that in order to draw crowds the pro who had won the previous head-to-head had to face the top amateur, newly turned professional. But Gonzales claimed that inexperience cost him victory in their series in 1949, and that subsequently he was supposedly better than Kramer and should have played Segura in 1951 and Sedgman in 1953, instead of Kramer, who did and beat them both. A fourth drawback to the tour records is that in the late 50s the head-to-head matches had largely ceased to exist and were in part replaced by round-robin tours, and the records of these are very incomplete and open to dispute.

Surely, then, the fairest and most consistent standard is to judge the 'greats' on the major tournaments won, which always has been and still is the universal tennis measuring stick for deciding who is the No. 1 player. Fortunately there is a solution to the problem of judging the pros who were banned from the amateur championships. They held their own major championship tournaments, three in number every year, recognized among themselves as the truest test of ability and superiority, and known by tennis cognoscenti and some of the press as the most important events in professional tennis, deciding who was the 'king of the pack'—in other words, who was the world's top professional tennis player.

These three contests were the two tournaments in September during the 1950's and 1960's, until open tennis began, at Wembley in London and at Roland Garros or Stade de Coubertin in Paris and the U.S. Professional from the thirties to the sixties, held in various places, particularly Boston and Forest Hills.*

For those who complain that the three major professional tournaments were not regarded as the important ones by the pros, I quote the *World Tennis* reporter of May 1963, who interviewed Butch Buchholz, Rod Laver and Barry McKay in Cleveland at a tournament there:

Reporter: Don't the matches mean more in Cleveland than elsewhere?

Rod: A bit.

Barry: No, less—because they don't count on the tour standings.

Butch: Oh, I think they mean more, but of course it's not the same as the tournaments at Wembley or Paris.

For those who still doubt the ascendancy of these three tournaments it is useful to quote a New York *Times* headline of September 18, 1961, 'Rosewall Conquers Gonzales in 4-Set Tennis Final at Paris—Aussie Captures World Pro Title.' Any reading of tennis magazine files during the 1950's and 1960's will show that the winner of Paris, London and the U.S., combined with the regular touring matches, was regarded as the top player of that year. However, there are no reliable records of the day-to-day matches among the pros all over the world at different times. Therefore we are left with the three top pro tourneys as the only guideline.

Thus we have as a numerical base for the analysis of who really was the greatest player of all time: the previously mentioned Australian-French-Wimbledon-Forest Hills-WCT-Masters tournaments and the three great pro events, which of

---

* I exclude this tournament after 1967, when it became less important due to the return of the pros to the Big Four.

course disappeared with the introduction of open tennis, which in itself spawned WCT and the Grand Prix.

Rosewall won 26 of these tournaments—2 French, 2 U.S., 4 Australian, 2 WCT, 2 U.S. Pro, 5 Wembley and 8 French Professional. Laver, his nearest rival, captured 19, while Gonzales took 13 and Tilden 12, of whom it is only fair to add that he was well past his prime when some of these events were begun and never played in some of the more recent ones. It is interesting to give the records chronologically of the other players generally referred to as being members of the top ten: W. Renshaw, 7 (British, 1881-86, 1889); H. L. Doherty,* 6; W. M. Johnston, 2; Lacoste, 7; Cochet, 7; Vines, 5; Perry, 9; Budge, 8; Kramer, 4; Hoad, 4; and Emerson, 12. I point out that to be just to some of the older 'greats,' the absence of jet planes made it impossible for them to compete in some of the major championships. Rosewall has also won 8 Big Four doubles titles, including the Australian with Hoad in 1953 and 1956; Wimbledon with Hoad in 1953 and 1956; the French with Hoad in 1953 and with Fred Stolle in 1968; and the U.S. with Hoad in 1956 and with Stolle in 1969.

One of the intriguing outcomes of this compilation is that it supports indirectly Pancho Gonzales' old charge that Kramer unfairly prevented him from playing tennis because Kramer was afraid to play Gonzales again after Kramer won their first tour, even though from the standpoint of drawing crowds on the head-to-head tours it might have been economically unfeasible for Kramer to have played him in 1951, and possibly in 1953, too. Gonzales won Wembley in 1950, 1951, and 1952, and the U.S. Pro in 1953. Gonzales alleged that Kramer was reserving for himself the lucrative head-to-head tours. It is only fair to add that Kramer beat all he played and retired undefeated.

Finally, the claim that Rosewall is the finest player who ever lived is based on the same interpretations used in other sports.

---

* Reginald B. Lanier, a longtime resident of Newport, R.I., says, 'I think the Doherty brothers, H.L. and R.F., were responsible for tennis players becoming so well turned out. Before they came over from England to play in tournaments here, everyone was casually dressed for tennis. But they were immaculate. They even used to change their neatly pressed white flannels between sets.'

The champion of the leading golf tournaments is called No. 1. The winner of the most games as a pitcher—Walter Johnson, Warren Spahn, Cy Young—is described as baseball's greatest pitcher. The best hitter of all time was probably either Babe Ruth, the most homers until Hank Aaron, or Ty Cobb, the most hits, or Ted Williams, the highest batting average in a modern season. No one would argue that Rosewall has won more important tennis matches in history than any other man. Bill Tilden and Gardnar Mulloy won more matches of all kinds, but, as Rosewall gets older, he is catching up with them.

To anyone who now argues that Rosewall may have won more often only because he played so long but that he was never No. 1 for as long as other great players, I point out that modern records show Rosewall may have had the longest reign of any recent top player—1959 to 1965—longer than Laver's 1966 to 1969 or probably Gonzales' 1954 to 1958. However, using this basis of longevity to determine No. 1, it could be argued that either Kramer or Gonzales, though not both of them together, were world leaders for as long as Rosewall. If one assumes that Kramer as an amateur would have beaten the world's No. 1 pro, Bobby Riggs, in 1947, it could be said that Kramer started his reign in 1947 instead of in 1948, when he beat Riggs 69-20. If one sides with Kramer in his dispute with Gonzales, Kramer would rule seven years as the monarch of the courts. Alternatively, if one agrees with Gonzales, Kramer is reduced to four years and Gonzales climbs to eight. Or a third approach is to take the disputed years of 1951 to 1953, split them evenly between Kramer and Gonzales, and Kramer comes out at five and a half years and Gonzales at six and a half, which on this interpretation would give Rosewall a slight edge. There is also some conjecture that Tilden lasted as long as Rosewall at the top in that 'Big Bill' won Forest Hills from 1920 to 1926 and Wimbledon in 1920 and 1921 (not counting a comeback in 1929 and 1930, when he might be thought of as a co-No. 1), but Lacoste, Cochet and to a lesser extent Borotra between them took most of the Wimbledon, Forest Hills and French championships from 1926 through 1930, Cochet in particular winning Wimbledon in 1927, 1929, the French in 1926, 1928, 1930 and 1932, and the U.S. in 1928, so that it is a reasonably good guess that Tilden's domination may have been at most six years, compared to Rosewall's seven.

Equally as startling as these records is the ignorant treatment accorded to Rosewall by some tennis writers and commentators, often former stars themselves. Typical of the lack of appreciation of Rosewall is an article, 'Great Players of All Time,' by Allison Danzig, written as late as 1972. Danzig gives four lists of the ten greatest players of all time—three by individual experts and the fourth by a panel. In not one of them is Rosewall included. In Danzig's own list appears Roy Emerson, always inferior to Rosewall. Hopman, never a Rosewall fan, prefers Emerson and H. L. Doherty, the great English champion and one of the first tennis stars to gain international fame. Lance Tingay, a well-known British writer, eliminates Rosewall in favour of 'Wilding, Doherty, W. Renshaw and Hoad.' By the time they were both twenty-five Rosewall's record had clearly outclassed Hoad's.

It will also be said by supporters of other stars and opponents of Rosewall's pre-eminence that, though Rosewall was a consistent player, Gonzales, Hoad, Laver, Tilden, Vines, Kramer, Perry, Cochet and perhaps Connors—to name most of the other greats—were on their good days better than Rosewall on his best days. Rosewall was steady, they say, but on a particular day 'X' was brilliant. However, having seen Rosewall in a match at Wembley in 1962 and having watched him destroy Newcombe in the Forest Hills semi-final of 1970, it is my opinion that on those favoured days when both players were at the peak of excellence Rosewall would have beaten any of his great competitors.

Will Grimsley in his book omits Rosewall from his list of great players by implication: 'Most students of the sport rank Kramer with Tilden, Budge and Laver, in varying order, as one of the best players to pick up a racket.'

A *Sports Illustrated* writer said Rosewall would not be remembered as 'the best' but 'as the fellow who defied time and space—by taking up so much of the one and so little of the other.' The same writer described Rosewall's face, saying he was heavy-lidded, which is not true. His nose he called a narrow railing, which is an exaggeration. He does, however, have a wide, delighted smile occasionally.

Another example of the bizarre habit of almost all tennis writers to consistently underrate Rosewall is this sentence from an encyclopaedia of tennis, describing the 1953 Davis Cup finals, which Rosewall won for Australia in the key fifth match, the score being tied 2-all: 'Rosewall defeated Seixas in the final rubber in a five-set match which was an anticlimax after the gruelling Hoad/Trabert affair.' Anticlimax? The deciding match?

Another group which has persistently underestimated Rosewall often in recent years are those so-called experts, the tournament selectors, who seed the players. To be fair to them, their first error was in the opposite direction when they made the eighteen-year-old Rosewall No. 1 in 1953 (he was and still is the youngest player ever to be ranked No. 1 in the Wimbledon seedings, and thus No. 1 amateur in the world), and he never reached even the semis at Wimbledon. It is true that Sidney B. Wood won Wimbledon at age sixteen, but he won by default as his opponent, Frank X. Shields, was ill and defaulted. In 1954 at Wimbledon Rosewall was seeded third and reached the finals. In 1955 Rosewall was second and failed to reach the semis. In 1956 Rosewall was second and lost in the finals to Hoad. In his early years the selectors were more accurate, but in the 1970's, always expecting Rosewall to collapse with age, they ranked him fifth at Wimbledon (1970), and he got to the finals. In 1970 at Forest Hills Rosewall was seeded below Laver and Newcombe, but won. In 1971 and 1972 Rosewall was seeded second behind Laver at the WCT finals, but won. In 1974 at Wimbledon Rosewall was seeded ninth, but should have been listed as No. 2, as he reached the finals. In 1974 Rosewall at Forest Hills lost in the finals, was seeded fifth, but should have been second.

But let us look at Rosewall from the subjective viewpoint, constituting my own aesthetic, judgmental estimation of him. He is the outstanding player in tennis history, as I think the book will bear out, and, given one full day's rest between matches, he may be the best player currently.* Fortunately in

---

* However, in an extended five-set tournament with its gruelling test of endurance, often scheduling matches on successive days, one would have to give the edge to Connors.

the last few years more people, though still a minority, are beginning to recognize Rosewall. He is close to being the most popular player in the world for the public, except possibly in Australia, the reasons for which will be explained later. Fans at Wimbledon and Forest Hills have made him their sentimental favourite, and the French have always had a special regard for him. The Japanese prefer him over the others, and so on. I am not, of course comparing him with national heros such as Vilas in Argentina, Borg in Sweden, Nastase in Rumania, Vijay Amritraj in India, or Ramirez in Mexico.

The explanation for his international following is that he is a sports hero for our times. He is the supreme artist of tennis—the most beautiful player, the most graceful, the cleverest, and the one with the highest emotional attractions.

Rosewall is similar to Alan Ladd in *Shane*, the classic Western movie. Both are small men, with the same virtue and tension, the air of triumph and defeat, the quiet hero against insuperable odds, the one riding out of the sunset to befriend the hard-working family and shoot down the bigger, tougher, more numerous bad men, the other walking onto the tennis court alone to show how hard work and courage and clean living and that magic of speed, like Shane's trigger reflexes, can conquer the taller, heavier and stronger opponent. Even down to their modesty the parallel holds. Each figures that God has sent him down to do a job, and it's not for him to ask why but to do his best. Rosewall is an old-fashioned hero in a modern setting playing a popular game—a real hero.

There are other cultural parallels to Rosewall. He is like a bullfighter, matching his speed, brain and courage in artistic motions against the heavier, dangerous opponent. His skill with the racket is comparable to that of the matador's with the cape and sword. There is even a similarity between him and Charlie Chaplin. Rosewall is a serious person, but the confrontation of the small figure against impossible odds, the power of the machine, is a theme in common.

As a tennis player he has the best backhand, and among the best returns of serve, lobs and volleys in world-class tennis. Most other great players are superior in only one, or at the most two, strokes—Gonzales, his serve, Kramer, his forehand

and second serve, Budge, his backhand, and Tilden his ground strokes with their heavy spin. Rosewall's backhand is a study in fluid perfection—an effortless swing from back to front, weight exactly distributed, the racket face slightly open, giving underspin and control. U.S. Davis Cup captain Dennis Ralston observes that Rosewall keeps both feet on the ground when returning serve. His forehand return of serve is only weak in comparison to his backhand return of serve. Otherwise it is first-class. The key is Rosewall's lightning reflexes. Billy Talbert, former Davis Cup captain and one of the great doubles players, has said that Rosewall is among the most accomplished in the art of the drop-shot. Rosewall's volley is more sharply angled or fired deeper to the baseline than any other player's. Gene Scott says there is no high forehand volley to compare with Rosewall's. A key technique of Rosewall's on an important point is to rush the net on returning serve, often volleying back the server's volley.

Contrary to popular opinion, Rosewall's serve is a great deal better than most international tournament players', and his second serve among the best in the game because of its low trajectory, the quickness of his delivery, and the cunning of his placement. His arch-rival, John Newcombe, has observed that your game is as good as your second serve. Rosewall's No. 2 delivery, with its accuracy, depth and punched low trajectory, is the equal of Gonzales' second serve, with its graceful curve, or Laver's twisting spin on his second serve. Rosewall is not physically capable of an explosive serve like Roscoe Tanner's or Mike Sangster's or Colin Dibley's—no man or woman standing less than five foot seven, weighing 140 pounds, can hit 'the bomb.' But his first serve is like a boxer's jab. Sometimes it draws blood, sometimes not; sometimes it stings; sometimes it's a tap but it is invariably well placed. Occasionally he aces, often he hits it hard enough to force an error, frequently the return is soft enough to be volleyed dramatically and violently away.

Considering Rosewall's size, his achievement is even more impressive. It was the original intention of this book to say that he belonged among the top five players of the century, and that pound for pound—to use boxing terminology—he was the best ever. However, as stated above, investigation showed that regardless of weight, he has been and is the quintessential tennis star. Nevertheless, in a game where height and reach are useful, Rosewall's accomplishment is all the more admirable and amazing. By comparison Kramer was 6' and weighed 170 lbs., Laver is 5' 9½" and 150 lbs. Connors 5' 10" and 151 lbs., Gonzales, Tilden and Vines were well over 6'. Rosewall is under 5" 7" and weighs 140 lbs. Only Bitsy Grant and Cochet can challenge him regarding size.

It will also be asked why Rosewall never won Wimbledon. Though a minor reason might be nerves on his part when he missed his two best chances in 1954 and 1970, and possibly '56, the basic explanation, which applies equally to Gonzales, is that as a professional from the age of 22 to 34, when he could have won Wimbledon several times, he was not permitted to play. His loss to Roche in 1975 turned on a disputed point, a match that could have gone either way.

Rosewall, whose middle name is Robert, was born November 2, 1934, in Sydney. At the time he was born his family lived in Hurstville. After about a year they moved to another combination house-store, and Robert Rosewall bought three clay courts located behind the house. Unlike the situation in America and England or the rest of the world, tennis was a leading social pastime of the lowest economic groups, which is why even today courts will be seen scattered around the poorer areas of the city. Before TV and rising land prices diminished Australian enthusiasm for tennis, a tennis court would be found behind probably at least one house per block in the 1930's. Usually they had lights, making tennis a popular night-time game. Ken remembers 'as a beautiful sight,' flying over Sydney as late as the fifties and 'seeing thousands of little lights twinkling from the night tennis.'

Mr. Rosewall's three clay courts were rented out to the public and provided an additional source of income. When he entered the Australian Air Force in the Second World War, he had to sell the courts, but Ken continued to play on them 'exclusively' until he was eleven.

Both Rosewall's maternal grandparents and paternal grandmother lived with them, and, having seen their various homes, I would guess that living conditions were cramped.

Ken does not know when his ancestors came to Australia; he

thinks most were Scottish, though Rosewall is a Cornish name.
His father's father died when Mr. Rosewall was a boy, and Ken
does not know what his occupation was. His mother's father
was employed in the Sydney transportation system.

Early Morning Tennis

In the early mornings when the sun was rising Bob Rosewall
and his tiny six-year-old son would walk onto the clay courts
behind their red-brick house, one of many identical homes in
the suburb of Rockdale. The night before the young Rosewall
would have laid out both his and his father's tennis clothes.
After two or three hours of practice they would stop and the
older Rosewall would go into his grocery store.

Mr. Rosewall (who as a young man worked as a clerk in a big
Sydney department store, and in fact returned to this
occupation for a few years prior to his recent retirement) had
studied tennis strokes for years from books, manuals and
observation as a fan and player. He himself had first started
playing in his early twenties and immediately fell in love with
the game. One day he was worried that his son was not being
properly taught since he was not a professional. He took the
boy to a pro, who said, 'His strokes are fine. You've taught him
exactly right. There's nothing I can do for him.' The elder
Rosewall drilled him, but pleasantly and without coercion, in
all aspects of the game. The small, thin youngster, he realized,
would not be able to overpower his opponents. He would have
to be able to do everything perfectly. Mr. Rosewall noticed his
son was becoming a good player at the age of eight, but he said
to him, 'Ken, if you quit rugby and cricket and concentrate
exclusively on tennis, I think you have what it takes to be a
champion. Or you can be good in all sports but champion in
none of them. Think it over for a week, and then let me know.'

The boy hesitated and worried for three days. He loved
tennis. Yet he enjoyed rugby and cricket. One evening he came
into the living room in that curious style of uncertainty and
yet conviction, and said to his father, 'Dad, I want to be a
champion.'

By the time Rosewall at age ten had finished his homework
and tennis practice he was so tired he was half asleep. His idol

was Frank Sedgman, one of the great Aussie stars in the late forties and early fifties, though his first hero was John Bromwich, one of the best doubles players of all time. When the Rosewalls gave up the house by the tennis courts and moved to another one in the same district, Rosewall's father would put the boy on the handlebars and cycle him to the court.

In a newspaper interview published in the 1950's Rosewall's mother denied that her son was 'teethed' on a racket, though agreeing his baby carriage often contained her rackets when she went to a tournament. She said, 'Kenny always went to tennis with his father and me, even when he was a baby in arms. We never left him at home. He had his own racket when he was only three. We didn't buy him a special racket but cut three or four inches off the handles so that he could grip it. He would spend hours a day hitting an old ball against a brick wall. When we had finished our matches Ken would race around to one side of the net and demand that we hit the ball to him. He was so small and fat that you had to stand on your toes to see him. He probably didn't hit them very straight at that time, but every now and again he used to send back a "whizzer". At that stage, because the racket was so heavy for his little arms, Ken gripped it with both hands. He used to get up at 5 A.M. to play his father, and he never wanted to stop.'

'Now I've met your father, but can you tell me what your mother was like?' I asked. Rosewall let out a sudden whoosh of air from his mouth, exhaled with shock and surprise at the question, the first of the morning, and then said happily and pleasantly, 'My mother was a gentle woman who gave me a lot of support other than the practical side which was my father's speciality with his great interest in the game. There was never much money, and they made many sacrifices, especially when I was a teen-ager going to tournaments. Maybe she spoiled me a little. My mother flew down to Melbourne for my first trip away from Sydney when Lew Hoad and I played in the Victorian championships. She stayed with relations, and Lew and I had our first experience of bunking in a YMCA. She was a slim, quiet woman.

'I have 20/20 vision, and I can see the ball and the direction it's going earlier off my opponent's racket than other players. It's partly inherited and partly all the hours and hours of practice as a boy with my father.

'When my father taught me, he had read in books that ground strokes should be emphasized. That was the way the game was played in those days. I always had a pretty good overhead, but in some things I'm left-handed, and can throw a ball twice as far left-handed, even though I play tennis right-handed. Maybe that's why my serve always was a weakness.

'I think my drive to succeed comes from inheritance and from environment-training by my family.

'All the good Australian players—Anderson, Hewitt, Laver, Newcombe, Roche, Emerson, Alexander—come from hard-working families of low-to-middle income, though I am not saying good players can't come from rich families. Crawford, Bromwich, McGregor, Pails, Stolle, Cooper, Hartwig and Dent came from middle-income backgrounds. John Newcombe's father was a dentist, and though in some areas dentists are very well paid, I would still regard the Newcombe background as a middle-income one. Young John Alexander, Ian Ayer and Clive Wilderspin had similar upbringings.

'The reason I got to the top is due to many sacrifices by my parents and then later by my family.'

Some American observers have maintained that the early school-leaving age of fifteen and the lesser emphasis on college education was to the advantage of Australian tennis players, though American boys and girls are given much opportunity to practise tennis while in high school and on scholarships to universities.

Early clippings show Rosewall winning tournaments at the age of nine. He weighed only seventy pounds and was four feet four inches tall. Already the Sydney papers were calling him 'clever,' remarking on his perfect shots, though one said his tennis was 'passive.'

Ken remembers, 'When I was a youngster of eleven, twelve or fourteen, I used to go to bed at 8 P.M. and get up at 4.30 A.M. to play tennis with my father at 5 A.M. before he went to work and I to school.'

Ken and Lew

The relationship with Lew Hoad began when they were both

twelve years old. They met in a local tournament in Sydney. It was the first time Ken and Lew had ever set eyes on each other. Hoad, of course, even then was bigger and taller. Hoad came from a family of several brothers. Rosewall was the only child. Ken remembers, 'I went about it as though I were playing for my life. Even at twelve Lew was an aggressive player. I was the consistent one, and although I did not have much pace, I placed the ball fairly well. As for my net game, I pooped my serve in and then retreated. I beat Hoad 6-0, 6-0. The next time I won 6-2, 6-3.'

Meanwhile, the same day in 1946 as Lew and Ken's first match, Jack Kramer and Ted Schroeder (subsequently winner of Wimbledon in 1949), having just finished winning the Davis Cup for America over Australia, were invited by their hosts to drop by at a local tournament, where they saw Hoad and Rosewall battling each other in the finals for Australian boys twelve and under. Ted said, 'Jack, what do you think of them?'

Kramer replied, 'We better get the hell out of the way before these kids get much older because they will be beating our ears off.'

Ted Schroeder encouraged the twelve-year-old Hoad after losing 6-0, 6-0 to Rosewall, 'Don't worry, kid, you'll beat him some day.'

Subsequently Hoad lost another match 6-0, 6-0 to Rosewall and reportedly gave up tennis as a result. However, Hoad tried tennis again, and a few years later beat Rosewall for the first time in the New South Wales Championships in Sydney. Their rivalry had begun.

In 1963 Jack Kramer told Ed Hickey, vice-president of the New England Merchants Bank, an old friend of Rosewall and an active supporter of pro tennis in the sixties, of this memory of Kramer's eighteen years earlier. Hickey asked Kramer who had won the contest then between the two twelve-year-olds. Kramer said, 'It's just like it generally is, Lew Hoad makes all the miraculous shots and Kenny wins all the matches.'

There is a charming film of Hoad playing tennis at twelve, a one-minute cameo in the middle of a long film about Australia's glorious victory some years later over the U.S. in the 1953 Davis Cup. The movie shows an angelic blond-haired Hoad, smiling happily, swinging a racket half his size. The fascinating thing about the film is not only the sentimental pleasure of recognizing the older Hoad's features in the boy but just how extraordinarily good he, and by implication Rosewall, was at that age. Despite the giant size of the racket, the swing on both forehand and backhand is perfect and the ball is solidly hit in the centre of the racket. To add to the allure of the cameo, the youngster is obviously enjoying every minute of the filming, exuding a delightful warm personality—a side of Hoad which did not appear often on the court in later years.

Besides encountering Hoad for the first time, Rosewall was soon to make an even more important acquaintance. Rosewall and Wilma McIver met at a junior tournament when both were fourteen. Wilma remembers fondly in that clear voice which ripples like a mountain stream, 'We met at the age of fourteen in an interstate tournament. He used to write me and send me chocolates.'

The McIvers lives in Brisbane, several hundred miles north of Sydney. Wilma's father and uncle, who were brothers, had emigrated from Stornoway on the Island of Lewis in North-West Scotland as young men and married two sisters. Mr. McIver was employed as an engineer servicing agricultural equipment around Australia.

Rosewall reminisces, 'My first hero was John Bromwich. He was one of the best doubles players I have ever seen. When I was fourteen, I was asked to be his partner in a tournament in Orange. I was so eager I would have walked the two hundred miles from Sydney to Orange.

'Orange is a city about two hundred miles west of Sydney and has always been a strong tennis area. We reached the finals, and there we met Jack May, who is now a senior executive with Spalding in Australia, and Henry Lindo, who was actually involved with the coaching of John Newcombe for some time and is now quite a good friend of mine. We won. I also won the junior singles, but because of the hectic schedule of matches I withdrew from the men's singles, where I was due to play May in the semi-finals, on the advice of my father and mother, who were with me at the time.

'My second hero was Sedgman. In 1949, because of my connection with Slazenger's, when I was fifteen, I played with

Ken McGregor in a doubles against Sedgman and George Worthington. My serve was pretty weak and my volley was not sound or safe. We lost 3, 4 and 3. Mac was six feet two and a half inches tall. Sedgman and Worthington were both six feet. I was slightly embarrassed. In my tennis shoes I was five feet.'

The young Rosewall was starting to travel outside Sydney to other cities and suburbs of eastern Australia as his tennis skill and fame grew. Commensurately the number of temptations increased.

'I come from a non-drinking, non-smoking family. I never drank, and when I was fifteen or sixteen on the interstate competitions with Lew and George Worthington, our No. 1 player, who later died of cancer and who liked to have a few beers, George would urge me to have a beer following a match. I said, "No, thanks. I'll have a lemon squash," and he'd tell me beer had some good ingredients for one's health. Then I married, and after I turned pro I started to have one or two beers after a match as I thought it would relax me.'

'You think pro tennis drove you to it?' I asked.

He laughed.

Rosewall finished school at fifteen, which was the school-leaving age in Australia. His marks were average, not due to any lack of intelligence but because of his preoccupation with tennis. However, Robert and Vera Rosewall thought it advisable that he receive a training in business, as in those days a tennis career was short and positions as coaching professionals were few and poorly paid. This was and still is a curious anomaly of Australian tennis, where private lessons are rare and the relatively few working pros give classes at various clubs representing different income brackets and at private schools in their area, going from one to another. The lucrative club professional jobs available in America with the well-paid individual instruction do not exist in Australia.

During that period of Ken's life, *The People,* an Australian paper, said, 'Some time ago Rosewall was upset because, after a year of learning the piano and showing promise at it, he had to give it up because he could not take enough time off from his tennis to practise his music properly.'

As his parents wished, Rosewall entered a business college.

He failed to become an accountant, studying at Metropolitan Business College in Sydney. 'Ken used to bring his racket to class. He was always on his way to play tennis,' said an official of the college, housed in a rundown six-storey structure, the paint flaking off the walls.

Junior Champion

Before Rosewall was fifteen, people were predicting he would be a champion. Ken remembers, 'In 1949 Peter Cawthorn was leading me 3-1 in the finals of the Australian Junior Championship on the centre court. He was nearly nineteen. I had just turned fifteen. We had to stop because of darkness. Then it rained for five or six days. It must have bothered him. He, not knowing my game, played my backhand. Then it stopped raining. When we went out to a side court, watched only by the linesmen and the other juniors who were there to practise ten days with the Davis Cup team like me, as we could not play any longer on the centre court, I won five of the next six games.' At fifteen he had won the Australian Junior Championship—the youngest ever. Newspaper after newspaper as well as adult tennis stars were predicting he would be 'a great player,' one of the rare times such forecasts proved accurate.

Around this time Rosewall was asked to play in an exhibition doubles with Ken McGregor, Frank Sedgman and John Bromwich. The spectacle was of some amusement to the onlookers and embarrassment to the grown-up players, as they each stood over six feet, while Rosewall by comparison seemed even shorter than he was.

Ken remembers, 'In January 1951, Bromwich and I played Sedgman and McGregor in an exhibition doubles at Manley, which is a suburb on the north of the harbour about seven miles from Sydney. Manley has a grass-court club, and the seaside event is very popular there, as it's beside the ocean, and between matches the players can relax on the beach. Sedgman, McGregor and Bromwich had come back from America, where they had won the Davis Cup some months earlier. Sedgman and McGregor were the two leading players, and Bromwich had won the Cup doubles with Sedgman.

Bromwich and I lost the exhibition. I was about five foot, five and a half inches tall, and I only grew an inch or so after that; so that I now say I'm five foot seven inches.'

Adult players often hoped to avoid meeting Rosewall in tournaments, not wanting to be beaten by a boy shorter in height. Coincidentally or not, an older Australian star, Billy Sidwell, winner of the U.S. doubles with Bromwich in 1949, and a doubles runner-up at Wimbledon in 1947 and 1950, removed one of his shoes for twenty minutes to relieve cramps while playing the sixteen-year-old Rosewall in a five-set match.

At that time Lennard Bergelin was one of the world's best players. Near the end of 1951 he arrived in Australia as the star of the Swedish Davis Cup team, which would meet Australia in the Cup matches, the winner to confront the U.S. Bergelin, a tall Swede with a face reminding one of two adjacent mountain ranges, was years later to become the coach of Bjorn Borg. During some tournaments prior to the Davis Cup match with Australia, which were used by all the teams as a sort of practice warm-up for the great matches, Bergelin drew in the round of 16 in the Victorian championships at Melbourne a relatively unknown boy, Ken Rosewall.

'When I beat Bergelin 6-1, 6-2, 8-6 at the age of seventeen, he was a top world player, and the year before had won both his Davis Cup singles over Australia, but he was up against the same problem against a young player that I am now. The newcomer knows much more about the star than the other way around. The young player has nothing to lose and is loose. The pressure is on the star. Many juniors have victories over established players, but then they move into adult ranks, and they can't keep it up. Bergelin had arm trouble that day, too.'

The loss caused a sensation in the sports pages of the Australian papers. The New York *Times* said, 'Bergelin was so disgusted when the game was over, he brushed newsmen aside and refused even to grunt.' This humiliation may have discouraged Bergelin, for the Swedes were easily eliminated by the U.S. in the subsequent Cup contest between the U.S. and Sweden. Australia then beat the U.S. in the finals.

But Rosewall had yet to show that he could compete against the best juniors outside Australia.

The USLTA sponsored Ham Richardson, America's first-ranked junior, regarded as the outstanding young prospect in the world, on a tour of Australia. Richardson stood over six feet, with a handsome face, curly blond hair and a slightly uplifted nose, seeming to show his superiority.

Ken remembers, 'Ham Richardson's game didn't seem to improve from the time I first played him at the beginning of 1952 until 1956 when I turned pro. I don't know why. He was a diabetic. He had a very good backhand, which he hit easily, that was flat and deep, and he had a good serve, but he didn't move very well. Except for the first match, I usually beat him.'

To be fair to Richardson, I point out that he played Davis Cup for the U.S. against Australia in 1955, playing one singles match, losing to Rosewall after Australia had won the first three matches, 6-4, 3-6, 6-1, 6-4; and in 1958 in the doubles, playing with Olmedo, defeating Fraser and Anderson 10-12, 3-6, 16-14, 6-3, 7-5. The U.S. won the Cup that year 3-2. But the general feeling in the tennis world, which I shared, was, as Rosewall implied in his observation above, that Richardson never lived fully up to expectations, though he did achieve a No. 1 ranking in the U.S. for at least one year.

Ken remembers, 'Ham Richardson came out here ranked No. 1 junior in the world in 1951, and played Lew Hoad and me, and when he left was No. 3.'

2

Rise to Stardom

Enter Harry Hopman

By early 1952 Rosewall, who had turned seventeen a few months earlier on November 2, 1951, was sufficiently good to merit selection for the Australian Davis Cup team, which would tour Europe and America through the spring and summer. Hoad was also chosen. It was an extraordinary honour for men/boys so young. The stars, of course, were Sedgman, McGregor and Mervyn Rose. It was Rosewall's first real encounter with Harry Hopman, an outstanding doubles player of the past, team captain and Australian journalist. He had met him about a year earlier, and in light of later controversy as to whether Hopman really discovered Hoad and Rosewall, it is significant that Rosewall says, 'When I first met him at the age of fifteen, my strokes were almost fully developed.' It also seems obvious from the highly organized Australian system of amateur tennis that Rosewall would have been selected for the Cup team on the basis of his remarkable wins in the various state championships, the Junior title, and the upsets of the grown-up players.

Rosewall's ill feelings towards Hopman may be traced back to an amazing incident in 1952 revealed curiously enough in Hopman's own book, *Aces and Places*. The suppressed violence of the tennis world comes out in the crude camaraderie and rough jokes among the stars. Hopman wrote, 'Rosewall was really a baby in the team that year, so I asked Ken McGregor, sitting beside him in the car, to punish him. "Big Mac" put a headlock on him, chiefly, I think, to hear the little fellow's cry of "Help me, Lew." ' Hopman's behaviour in this incident was truly startling, besides being crude. If Rosewall was indeed a 'baby', punishing him was hardly the way to mature him. As Rosewall was possibly the most talented junior player in the world, known also for his polite, co-operative behaviour and a better player than most adult tournament players, he deserved respect. But Rosewall could scarcely protest as Hopman helped to control the tennis establishment without whose support a young player without money was virtually lost.

A man who met Rosewall during the 1952 French tournament remembers, 'He was shy, reserved. He was very gentle. Hoad was quite different—much more confident and aggressive.' A Sydney psychiatrist said, 'In the early days after a match before the microphone Rosewall was so nervous and tight it was almost painful.' A Sydney businessman remarked, 'Hoad was a bit of a lad. Rosewall comes from a generation when the sports hero was supposed to be cool and quiet. Jack Brabham, the racing driver, was another example.'

Moving on to England, Rosewall attracted attention in the tournament at the Queen's Club in London, which in those days always preceded Wimbledon. Gardnar Mulloy remembers, 'When Ken beat me at Queen's, the press in interviewing him remarked that he played well to win, and Muscles [Rosewall's nickname] responded with, "Well, I ought to beat Mulloy; he's older than my father." '

Though a few days later Mulloy beat Rosewall in four sets of the second round at the 1952 Wimbledon, after Ken had beaten British junior champion John Barrett 6-2, 6-2, 6-0 (Barrett and Rosewall were to become close friends and still are), Gardnar proved a good prophet: 'I think Rosewall will go further than Hoad because he also has the guile and strokes to finish off openings he makes. Hoad appears unable to beat his opponent until his third or fourth stroke.' What really caused a sensation, though, came when Rosewall and Hoad beat the No. 2 seeds, Mulloy and Savitt, in five sets in the doubles. Savitt had been the Wimbledon champion in 1951, and was seeded No. 1; Mulloy was four years older than the combined ages of the seventeen-year-olds, but one of the world's all-time finest doubles players. Mulloy remembers, 'Savitt and I had *match point* on Rosewall's service to me. He missed the first serve. Then on his second serve I hit my forehand return weakly in the net. Savitt, rightfully, yelled at me, and we exchanged a few words and lost the match!'

Rosewall described to me a key shot, which came as the first winner in the last game, score 6-5, fifth set, Hoad serving, while we were talking about his famous win over Laver in 1972. I was saying, 'I remember in the WCT final '72 Laver in the first set, when smoking along, was forced to run back by a perfect lob of yours which landed in the corner to his backhand, and he swivelled around and whipped a backhand down the line while you were at net.'

'When you get a lob like that,' Ken replied, 'you can either try to lob it back and stay in the game or go for a brilliant shot. Some players are only able to take a stab at it. I recall in 1952 at Wimbledon in the doubles on the Centre Court, the first time I played on it when I was seventeen, Hoad and I were playing Savitt and Mulloy, and they hit a very deep lob more on my side, and I went back for it and twelve to fifteen feet behind the baseline I hit as hard as I could a backhand which flashed down the middle between them.'

This was the turning point, and Mulloy and Savitt exchanged some angry words after it. So impressed were the Americans, moved by the amazing spectacle of their young opponents, that both grinned on occasion after a dazzling Rosewall placement or a Hoad smash. This was their usual technique: Rosewall would make brilliant speedy-angled shots drawing the heavier Americans out of position and Hoad would pound away the soft return.

On the basis of their Wimbledon record there was considerable excitement in the American tennis world the summer of 1952 awaiting the arrival of the 'babies', as the British press had dubbed them.

One of the tournaments they played in the U.S. before Forest Hills was at Orange, N.J. This was the first time I saw Rosewall play. It was a day of bright sunshine, and the grass at the country club looked especially green in contrast to the dry, parched look that the New Jersey countryside has by August of a summer. On one side of the net in a doubles match were Sedgman and McGregor, on the other the two

newcomers, Rosewall and Hoad. I remember the expressions
on the two adult stars' faces—amusement, respect and a little
awe, though they were confident of winning, as in fact they did
in the third set after splitting the first two. But the surprise on
Sedgman and McGregor's faces is easily understood when one
realizes that Sedgman and McGregor were the No. 1 and 2
amateur players in the world, and would soon turn pro to face
Kramer and Gonzales, and here they were being given a battle
by a couple of seventeen-year-olds who were so precocious it
was a little frightening, which was why Sedgman and
McGregor often smiled at each other after a dazzling rally. But
the player who most stood out in my memory, who in fact
impressed me more than the others at the time, was Rosewall.
It was not the anger in him which struck me, as Hoad, sullen
and relaxed, was the hostile one of the pair, but the repressed
violence which erupted in the fastest reflexes I have ever seen
on a tennis court, including Connors and Borg of today. When
a ball came to him he seemed to take it as a personal attack and
react like a bullet shot from a gun, volleying it away, the
violence exploding in the shot, yet beautifully controlled.

'You said you came from a poor- to middle-income family.
How did you feel about the upper-class country club world into
which you were thrust as a young tennis player?'

'That doesn't apply to Australian tennis, but outside of
Australia I was impressed, but I tried not to let it affect me.'

At Forest Hills the young Rosewall met Vic Seixas, who was
seeded No. 1 and expected to win the national championship,
in an early round. Seixas was twenty-nine years old. Rosewall
had seen him play tennis in November and December of 1951,
in Australia. 'McGregor advised me before the match against
Seixas in 1952 that, if I hit a shot to his backhand and came to
net, Vic would probably return down the line. Thus I was
able to successfully anticipate and volley the ball with my
forehand.

'I used to play Vic Seixas' forehand, which he sort of scooped
up and the ball would come over high, and, if you were quick,
like Sedgman and me, you could get to it for a volley.

'I never had much trouble with Seixas' game. His serve and
forehand had a lot of topspin that bounced high and gave me
the angle so I could hit cross-court.'

Rosewall beat Vic Seixas 3-6, 6-2, 7-5, 5-7, 6-3 at Forest Hills in 1952. Seixas was quite upset after the match. Hoad beat Larsen—another surprise. America's Cup hopes had 'hit rock bottom'.

Photos show Rosewall looking about fourteen. Red Smith described him as having the 'immature features of a Boy Scout'. After his win over Seixas the following dialogue occurred between Rosewall and the American press:

'Did the match go as you expected?'

'Nope.'

'Why not?'

'I dunno. I hoped to do well.'

'Did you go out there thinking you could beat Seixas? Not hoping you could, but believing you could?'

'I didn't think I'd beat him.'

'What happened?'

'I dunno. He didn't play too well.'

'What was the best part of your game?'

'Mr. Hopman will tell you.'

One American columnist wrote: 'Bless me if this kid from the Antipodes did not have the nerve to beat our Vic Seixas in our own national championships, pat our No. 1 player paternally on the back and then grab two bottles of Coke and amble off the court drinking from alternate straws.'

Seixas, now a successful businessman in Philadelphia and star of the senior tennis circuit, remembers with a slightly dry tone his matches against Ken. Seixas has blue eyes and grey in his dark curly hair but looks very similar to the Seixas of his youth. There is something almost cold, chilling in his blue eyes, but one cannot help liking him. Seixas has that quality of the leader, where you want to get close to him but can never get close enough. He said, 'In those days Hoad, Trabert, Rosewall and I were together a lot. We never could understand how I could usually beat Hoad and lose to Rosewall, Rosewall lose to Trabert, and Trabert usually win over Hoad. Later Rosewall became better than all of us. I tried everything against him, as you do when you lose. I tried playing his forehand, but I think it usually doesn't work if you have to change your own game. I tried rushing the net. I was seeded No. 1 at Forest Hills in 1952 when he first beat me at the age of seventeen. Though I almost always lost, I always played well against him, and I liked his style. As regards who wins a match, some styles work better against one player than another. Mine obviously usually lost to him.'

In the next round at Forest Hills, 1952, Rosewall opposed Mulloy. By the third set Mulloy was visibly 'tiring, slowing up his footwork, and losing control' even before the rest period, but then Mulloy changed his tactics, using slice to Rosewall's backhand and hitting down the middle to go to net, and Mulloy won the fourth set, while in the fifth Mulloy, softening his game from fatigue and intention, extracted errors from Rosewall, 'who had been showing signs of fatigue in the fourth set'. Mulloy won the match. So quick was Rosewall at the age of seventeen that Mulloy hit a freak cut-shot which bounced back across the net and Rosewall shot around the net to get to it.

Describing this match years later, Mulloy wrote me, 'Rosewall had me 4-2 in the fifth set, and I won it 6-4. I remember the point that gave him the lead for 4-2. I went in for a drop-shot which I barely reached, but in doing so I touched the net, which was not detected by the officials. My conscience bothered me; so I called it on myself. Afterwards all my friends told me I was crazy to give away a point like that—would the players today do the same?'

During one of our interviews in Australia, in December 1974, Ken recalls, 'Gardnar Mulloy had a good all-court game with a serve without much spin, which one could handle easily, but with a good fluent swing, not taking much effort, and that's one of the reasons he's lasted so long. His game's still the same. He had a good forehand, which you can still see today. His other great assets were his desire to compete and the very good condition he was always in. He grew up when there were a lot of what you might call "odd-bods" playing all over the world, and he became a tough competitor. Because he learned on clay, he might have been a little better there than on grass.

'The Australian press can be very critical on some players, and I remember seeing him lose to Bromwich in the Australian championships at White City stadium in Sydney, and Gardnar was unhappy with his play and the reaction of the crowd, and the press gave him a hard time over his behaviour in some ways on the court. Tennis has been Gardnar's life, and he's still in very good training as a senior.'

After New York the Aussies went to California for the Pacific Southwest tournament. In Los Angeles Rosewall and the team were at a lunch at which was present a Hollywood starlet. His teammates kidded him into posing for a photograph with her. An Australian newspaper said he had 'a wide, fixed grin of embarrassment', and quoted Lew Hoad as saying Ken 'had blushed furiously throughout and, under the table, had screwed his table-napkin into a tight knot'.

According to an article by Nell, Hopman's wife, Rosewall carried on tour eight photos of Wilma. The one on his bedside table was regularly hidden by his teammates. On another tour a few years later his Aussie teammates kidded Ken because he talked most of the evening with Debbie Reynolds at a Hollywood party. Debbie Reynolds was somewhat similar in appearance and character to Wilma.

Returning to Australia in the fall of 1952, Rosewall was reunited with his family, who were delighted with his victories. He rested briefly before continuing the tournament circuit in Australia, which was starting up with the onrush of summer and the various state championships, leading up to the Australian Championship at the end of the year. During this period Ken was given an easy clerical job at the Slazenger office in Sydney in exchange for Rosewall playing with their rackets and participating in Slazenger promotional activities. However, amateur rules then prohibited the company from advertising his name on their equipment. Hoad was employed by Dunlop, and they were allowed several afternoons a week off to go to the gymnasium or play tennis outdoors. There were no indoor courts in Australia, which is still true.

The physical training in weight lifting was supposedly encouraged by Hopman and the other powers of the tennis world there to strengthen Ken's muscles and durability. Superficially he appeared too slight and frail, though the heavy muscles in his legs and arms must have been largely developed by then. Around this period he acquired the nickname of 'Muscles' from the other players, an affectionate joke demonstrating his supposed lack of them. The exercises lasted for only a year.

Rosewall played excellently in the early rounds of the Australian Championship, eliminating Seixas (as usual) in the semi-finals. In the Finals he met the favoured Rose, a dark-haired, sharp-faced left-hander with a nice clipped style of play. Ken says, 'Mervyn Rose was under a lot of pressure, as suddenly he had gone from No. 3 to No. 1 when Sedgman and McGregor turned pro, and he did not want to lose to a seventeen-year-old. I had been doing nicely in the tournament, having beaten Seixas in the semis. Rose had beaten me in five sets a year earlier. I won ten of the first eleven games, and he never could get into the match. His backhand was weak, but he was very quick at the net, and he won the Paris tournament in 1957 rushing to the net, which is an extraordinary accomplishment on clay. Though Rose's backhand was weak, in doubles he could chop his return and come in to net, covering up the weakness. I was quite excited to win the Australian championships in January 1953—the youngest ever.'

After Rosewall had beaten Rose 6-0, 6-3, 6-4, Rose said in the locker room to the press, 'I've had it. . . . The little devil would have got the ball through the eye of a needle today. I'll repeat what American Vic Seixas said when Rosewall beat him in the semi-finals on Thursday, "It is no disgrace to be beaten by this kid." '

Rose, a top-ranked world star and supposedly Australia's best, then gasped, 'What will he be like in another couple of years?'

Before leaving on the 1953 world tour, Hopman vigorously trained Rosewall. Usually in Melbourne for two weeks before leaving on a Davis Cup tour he put him through gymnasium exercises, including weight lifting. There would also be running outdoors.

One of the first countries the Australian team visited on their 1953 world tour before reaching France and England was Italy, where they would play in the Italian championships. In Rapallo, Hopman told Rosewall, 'You're slovenly and slow-footed and your timing is off as a result.'

Rosewall replied, 'No. The tension in my racket's wrong.'

But Hopman made him practise his volleying and ground strokes.

Rosewall was the first member of the team to leave the TV room or lounge on tour and go to bed. Hoad would be the last.

Despite the hard work and Hopman's supervision, tennis was always fun for Rosewall. Perhaps it was too much fun for Hoad sometimes. Hoad probably became bored with the sport too on occasions, resulting—among other things—in lapses of concentration, which took varying forms, at least one of them entertaining for Rosewall, though in this incident one can sympathize with Hopman's task of moulding serious players out of his young stars. Ken remembers, 'Of course Lew's only real weakness as a great player was lapses of concentration. As far back as 1949 I remember we would be playing doubles together, and Lew would become interested in the match on the next court. He would persuade me to watch it, and before we knew it, we would have lost a string of games. This would upset our advisers, but it didn't bother us at the time.'

Entering the French championships in 1953, Rosewall was eighteen. His training on the clay courts of Sydney would help him slightly, as the French tournament is played on the red clay characteristic of continental Europe. Defeating a series of lesser players, he faced Seixas in the finals. Seixas was much the older player—famous, experienced—though in their first few meetings, Rosewall had always won. Seixas was far more familiar with the atmosphere of a big final than Rosewall. Yet Seixas was not considered an outstanding clay-court specialist.

The first game broke Seixas' heart. Rosewall hit four winners in a row—a sizzling forehand down the line, then another cross-court. Rosewall played a perfect drop-shot—the third point. The fourth point and a love game against Seixas' service came from a flashing backhand.

From then on it was downhill all the way for Seixas. Though Seixas played well, nothing worked. He tried the net. He would hit a wonderful volley which Rosewall would not be able to reach, Seixas hoped. But Rosewall would somehow get to it, hitting a passing shot. Then Seixas tried to throw off Rosewall's timing by deliberately slowing the speed with which he hit the ball back. Rosewall's errors increased, but not enough. Seixas made a supreme effort and won the third set. Hopman, who was watching the match, had coached Rosewall to rest a set if he was in trouble and let the other man wear himself out. Rosewall won the fourth set and the match. The score was 6-3, 6-4, 1-6, 6-2. He was the youngest player ever to win the long, exhausting test on the red clay courts of Roland Garros.

Rosewall had another triumph in the French championships when he and Hoad beat Mulloy and Budge Patty, the Wimbledon winner in 1950, in the finals of the 1953 men's doubles. Mulloy recalls an incident in this match: 'In the finals of the French doubles at Roland Garros (I was playing with Budge Patty), Rosewall put up a short lob to me. As I smashed it, Hoad charged the net, and the resulting smash of mine hit Lew flush on the nose. He bent over with blood streaming down, and he was obviously in pain, and Ken came over and said, "If you'd had enough sense to duck, the ball would have gone out, and we'd have won the point!" Later it was determined Hoad had a broken nose.'

Even at Wimbledon Hopman, ignoring rainy weather, which suspended that day's play and the request by Rosewall and the others for a day's rest for shopping and movies, would insist on a jog in Hyde Park. In practice Hopman made Rosewall try to pass two men at the net. Rosewall had to play net against two in the backcourt. Working on their skills in doubles, Rosewall and a partner would fire net shots back and forth against two on the other side of the net.

Sedgman said that in the fifties Hopman taught Rosewall a rocking motion on the serve, somewhat similar to the way Frank Parker served, whereby the server starts on the left foot, rocks back to the right, then goes into the swing in order to obtain rhythm, but Sedgman said that he, Sedgman, gave up on the technique, concluding it was 'wasted motion.' Sedgman also said that Rosewall kept his elbow close to his body just before hitting, but that his serve would be better if he raised the elbow above the right shoulder, which is the style used today by John Newcombe and which Ken himself now uses.

Being seeded first at Wimbledon when you are eighteen is an extraordinary honour.* In June 1953 Rosewall faced a minor

---

* At Wimbledon, 1975, Rosewall was seeded second.

Australian player, Jack Arkinstall, in an early round. Arkinstall found a weakness in Rosewall's forehand but eventually lost the match more from surprise than Rosewall's effectiveness, as Arkinstall wasn't even ranked in the first twenty in Australia. The score was 4-6, 3-6, 6-1, 6-4, 6-2.

Halfway through the tournament Rosewall came up against the Dane Kurt Nielsen. The morning of the match Rosewall suffered from a stomach upset, induced by something he had eaten the night before. During the match he was fed glucose to restore his strength. Ken recalls: 'Nielsen lacked the killer instinct, so they say. He had temperament problems, though he was always calm when I played him. He had a big serve, which he could hit all day, and after three hours his serve would be just as strong. When I lost to him in the quarter-finals at Wimbledon in 1953, 7-5, 4-6, 6-8, 6-0, 6-2, and again in the semis in 1954, I did not know I should have come into net and utilized my good volley and quickness and overhead. I had not been told that was the way to play. Harry Hopman's failure was in not recognizing that I could play the serve and volley game as well as any of the other players, allowing for the fact that my serve was nowhere near as fast. I should have been encouraged to play this way at an earlier stage, and I do believe that many matches that I lost, particularly those to Kurt Nielsen and to Drobny as well in the 1954 Wimbledon final, I would certainly have been in a greater position to win. After moving into the pro ranks I was able to prove I could play a serve-volley, more aggressive game.'

The London papers called Rosewall 'Wimbledon Mystery Man' during his weak showing in Wimbledon 1953.

Returning to Australia in the spring, which was autumn in the northern hemisphere, Rosewall continued his romance with Wilma, the pretty girl from Brisbane. One day in October he sent her a telegram, 'Sorry Havent Written See You Tomorrow Love Ken.'

The People, an Australian paper, also said Rosewall at age eighteen would rather listen to classical music at home than escort a girl to a local dance to which the whole family went. Explaining his relative lack of enthusiasm for the local girls when Ken was thinking of Wilma, his mother pointed out that the girl was 'a partner not a romantic interest.' The paper said,

'He seems to enjoy himself normally on these outings.'

Soon a very important test was to face Rosewall and Hoad—the upcoming Davis Cup matches between the U.S. and Australia. Since Kramer and Gonzales' elevation to the pro ranks in the late 1940's, Australia, led by Sedgman and McGregor, had won back and held the trophy for three years running, 1950 to 1952; but then Sedgman and McGregor turned pro, and by the fall of '53 it was considered almost certain that the U.S., starring Vic Seixas and Tony Trabert, both adult, experienced players at the peak of their game, would regain the Cup. Though Seixas had a losing record against Rosewall, he had won Wimbledon that year, and Trabert, Forest Hills. What chance did two teen-agers backed up by Mervyn Rose have against this formidable pair?

Although the Davis Cup was and is watched in the U.S. with intense interest by tennis fans, the trophy assumed larger proportions in Australia, where it had become a matter of national pride and honour, thrilling most Australians, who regarded themselves as a tough race, overcoming any sense of inferiority about their alleged lack of culture and crude ways. As someone once rather unkindly wrote, 'Australia is a continent surrounded by water and inundated with athletes.'

The 1953 Davis Cup film, including sequences from play as early as Sir Norman Brooke just after World War I, shows how tennis has progressed since the 1920's. The strokes are relatively clumsy compared to today's grace, the pace slower, the net game infrequent.

However, Ned Chase, the American author of an instructional book on tennis, winner of many club tournaments, and once an assistant pro for Gardnar Mulloy, says, 'This is not necessarily so. Those of us who have seen Doherty, Crawford, Vines and Tilden insist they would have been the equal to today's top stars.'

The film shows Rosewall very nervous and tight in the second match against Trabert. Hoad had won the first over Seixas. Rosewall was under enormous pressure with all of Australia watching, including the Prime Minister in the stands. More often than not, his shots are out, sometimes by a few feet, other times by only inches, his service tentative. He lost 3-6, 4-6, 4-6.

Rosewall's face was covered with gloom and depression after he was dropped from the doubles. The film shows Rex Hartwig, who replaced Rosewall in the doubles because of Rosewall's uncertain performance in the singles, losing the doubles, his head in the clouds, his shots sometimes in the court. Some years later Hartwig admitted to Gonzales that out on a tennis court he had no idea what he was doing.* The film shows Hoad beating Trabert and then rain postponing the deciding match between Rosewall and Seixas to the next day.

When Rosewall's mother flew from Sydney to Melbourne, her ticket paid for by an Australian tennis club, for his match against Seixas, she said, 'I know he will do well if he knows I am near.' An article in *Sports Novels*, March 1954, said Rosewall had suffered from eczema since the age of four. 'His mother told me that at times the eczema itch would travel right up as far as his shoulders, to his legs and arms. . . . Ken was suffering excruciating agony with eczema itch in his feet and ankles during the 1953 Davis Cup.' To this day the rash still bothers his ankles on occasion. The New York *Times* reported in September 1953 that Robert Rosewall had said Ken was excused from Australia's three-months' compulsory military training due to 'chronic dermatitis—inflammation of the skin around his ankles'. Rosewall had searched throughout the European and Australian continents for ointments and other treatments.

It's up to you, Ken

The morning of the match he woke up in the hotel room he shared with Hoad to read banner headlines of 'IT'S UP TO YOU, KEN.' The film showed Hoad throwing a pillow at Rosewall and Rosewall playfully taking a swing at Hoad. Cameramen were obviously crowding into the bedroom. Rosewall remembers today, 'I had lost to Seixas in the Victorian championships in November 1952, which he went on to win. I had of course

---

* Gonzales told the New York *Times* in an interview with Dave Anderson in 1970, 'Rex Hartwig was a strange player. He was in a fog out there on the court. He once told me, "I don't know what I'm doing," but he could hit a backhand volley perfectly every time. He was amazing.' Hartwig won several major doubles championships

beaten him earlier at Forest Hills, and subsequently I had won
again in the '53 Australian championships and the finals of the
'53 French.'

Rosewall has since said of the fifth and deciding match in
Davis Cup play, 'The eyes of the world are on you; your
country's hopes rest on perhaps a shaky second service or a
backhand that may break under continuous pounding. Your
knees shake, your heart pounds and you breathe painfully.'

And yet in the match the speed and precision came back, and
though he was obviously still tense, he was less insecure and
the shots were fast, angled, the serve deep, Seixas wrong-
footed and outrun. It was a tribute to Rosewall's courage,
having just turned nineteen, in the face of his flubbing his
opening singles, that he beat Seixas in four sets, 6-2, 2-6, 6-3,
6-4. Australia went wild with the result. After the victory his
mother said, 'I feel all-in. I'm very happy Ken won. It's the
loveliest day I've ever had.'

'After I beat Seixas, the fans threw their cushions onto the
court,' Ken told me years later. 'I was a little nervous in my
first Davis Cup match. . . . Trabert played better on other
occasions, but his game was solid that day and he beat me.

'Rex Hartwig was a very good player, but he preferred
doubles. I think he liked to have someone backing him up,
whom he could talk to. Rex is now a sheep rancher about a
hundred or so miles outside of Melbourne.'

At the end of 1953 in *World Tennis* magazine one writer
ranked Rosewall No. 1, two listed him as No. 2, one tied him
with Seixas for second, and three placed him as No. 3. Though
Rosewall was only nineteen, he received the Canadian British
Commonwealth award to the sports athlete who had made an
outstanding achievement during the year. Accompanying the
Hubert Parry Memorial Medal was a letter to Rosewall which
included the following '. . . the game of tennis was Sir Hubert's
favourite pastime and, at the risk of sounding morbid, I might
say he suffered his fatal attack while playing a few sets at the
age of seventy'.

The 1953 Davis Cup had marked a turning point in the
competition between Rosewall and Hoad as to who was the
better player. From the time they had first met as boys seven
years earlier, Rosewall had dominated Hoad, but Hoad had

caught up and equalled Ken by the close of the year, winning both his Davis Cup singles. Hoad's power game, featuring the rush to the net, was starting to give him a slight edge on some days over the smaller player, who, though very agile as a volleyer, persisted in playing mainly from the backcourt. Why Rosewall failed to take advantage of his renowned quickness has been made clear in the preceding pages.

Following the Davis Cup, Rosewall entered the Australian Championship. Perhaps Rosewall would regain his ascendancy over Lew, but Hoad could not play as he had been called up for three months of national service. Hopman then maintained that the reason Rosewall lost the 1953 Australian Championship to Rose was that he failed to turn up for a practice, as Hopman had advised him to do on seeing him beat Ham Richardson sloppily in an earlier round, and went instead to a movie with Wilma. Rose beat Rosewall in five sets in the semis. Hopman used this incident as an excuse for laying down the law to young tennis players.

Ken's failure to win the Australian Championship in 1954 was attributed by the newspapers to his being in love with Wilma. Hopman, whose expression of happiness at Rosewall's great win over Seixas in 1953 had seemed less enthusiastic than one might have expected (I watched Hopman's face in the 1953 Davis Cup film, when Hopman stood beside Rosewall after his victory), declared in what might be described as another bit of his own image-making as the wise father-genius of the team, 'I hated to see him play poorly, but heck—a young fella's got to fall in love.'

In the early part of 1954 the Australians set out on their annual tour of the big championships. Rosewall met and defeated almost all of the well-known stars of that period including Art Larsen, the American No. 1 and the Indian No. 1, Krishnan. Larsen, a lefty, whose rackets were strung with nylon, was a very unusual character, with a kind of happy vague expression on his face, blond curly hair and a slim, almost delicate-looking body, but he had a shrewd, deceptive all-out game. Several years later his career, and almost his life, was destroyed when he was injured in a motorcycle accident, but he had—to everyone's surprise—won the U.S. Championship in 1950, defeating Herbie Flam in the finals, after Gonzales had risen to the pro ranks.

Ken remembers, 'Art Larsen had the same game as me, but I was a little quicker than him. Some people regarded him as a strange fellow as he used to party all night, but then sometimes he'd wear out the guy who'd gone to bed early. His nickname was "Tap", because, I think, he'd tap the court with his racket or the umpire stand or he'd turn his head away from the court. He had a nervous desire to tap everything.'

When Rosewall beat Trabert in five sets in the 1954 semi-finals of Wimbledon, Trabert's left foot was a mass of blood and blisters from the running he received from Rosewall. His wife, Shauna, was nearly reduced to tears in the last set as their hopes for turning pro and a home of their own were shattered for one more year. Rosewall now faced Jaroslav Drobny in the finals.

At Wimbledon, even when he wasn't playing men's doubles or mixed doubles or singles matches, Rosewall was practising. After he took the last two sets off Trabert, the current U.S. champion, giving up only two games, Hopman said, 'I don't think anyone can play better than that.' This was just before the big final against Drobny, who had saved his energy during the two weeks by avoiding the doubles and slouching in an armchair watching TV or reading detective stories.

Ken says, 'I went into the final against Drobny planning to play his backhand. I was badly advised. Harry Hopman was the team coach. I'm not saying he badly advised me, but you have read that he went out and found Lew Hoad and me and developed me. . . . He did try to help my serve, but he had no effect on my backhand or forehand.

'Dumb is the way I'd describe my game against Drobny. . . .'

'You were only nineteen,' I said.

'I should have come to net more on my serve and return of serve. I'd serve to his backhand, and instead of following it into the net, I'd wait on the baseline, and he'd hit a soft deep return and come in to the net himself, knowing I wouldn't come in, which if I had would have surprised him and is a good tactic. His backhand was a defensive one and weaker on grass than on clay, where he had more time to attack with it. Similarly I should have returned his serve and followed my shot into the net, which is a good tactic and also would have surprised him. It unnerves the server. Also I hit too many lobs to his backhand side, because he moved well for an overhead, instead of hitting a passing shot or dink to his backhand volley. He had a very good action on his serve, which you can even see today when he plays despite the round "tyre" around his waist. It wasn't as fast as Laver's serve, but a little more consistent and slightly less double faults. But Rod's other strokes were definitely better, faster and with more variation. He was the better player.'

Was it also nerves that cost Rosewall the Wimbledon championship in 1954? Rosewall was the more nervous of the two coming onto the court. He was stiff and tense in the first set, although Drobny lost his serve for 0-2 after two double faults. Drobny used a left-handed spin with wonderful length and angles, showing a determination thick enough to cut with a knife. Rosewall had the best return of serve in tennis, with the delicate discerning touch of a Cochet or a Riggs and the ability to thread the ball through the narrowest of openings.

In the last set (Drobny won 13-11, 4-6, 6-2, 9-7) Rosewall seemed exhausted—a limp little figure bent almost double over the baseline as he waited for service. (The appearance of exhaustion was to become a theme in Rosewall's career.) Drobny was thirteen years older, wore glasses and had lost the sharpness of youth in his game. One writer described him as having 'a paunch', though a photo does not support this.

By the last point Drobny was becoming tired, too. Because the Czech led two sets to one, 8-7, his ad and match point, and he would feel the need to end the match then and there, Rosewall expected a fast curving serve followed by Drobny coming to net. But Drobny hit a soft serve sharply angled to Rosewall's backhand. Rosewall had begun his swing. He was surprised. His timing was off and he tried to compensate, but the ball went into the net.

By the end of the finals Rosewall looked more tired than Drobny. The Centre Court audience had largely supported Drobny because of the latter's age and underdog status—he was seeded far down the list—and their awareness that it was probably his last chance. In the light of the cold war at that period there was a measure of anti-communism in the spectators' enthusiasm for 'Drob', as he was an expatriate from Czechoslovakia. Hopman vigorously criticized the British crowd's partisanship in the Australian newspaper for which he wrote, arguing that loyalty to the empire should have been more important. This, of course, set off a new controversy. Some long-time observers said it was the best-played final of all time.

During that period Hopman said Rosewall and Hoad at nineteen were much superior to Sedgman at the same age, but Hopman was never partial to players formerly under his tutelage who had turned pro, as Rosewall and Hoad would discover a few years later when they became professionals.

One of the reasons for the dissension in the Australian tennis world prior to their team's encounter with the U.S. in the 1954 Davis Cup was the shabby treatment of Rosewall-Hoad and Co.—possibly one of the results of the class system—by the tennis authorities. While the American team travelled by limousine, ate in the best restaurants and were amused by pretty girls and gracious hosts and hostesses, Rosewall and his teammates had to pay for their own lunches in the L.T.A.A. tent and travel by public transportation on the Melbourne trains. The tennis establishment made £20,000 on the matches, and meanwhile Sedgman and McGregor were sometimes earning £1,000 a night as pros.

Nevertheless, Rosewall and Hoad were expected to retain the Cup for Australia. One of the reasons was that by late 1954 Rosewall had scored his eighth straight triumph over Seixas, winning in December in the Victorian finals at Melbourne.

Tony Trabert, possibly a more impartial observer than Hopman, wrote in a *Sports Illustrated* article before the 1954 Davis Cup that he did not think Hopman made the difference of a point a game when advising Rosewall and Hoad. But Hopman implies in his own book as clearly as possible that he deserves much credit for their success.

The 1954 Davis Cup film shows that Rosewall was fantastically fast in those days. His reflexes were like a trigger going off. Side to side, forward-backward, up-down, instantaneous reaction. At the age of nineteen he looked boyish with a short haircut. His serve was jerky, the forearm and upper arm stiff on the backswing, the racket and arm halted before swinging to hit the ball. His feet were like those of a ballet dancer—millions of little steps, dancing, dancing here and there, all over the court.

At White City stadium in Sydney, a vast, ugly structure of tubes and seats was built, bringing the seating capacity to 25,000.* The ladies all wore hats. The Australian officials and tennis backers were mostly stocky, round-faced men with an innocent hearty vigour towards life.

The Americans, such as Talbert, Trabert and Seixas, looked cooler than the Australians. The good sportsmanship on both sides was evident, a pleasant contrast to today's big business and commercialism.

Trabert had very graceful strokes and a powerful fluid serve. He looked every inch the athlete. Despite his handsome face, there was something slightly unattractive about Seixas' behaviour on the court, with his dark hair seeming to add to his angry demeanour of righteousness. In the film, Hoad is an easygoing, likeable boy with short punchy strokes, though another observer of Hoad's play over the years describes his strokes as 'lovely, powerful and perfect.' Hopman's voice has a curiously whining, rasping quality, but this impression may be due to a distortion in the film soundtrack.

But it was Rosewall's fire and hard determination, concealed and suppressed, which were to mark him as the future great champion, though his serve left something to be desired. Rosewall was, of course, already one of the top stars among the amateur players.

One hundred and twenty million TV viewers around the world in countries such as England and America watched films flown out of Australia the day of each match. In the first match Trabert, playing solidly and gracefully, overcame Hoad 6-4, 2-6, 12-10, 6-3. Then came the major surprise when Seixas, playing with determination, attacking more successfully than he ever had before in his previous matches against Ken, showing an accuracy of placement superior to his earlier efforts, upset Rosewall 8-6, 6-8, 6-4, 6-3. In the doubles the American pair of Trabert and Seixas won over Rosewall and

* The crowd for the match on December 27, 1954, was 25,578, the largest crowd in tennis history for a regularly scheduled event, excluding the freak King-Riggs extravaganza in the Houston Astrodome.

Hoad 6-2, 4-6, 6-2, 10-8. The Cup was now in American hands and, though it was small consolation, Rosewall defeated Trabert 9-7, 7-5, 6-3, and Hartwig, replacing Hoad, conquered Seixas 4-6, 6-3, 6-2, 6-3, in the non-deciding single matches.

After the defeat of the Australians, the Sydney and Melbourne newspapers, demonstrating their special talent for blunt criticism, blamed Hopman's 'iron discipline' as the cause of their defeat. Rosewall and Hoad were only twenty, and should be allowed more time with their families and for leisure activities. However, Rosewall now says, 'I don't think Hopman overtrained or overtennised us. That was something the newspapers built up. He had to be strict with such a young team, but he was a little overstrict.'

Ken remembers, 'It's rather difficult to say why these things happen. It seemed up to the time we went out to play the Davis Cup matches of 1954 that both Lew and I would be successful in our matches. Of course, it was a very big occasion. Lew and I were playing in our hometown of Sydney, where we grew up and obviously knew so many people. It was the biggest crowd ever to see tennis up to that time—25,000 or so. I think in Lew's match with Tony, which was the first match, he was somewhat unlucky. It seemed as though he was on the verge of leading two sets to one, and all of a sudden the match changed around. In my match against Vic Seixas on that day I suppose he played as well as he could under those circumstances, and I just was not able to adapt to that type of condition and be able to play the type of game I wanted to. I suppose Tony and Vic were keyed up for those matches, having lost the year before when they were certainly favoured to win. I suppose you could say they were out to get us.'

Hopman's stern control of Rosewall and the others surfaced again. After the matches Rosewall did not want to play an exhibition against the Americans.

Said Hopman, demurring, 'Rosewall's had an easy season and the LTA is not asking too much of him.'

Another Australian official added, 'He was committed to play. His employers said he was available.'

In the Australian Championship at the beginning of 1955, that year played on the heavier grass of Memorial Drive in Adelaide, there was great tension in the air in the finals between Hoad and Rosewall. Rosewall was determined to win back the No. 1 position. From the age of twelve on Rosewall had dominated Hoad. In 1954 Hoad had caught up with Rosewall. In the finals, which Rosewall won, Rosewall was starting to come to the net on his serve more and more frequently. The score was 9-7, 6-4, 6-4.

But the rest of 1955 was to be Tony Trabert's outstanding year as an amateur; he won the French over Davidson 2-6, 6-1, 6-4, 6-2, captured Wimbledon over Nielsen 6-3, 7-5, 6-1 and the U.S. over Rosewall 9-7, 6-3, 6-3. Interestingly, though, it was the second time Ken had reached the finals of either Wimbledon or Forest Hills, the most important tourneys, which Hoad had yet to do. Of course, Trabert's excellent streak, only one short of the Grand Slam, was to earn him a contract with Kramer in 1956, leading to the disastrous defeat by Gonzales in their head-to-head tour, 74-27.

Recalling their amateur days together, Rosewall said with typical understatement and special consideration for an opponent and friend, 'My record against Trabert as an amateur, as I remember, was two-to-two in major events. I lost to him in the '53 Davis Cup, beat him in the Wimbledon semi-finals in 1954, won again over Tony in the '54 Davis Cup in the fourth match when they were leading 3-0, and lost to him in the Forest Hills finals in '55 just before he turned pro.

'Tony Trabert had an edge over me as an amateur, though we only played six or seven times, but as a pro I won a few more than him, though Tony was less active then.

'One of Tony's weaknesses was that he shifted his hand too much from the forehand grip to the backhand. He may have developed this habit because he learned to play on the clay courts of the American Midwest, where the ball, as on all clay courts, has a slower bounce. He moved his hand far enough so that he placed his thumb solidly on the back of the handle. The result was that on a slow surface he hit a fine solid backhand, as he had time to get to the ball. He made a low backswing and followed through on high, giving the shot top spin. This was fine. But on grass the ball comes in low and fast. And some of us—you have to be an extremely high-class player to do this—found that if we took a fast ball early enough and hit it fast and deep to Tony's backhand it could embarrass him as he was not able to prepare early enough.'

In October 1955, there was considerable excitement in Australia as to whether Rosewall and Hoad would accept Kramer's offer. Robert Rosewall favoured it. Kramer had already obtained their signatures on letters agreeing to the terms of the contracts, but they were invalid as they were under twenty-one. Hoad's parents felt the offer was too low. Then Slazengers and Carnation Milk gave Rosewall soft jobs with good pay. When the 'tennis twins' decided to remain amateur, the radio stations throughout Australia interrupted their programmes for a flash bulletin.

Rosewall and Hoad had turned down offers of $45,000 each from Kramer. Rosewall was given a new five-year contract by Slazengers, and Carnation Milk promised him a job, bringing his earnings up to $5,600 a year. Hopman says in his book that he arranged the Carnation Milk job for Rosewall.

Ken recalls, 'I used to represent Carnation Milk. I joined them as an amateur in 1955 when everyone thought Hoad and I might turn pro. I continued with Carnation when I turned pro in 1957. One year every twelfth can of Carnation Milk would have a recipe I'd recommend. I used to do radio interviews for them.'

I said, 'I guess the idea was that Australian mothers would feed their babies Carnation milk and they'd grow up to be a star like you.'

'Yeah,' he said laconically. 'A lot of it was used for baby-feeding.' To this day the daily routine of the Rosewall household is interrupted one morning a week by the sound of the buzzer, announcing the arrival of the local Carnation salesman with a delivery of a free case of milk.

Ken and Wilma were engaged on November 5th, 1955. She was a stenographer. The engagement was announced at a barbecue party in Brisbane given by the Queensland Lawn Tennis Association as a welcome to all the players for the state championships at Milton.

One of the most devastating Aussie defeats of the U.S. was in the 1955 Davis Cup in December, the score 5-0, Rosewall winning both his singles. He defeated Seixas 6-3, 10-8, 4-6, 6-2, and Ham Richardson 6-4, 3-6, 6-1, 6-4; while Hoad also beat Trabert and Seixas in his singles, losing only one set to each of them. In the deciding doubles Hoad and Hartwig narrowly conquered Seixas and Trabert 12-14, 6-4, 6-3, 3-6, 7-5, and this match may have awoken Hopman and the Australian selectors, who determined who played the matches, to the likelihood that Rosewall and Hoad were really the strongest combination after all. Rosewall, Hoad and the other members of the team received a ticker tape parade in Sydney after the Davis Cup win. The New York *Times* reported some months later that the USLTA, in desperation over America's Davis Cup losses to Australia, published a comic book to encourage more youngsters to play tennis.

Visitors to Sydney from other parts of the world were often taken to the Rosewall shop to see Ken's father at work there, the native Sydneyite host pointing out that this was where his son had started life, and it was not unusual to see in a Sydney newspaper a photograph of Ken helping his father behind the counter beneath hundreds of cans of food, some of them presumably Carnation.

Rosewall was listed as No. 2 for the year behind Trabert, ahead of Hoad, No. 3, by Edward C. Potter in *World Tennis* magazine.

To astute observers of the tennis scene another aspect of Rosewall's character emerged, demonstrating his interest in religion and his faith. A newspaper clipping of March 12, 1956, quoted Rosewall as saying he read the Bible daily, though due to tennis and travel he could not go to church often: 'The Bible gives me confidence, hope and courage—all of which are applicable to the great game of tennis.' This side of Ken's personality was keynoted again many years later when Bud Collins observed wisely, 'For Ken, tennis is a religion. To Rosewall, Nastase's behaviour on the court must be like a bad comedy act being brought into church.'

Meanwhile, at the beginning of 1956, his greatest year, Hoad was starting his run for the Grand Slam, winning over Ken in four sets in the Australian Championship final. The competition and pressure building up between Hoad and Rosewall at this time must have been fairly intense. Typical of pettiness in tennis was Hoad's saying that Larsen, Patty, Drobny, Sedgman and Savitt were better players than Rosewall, according to an interview with Hoad in the July

1956 issue of *World Tennis*. Rosewall did not enter the French Championship, and Hoad then won the French title, dismissing Sven Davidson in the final.

When Seixas lost to Rosewall in the Wimbledon semi-finals in 1956 in five sets, 6-3, 3-6, 6-8, 6-3, 7-5, Rosewall was praised for his comeback by the British press. Rosewall had been far behind in the match and had rallied, though it could be argued that Rosewall's comeback was only to be expected because of his domination over Seixas in earlier encounters. The English newspapers attacked Seixas for throwing his racket after the loss, shrugging off Rosewall's arm at net, putting his hands over his ears when the crowd applauded Rosewall, shouting at a linesman and yelling, 'Shut up' to the section of the crowd that booed him. This was Seixas' tenth loss to Rosewall in twelve matches, and the match provoked the *Daily Mirror* sportswriter Peter Wilson into one of the more absurd bits of sportswriting, if it can be called that: 'My hands are shaking, my heart is pumping, my voice is cracked as I try to write this story for you.'

When Rosewall and Hoad faced each other in the 1956 Wimbledon final, Hoad had already won the Australian and French tournaments that year. Rosewall still had the edge on him in major tournament victories, having taken the Australian twice, in 1955 and 1953, and the French in 1953. Hoad wrote in his autobiography that in the first set 'Rosewall was far more nervous than he normally had been in our matches.'

In the first set they reached 2-all. Then Hoad flailed three forehands into corners against Rosewall's serve. He had broken him, and the set was soon his.

The second set saw a Rosewall revival, Rosewall hitting a cross-court winner from outside the court, guiding lobs to the vicinity of the baseline, whipping passing shots around Hoad at net, to win 6-4.

The third set fell to Hoad, as Rosewall double-faulted and fell twice on the court, despite a beautiful stop-volley which helped him to hang on to 5-all, when Hoad broke him again.

In the fourth set Rosewall, behind two sets to one, confronting defeat, fired a backhand down the line in the second game and chopped a stop-volley in the fourth game, both games on Hoad's serve, both won by Rosewall. He now led 4-1, but Hoad hit a series of his pile-driving flat serves and Rosewall made more and more errors, and Hoad was the winner, 6-2, 4-6, 7-5, 6-4. Their conversation at the net after the last point went as follows:

'Bad luck, Ken.'

'You were too good for me today, Lew.'

The crowd had whistled in amazement at some of the points. The Centre Court was of course packed. But Hoad was now indisputably No. 1 in the amateur ranks, and he, not Rosewall, received the congratulations of Princess Margaret and Sir Anthony Eden and the warmer accolade of Australia's Prime Minister. Hoad wrote in his book published two years later that the way he beat Rosewall in the 1956 Wimbledon final was taking his serve as early as possible and hitting it hard.

Forest Hills '56

In a *World Tennis* magazine Popularity Poll at Forest Hills in 1956 Savitt was rated No. 1, Hoad No. 2, Seixas No. 3 and Rosewall No. 4. In the round of sixteen Rosewall typically lost the first set to 'Huge' Hugh Stewart, who was 6′ 5″ tall, before winning the second 9-7 and the remaining two easily. Then came one of the most famous matches in Forest Hills history.

Dick Savitt only played on weekends, preferring his job in the oil business to tournament tennis, to the surprise of other tennis stars. Rumour said that Savitt found the pressure of big matches too nerve-racking. He hadn't played at Forest Hills since 1952. He had won Wimbledon in 1951.

Savitt stayed back and made it difficult for Rosewall to come to net. Even if Rosewall guessed where the ball was going, Savitt hit his hard, heavy ball there anyway. Rosewall, advised by Hopman and aware of Savitt's lack of tournament play, drop-shotted and lobbed to tire Savitt out.

The big burly player was behind 4-6, 5-7, 3-4 and 0-40 on his serve, when he hit three aces, won the set 6-4, the next one, 10-8, and the crowd was in a frenzy of excitement. Rosewall, who hadn't won a major championship since the Australian in January 1955 and was now displaced in the public eye as the most promising Australian star or world star for that matter by Hoad, was about to be pushed further down in the world rankings.

Rosewall was so upset as Savitt made his comeback that he flung his racket to the ground. He also tossed balls over his head. The crowd was fiercely pro-Savitt.

But he had run Savitt all over the court, and in the fifth set, Savitt, out of training, collapsed, 1-6.

Ken recalls, 'I remember at the end of the fourth set or the beginning of the fifth a few boos or, more likely, a number of groans coming from the crowd when I took off my regular shoes and put on spikes. Similar to some matches of mine these days, where I'm the sentimental favourite, Dick was the popular one with the crowd, being a local player and coming out of semi-retirement. With his good ground strokes I was reluctant to come to net, but I was aware of his being slower afoot than me. He was a big man, and our games were not really similar. He used little spin, except on the second serve, whereas I hit the ball with more spin, particularly on the backhand.

'Dick was a nervous player for big matches. When he came to Australia in 1951 or 1950, he had a very bad time with foot-fault calls. The rule has changed, but in those days you had to keep one foot, in other words the same foot, on the ground all the time, but he would take a little step with his left foot and then swing the right one onto the court.

'Savitt hit a heavy ball because he followed straight through with a long swing, almost like a scoop. This gives the ball more weight as it's on the racket face longer, whereas when it's hit with a lot of wrist, which is the way Laver plays, it is a lighter ball as it's on the surface less time. His net game was not good, and I would draw him to net by hitting shots angled to the middle sides of the court and then pass him or lob him.'

Entering the finals against Lew Hoad, Rosewall looked beaten before the match began. According to *Time* magazine, one observer remarked, as Rosewall came on the court with the husky Hoad, 'He's a sure loser.' He lost the first set to Hoad.

By the end of the first set Rosewall's face had turned in-to a curious frown, gradually emerging into a muted expression—as Rosewall's emotions were never on the surface—of wonder. He had discovered on this day he could handle Hoad's service. He had discovered Hoad's net game was far from perfect. He noticed Hoad's overhead was bothered by the wind. In fact, Hoad's smashes were often downright sloppy.

He realized he would have to change tactics. Hoad was pounding in those hard flat serves which went by Rosewall like they'd been hit by a pile-driver, and Hoad was following his serve into net when Rosewall did get the ball back, and Hoad was taking the net on Rosewall's serve with his heavy topspin forehand and backhand.

Rosewall started to employ his careful strategy against Hoad, accuracy and speed, taking the net more and more often, throwing well-disguised drop-shots and tossing surprise lobs at Hoad, who scampered back to flail futilely at them. Rosewall struck the white chalk time after time with his long lightning drives.

So Rosewall, previously considered a backcourt player primarily, though he had recently been rushing the net a little more, utilizing his excellent volley, started to take the net against Hoad on his serve. Rosewall's fantastic speed enabled him to tear across the grass to volley Hoad's powerful returns. Rosewall punched the ball on the volley past Hoad for winner after winner. The score was 4-6, 6-2, 6-3, 6-3.

In the locker room of the West Side Tennis Club, Rosewall described his emotions after beating Hoad, thus depriving him of the championship and the Grand Slam. Ken remembers, 'I was choked.' Throughout their amateur days they had been roommates on tour.

The New York *Times* praised Rosewall for his patience after the match with autograph-seekers and cameramen, and mentioned that he borrowed a pocket mirror to comb his hair before being photographed, 'just in case my fiancée sees the pictures'.

Don Budge wrote in *Winning the Big Four* that Hoad lost to Rosewall at Forest Hills in 1956 because Rosewall had the advantage of a tough match against Savitt, who served and hit as hard as Hoad, while Hoad had an easy run to the final, and Hoad arrived in the U.S. late, playing only at Longwood and thus not having acclimatized.

I said, 'I have read that Don Budge helped you with your

serve at the West Side Tennis Club in the late afternoon
immediately after you won Forest Hills in 1956, and also when
you first came to New York at the Brooklyn Heights Casino
club on the pro tour against Gonzales.'

'Let's put it this way. I'm the sort of person who, if someone
comes up and gives advice, I listen, but I make up my own
mind later.'

After the Forest Hills tournament was over, *Time* called
Rosewall an 'old-fashioned champ', lauding his ground strokes,
net play and court strategy.

A sports columnist in a New York newspaper, Melvyn
Durslag, now well known in Los Angeles where he is a
sportswriter for the *Herald-Examiner,* wrote on September 19,
1956, one of the cleverest analyses of Rosewall's early character to be found among the thousands of pages written
about our hero (perhaps Mr. Durslag was somewhat similar to
Rosewall): 'Rosewall,' he said, 'gives one the impression he
would prefer not being interviewed. Rosewall carefully edits
his conversation and gives no information unnecessarily.'
Durslag quoted Clifford Sproule, the captain of the Australian
Davis Cup team that year, as saying, 'He's a terribly shy one.
He is bold only inside the court.' Durslag then extracted from
Sproule a marvellous story about Rosewall meeting the
president of the Carnation Milk Company in Los Angeles.
Rosewall, of course, was employed very part-time by their
Australian branch. When the head of the company said, 'What
are you doing down there, Ken?' Rosewall replied—probably
all too truthfully—'Oh, not much of anything.' Sproule then
told Durslag, 'I took him aside afterwards and said, "Son,
when you talk to your boss, you have to blast your horn a
little." ' Durslag then obtained an interesting quote from
Sproule to the effect that 'only children' did not usually make
good tennis players, becoming 'exasperated' when losing
matches, but that Rosewall was an exception. However,
Durslag decided that 'Rosewall's detachment from worldly
matters' might be due to being in love with Wilma, to whom he
had written a hundred letters in three months. Cliff Sproule,
also an Australian Davis Cup selector in the early fifties, said,
'He's a chess player on the court.'

By implication Kramer preferred Hoad's tennis as a box-office drawing card over Rosewall's, despite Rosewall's victory: 'In tennis the whole game is built around service.' He offered Hoad $100,000 to take on Pancho, but added, 'I'll be glad to put Rosewall on salary, but Hoad is the gate.' He did concede, though, 'Outside of service Rosewall has the best all-round game of any amateur.' Additionally explaining Kramer's attitude towards Hoad and Rosewall, Ned Chase says, 'Hoad also won what was then the world champion-ship—Wimbledon,' though I maintain that from the viewpoint of the American promoter, thinking of the potential U.S. box office, the U.S. Championship was equally if not more important, as witness Gonzales' turning pro in 1949 though he never won Wimbledon, and Schroeder, who had won Wimbledon in 1949, being unable to turn pro (though Kramer, who was a good friend of Schroeder's and Schroeder's coach during the match against Gonzales, had hoped he would be able to), because he lost to Gonzales at the 1949 Forest Hills tournament in the finals.

Referring to the frequent charges of secret payments made to amateurs in those days, Ken remembers, 'I never received under-the-counter payments because I was always with the Australian Davis Cup team, and my expenses were paid by the Australian Lawn Tennis Association.'

I said, 'Why does Hopman say that you and Hoad did not practise well against each other?'

'We were very competitive, beating each other in matches, and in practice you just can't do what you like. In practice you have to co-operate with the man on the other side of the net, but Hoad and I had built up such a habit of trying to defeat each other in matches that we could not abandon the habit in practice, when instead of trying to hit the ball so your opponent can't reach it you must often hit it just where he wants it so he can practise the stroke.'

Though Rosewall had some trouble with his serve, he and Hoad beat Vic Seixas and Sam Giammalva 1-6, 6-1, 7-5, 6-4 to win the Davis Cup in 1956. Rosewall played the forehand court despite his better backhand due to a shuffle in teams one year earlier. He had been dropped from the Davis Cup doubles in 1953 and 1955 in favour of Hartwig and had joined up with Fraser, at which point he took the forehand because Fraser was a lefty. This had the advantage of giving him extra practise on his less effective forehand. Hopman then rejoined Hoad and Rosewall, but allowed Rosewall to stay on the right to continue strengthening the forehand.

Potter ranked Hoad No. 1 and Rosewall No. 2, though this was before the end of the year. Tingay did the same. However, in the last few months of 1956 Rosewall overcame Hoad in three straight matches on the Australian circuit. The Forest Hills victory over Hoad proved to be one of the two or three most important in Ken's career. It led to the contract with Kramer.

3

Learning to be a Professional

The Australian newspapers called it 'The Wedding of the Year' and 'Doubles for Life'. They were on the front page of a leading woman's weekly magazine, looking like pretty dolls. Photographs show Wilma often wearing a suit and a pillbox hat in the days before the ceremony, looking pretty, slightly surprised and very happy. Ken was a model fiancé in his dark suit, pleasure on his face. His marriage was much more orthodox than the Hoads', who had eloped at Wimbledon about eighteen months earlier, forcing Hopman's reluctant consent. In a London registry office there had been only two witnesses present to the union of Jenny and Lew, and the honeymoon had been in a London hotel. Thus the marriage of Ken, the other 'twin', was an opportunity for Australia to celebrate this happy event with the proper approval of church, society and press, and perhaps more important, a chance for the Australian public, who had long followed the adventures of their two brilliant representatives, to at least participate in a minor way as approving spectators, which they had not been able to do with the Hoads. The Rosewalls took on added attraction as a model couple: the attractive, loving young bride and the hard-working, likeable and very successful young bridegroom.

As can be imagined, the wedding itself was a major affair. Police and church officials warned beforehand that they would not tolerate a demonstration similar to the nuptials of a Miss Australia in the same cathedral a few years earlier, when the crowd tore the bride's veil and jumped over the pews. Eleven hundred guests crowded into the church or stood outside in the cathedral grounds. Lew Hoad, Hopman, and the Premier of Queensland were there. The Australian Prime Minister, Mr. Menzies, sent a telegram. Rosewall, according to the paper, drank four glasses of water to calm his nerves and walked to the front of the altar twenty minutes early. Wilma blew a kiss to the crowds outside as she stepped from the car.

Rosewall had just turned pro. Significantly, Wilma told the press: 'I am happy with Ken and as long as he is happy to travel the world as a tennis professional I am happy to go too.' This firm support was to play an important role in his future rise to the top of the tennis world. Ken remembers twenty years later, 'We spent our honeymoon on the Gold Coast, an attractive beach area, and we often go back there. The Gold Coast, five hundred miles north of Sydney, fifty south of Brisbane, is a popular beach resort area, twenty or twenty-five miles long, for summer and winter vacations, as it's so much warmer there than the southern part of Australia. Promoters gave it that name to popularize it.'

Pancho Gonzales

Following their honeymoon, Ken began to prepare for his head-to-head tour with Gonzales. But first he spent half an hour in the locker room trying to persuade Hoad to turn pro with him. Ken remembers today, 'Kramer had tried very hard to get Lew at the end of '55 and realized Lew was not so interested at the end of '56. Also Lew and Jennifer, who were recently married, had a wonderful opportunity in that they had been asked to tour the world, playing in tournaments together, as amateurs. Kramer was said to be cunning and elusive and very skilled in pro tennis business, and many thought it would be better for Lew to turn pro later. I tried to persuade Lew it would be best for both of us to turn pro together. Lew was one of the best players, but he got a bit bored as an amateur after that, losing to people he shouldn't have; but then he signed the contract with Kramer just before Wimbledon and went out and won it for the second year running. He was able to get used to pro tennis, playing Kramer, Segura, Trabert and myself before facing Pancho Gonzales at the beginning of 1958.'

Rosewall's defection to the pro ranks at the end of 1956

caused attendance to drop to 7,000 for the finals of the Aussie Championship in a stadium holding 15,000. Explaining the difference between pro and amateur tennis, Segura said, 'The pros pay tax.' Rosewall practised with Dinny Pails, a former Aussie Davis Cupper and a pro of the early fifties. Pails said, 'He doesn't win matches with his serve, but he doesn't lose any either.' Gonzales announced on arrival, 'I'll beat Ken in three sets. I'll demoralize that little fella,' while complaining of a sore hand. 'The last time I saw Ken play I was not impressed. I have heard since that Rosewall attacks the net much more now.' They had a prodigious match, which Gonzales won 6-3, 3-6, 6-3, 1-6, 9-7. Rosewall was nervous in the first set but he won the next night 7-5, 6-4, 14-12.

Gonzales proceeded to win the next five matches, all on grass, though the scores were usually close.

After the first few matches against Pancho, Rosewall began to work on his serves. During one match, with Pancho leading two sets, 4-0, a fan yelled to Gonzales, 'Come on, Pancho, let him have a courtesy game.' But Gonzales said afterwards, 'Ken reacted very well. He doesn't say anything and he tries real hard.' Rosewall remembers, 'On my first tour against Gonzales, I felt like I was being thrown to the lions. . . . I have to class Gonzales a notch above Hoad, although the latter is the greatest of all time when he is on. There was an enormous difference between Gonzales and the amateurs of that year. His ground strokes were solid and his only weakness seemed to be return of serve. There was an incident every time Gonzales played.'

Incident at Adelaide

After trailing 7-1, Rosewall finally took another to make it 7-2. Then came the Adelaide match before 13,000 fans. In that morning's newspaper, Gonzales had declared Rosewall didn't have a chance. Gonzales had said, 'Rosewall is struggling all the time to keep the ball in play, let alone make passing shots. He's a great little guy but I'm going on beating him night after night.' The crowd was quiet during the first two sets. Pancho hit a series of aces, powerful serves which were impossible to return well followed by skilfully placed ground strokes and volleys. The score had reached 4-6, 4-6 when Ken came alive, beginning to make beautiful passing shots, cross-court dinks and brilliant volleys. The crowd started to ridicule Pancho, who was six feet three inches compared to Rosewall's five feet seven inches, reminding Gonzales of some of his remarks.

One spectator yelled after Rosewall won a brilliant point, 'Ken still struggling, eh, Pancho?'

Gonzales yelled to the heckler, 'Why don't you come down and have a go yourself.'

Another shouted, 'Hey, Pancho, you having trouble keeping the ball in play?' Gonzales shouted, 'Listen, horsehead, you're very brave hiding among five thousand people. Why don't you come down here where I can see you?'

Gonzales became angrier and angrier. Then Rosewall evened the match, winning the fourth set with a flowing cross-court. The third and fourth set scores had been 6-3, 9-7. The match was now even. The tension had risen to the point where the audience erupted into cheers for Rosewall mixed with catcalls at the American. Gonzales, losing his temper, hurled his racket at the microphone by the umpire's stand with such force that it bounced into the stands. Pandemonium broke loose.

After the crowd had calmed at the umpire's urging, the fifth set began. But between points the Aussies continued to jeer and stamp their feet at Pancho's scare tactics and histrionics. Rosewall played the finest tennis of his life, ripping through Pancho's game, winning 6-1. One report said that Gonzales had seemed to throw away the last set because of his rage, but Gonzales refuted this afterwards, saying, 'Rosewall's play in the fifth set was the best tennis I've ever faced.' It may be surmised that Gonzales, at twenty-nine feeling the first twinges of age, found himself under enormous pressure from Rosewall to maintain his position as No. 1. He explained why he knocked over the microphone when hurling the racket at the umpire's chair. 'The mike was the only thing I could hit that couldn't sue me.' Kramer, anxious to conciliate all sides but doubtless pleased at the large crowds, said placatingly, 'Pancho has been trying hard to maintain his best manners before these Australian crowds, but apparently he blew off about three weeks' steam tonight.'

The Adelaide match proved to be a turning point, and

Rosewall won the next match. He had won the last three. But fortunately for Pancho, the play on grass was over, and the tour would switch to the indoor surfaces of America.

Normally taciturn or shy with the press, Rosewall unburdened himself to an Australian cartoonist, Jim Russell, who was an old friend, before flying to the U.S.

With typical understatement he said, 'The conclusion I reached very quickly is that Gonzales is the best tennis player in the world.

'I had to alter my old baseline game to cope with Hoad's power last year. I'm using the same game against Gonzales. I try a flat first serve to his backhand, then a net rush, gambling on my reflexes. When I'm not serving, I concentrate on hitting them low and wide.'

His interviewer-friend thought conditions were going to be even more unfavourable for Rosewall when they arrived in the U.S. and started to play indoors.

Rosewall reflected, 'On canvas or boards the bounce is truer than on grass. That will help my ground strokes. Then the absence of wind will be a benefit because I can place my volleys more accurately.'

Russell said, evoking the general pessimism about Rosewall's chances, 'But honestly, Ken, aren't you getting discouraged?'

Rosewall answered, 'If I were still an amateur I would be, but now I know that if I am beaten tonight I can beat him tomorrow by improving whatever failed me. The one hundred matches are going to be like one hundred finals. I am not discouraged at all.'

Gonzales said later, 'I hold no grudge against the Aussies for cheering Rosewall over me. It's a perfectly natural thing. But I'm trying to get Kramer to arrange an exhibition in Mexico City. If Ken beats me there, they'll kill him!'

Although the headline attraction was Rosewall v. Gonzales on the head-to-head tour, the contest held almost every night also featured a preliminary match between Segura and Pails, who played in the doubles; and when the occasional pro tournament occurred, other stars such as Sedgman joined the group.

Even when he was not playing, Rosewall was mad about

tennis, watching the other players such as Sedgman, Pails and
Segura, occasionally exclaiming in his modest way, 'Hey,
those are good points.' Rosewall's forehand improved under
the pressure of professional tennis. One theory was that his
forehand was weaker because he was a natural left-hander.

Rosewall arrived in the U.S. for the tour against Gonzales
with one suitcase. Wilma accompanied him, saying, 'I make a
point of being there when Ken plays and only occasionally
miss a match.' For a few days she stayed in California with
Gloria Kramer, Jack's wife, to take a rest from the intense
pressure she and Ken had been under. As a former
stenographer from Brisbane, she must have found the
adaptation to the frenzied life of a pro tour even more difficult
than her husband, who at least had been in the glare of
publicity during amateur days, though always under the
protective umbrella of the Lawn Tennis Association of
Australia.

The opening match was in New York's Madison Square
Garden. But first there were promotional activities.

Rosewall looked dazed from the trans-Pacific continental
flight at a press luncheon in New York the day after he arrived.
Two days later he was to meet Gonzales.

He said, 'Gonzales' first serve is more consistent than
Hoad's, although Lew's is as hard, and Gonzales' second serve
is both more consistent and harder.'

'What are you going to do with all the money you make?'

'Save it.'

Rosewall played TV star Steve Allen in a benefit to raise
money for Art Larsen, still an invalid from his motorcycle
accident. Allen took one half-hour lesson, his first, before
facing Rosewall.

Rosewall had never played on indoor courts before except
once at The Queen's Club in London and a few hours' practice
on another occasion at the Brooklyn Heights Casino Club.
Before the big match, he practised his serve with Don Budge in
the looming, cavernous court at the Heights Casino.

Touts got $15 to $20 a ticket for the pro opening between
Rosewall and Gonzales. There were 11,500 at Madison Square
Garden—a good turnout. Rosewall was so bothered by the
indoor court of canvas stretched over the ice for the first match

that he often hit the ball on the wrong foot. Even though it lasted only an hour, it was a curious contest. Gonzales was suffering from a cyst in his racket hand and only served at three-quarters speed, with the result that Rosewall served the only aces, four in all. Gonzales pushed the ball in rallies rather than stroked it, but his vast experience with indoor conditions was too much for Rosewall, and he won 6-2, 6-4, 6-2, exploiting Rosewall's forehand. Ken committed most of his 59 errors on the right side, while Gonzales erred 35 times. But it was to be a lesson for Rosewall, and from then on he cut down on his backswing on the forehand, eliminating much of its hook.

Ken remembers, 'On the U.S. circuit in those days almost all the matches were played with canvas laid over wood or ice and pulled tight with block and tackle. This sort of surface was very good for Gonzales' game. Although he usually served to my backhand on our head-to-head in 1957, one of his best serves was swung wide to my forehand, particularly in the No. 1 or deuce court. I didn't have the strength to pull it cross-court, whereas players like Hoad and Sedgman could do this and thus did better against Gonzales on the indoor surface, where he was almost unbeatable then. At the same time Jack Kramer, when he beat Gonzales in 1949 on their tour, with his consistent serve, particularly the second one, did very well with the serve swung wide to Pancho's forehand.'

Budge said sadly after Rosewall's loss to Gonzales in three sets, 'Rosewall is a beautiful player, but it will be a rough go for him on the American tour. Rosewall's serve seemed quite a bit better in our practice session, but not as good against Gonzales. He reverted back to his earlier form.' Rosewall also continued to suffer from a type of eczema that causes bad rashes.

A heckler repeatedly criticized Gonzales at Boston Garden. Gonzales said, 'You're entitled to your opinions, but I think you should keep them to yourself, so will you please shut up?'

Gonzales missed an easy net shot. The man yelled again.

Gonzales tossed a ball to hit it hard at the man, but held himself back momentarily and then struck it softly at the spectator. The man got up to leave and Gonzales ran after him, seizing him by the collar. A basketball player, Dick Hemric, standing nearby, walked over. 'You're not going to hit him, are you, Pancho?' 'No, I just wanted to let him know he wasn't an ideal spectator.'

Gonzales won 6-2, 5-7, 24-22.

By the end of May 1957, playing across America in numerous towns and cities, one night here and another there, going to bed late, driving on or flying to the next auditorium and hotel, Rosewall was breaking even with Gonzales in their matches. But Pancho had built up too big a lead in their earlier battles, and the final score stood at 50-25. He had won the head-to-head contest for supremacy. It was to be a temporarily costly loss for Rosewall, for it meant that he would not be asked to play the Mexican-American in the next tour.

I asked Ken, 'Who were the most sportsmanlike players?'

'All the Australian players I've known have been sportsmanlike, including Lew Hoad, who would get upset at himself but not at the crowd, the umpires or me. Mark Cox was, too. Jimmy Connors has improved a lot in the last year.'

'Who were the least sportsmanlike?'

Avoiding a direct answer, Ken observed, 'Connors' earlier troubles stemmed from Nastase, who got them from Tiriac.'

Returning to our discussion of the 1957 tour against Gonzales, Ken still remembers it vividly:

'When I first played Gonzales, I played an attacking game coming into net, which was the way he played. Gonzales' backhand was not that strong. He undercut it and hit it a little behind. So you'd try to play a shot deep to it. But he was always thinking one shot ahead while some players who hit a shot think it's going to be a winner and don't move any more. He liked to hit his backhand down the line and I would come in for the volley, but he was already moving cross-court. He placed his ground strokes not necessarily by trying to hit a winner but to set up the next shot.

'I tried to ignore his outbursts on the court, such as when he smashed his racket against the metal rod holding the microphone and broke the rod in half. There was a terrific uproar before the crowd of 14,000 in Adelaide. In Boston Garden he seized the lapels of the Boston Garden physician, Dr. Edward R. Brown. He died recently. He nearly died then, too. It was noticeable Gonzales' game would pick up after these explosions and my game would go off a little, losing concentration.

'I think Gonzales may have tried to physically intimidate me, frighten me, by his violence on the first pro tour. But he did it with everyone. He was naturally like that, and I don't think he did it deliberately. One day he could be charming, even to other players' wives, and the next he wouldn't give you the time of day.'

I said, 'It was a myth he ever retired. He would announce it and then be playing a month or two or three months later.'

'He's not the first to do that. He did play less though in '62 and '63, when he took that job in the Bahamas. But he left it in '64. He couldn't do anything else, and he needed the money. So he rejoined the pro tour.'

'Do you feel he was more explosive in his matches with you because you were short compared to him and he figured he had a better chance of scaring you?'

'It could be. There was some pushing and shoving with other players, though he never pushed me. He and Trabert were always at each other. He never tried anything with Hoad. Lew was very strong. Gonzales always looked as though he was going to fight, but I don't think he ever wanted to.'

'Why in an interview with him in about 1970 was he rating you below other stars, many of whom you were clearly superior to?'

'I think if you beat a man a lot, you tend to have a low opinion of his game, even if he is a very good player and beats about everyone else. I think that's why he said it.' He was referring to Gonzales' 2-to-1 victory in their tour.

'Do you think he harboured an old grudge because you were the one who ended his dominance?'

'I and others did.'

'Why do you think he gives you some credit such as praising your training habits and your always being in position for the ball?'

'He has to give me *some* credit,' he said with a laugh. 'He always did recognize my ability to move.'

Rosewall's first notable victory as a pro came at Wembley, in June 1957. At Wembley Gonzales first showed slight signs of slipping, losing to ageing Jack Kramer in a play-off match for third place 1-6, 6-4, 6-4. Rosewall beat J. Iemetti of France 6-1, 6-1 in the first round. He beat Peter Cawthorn 6-2, 6-1 in the second round. Rosewall beat Kramer in the semis 6-1, 6-3, 6-2, while in the other semi Segura beat Gonzales 11-9, 12-10, 6-4.

Rosewall's serve and net game had improved. He split the first four sets with Segura in the final. In the latter stages, Segura suffered from leg and hand cramps, Rosewall hit aces and cunning passing shots. He led 3-0 in the fifth. Segura came up to 4-4 before Rosewall won. Rosewall, holding the trophy representing his first big tournament win as a pro, looked very happy.

Around this time Vic Seixas, still an amateur, perhaps reflecting relief that he no longer had to contend with Rosewall, conceded just how good a player he was. Seixas said, 'He's the toughest opponent I've ever faced. He may not be the best tennis player I've faced, but his style gives me the most trouble.' Meanwhile, Lew Hoad had failed to win the Australian and French tournaments in 1957. His back was starting to trouble him. But he made a supreme effort and took Wimbledon again, beating Ashley Cooper 6-2, 6-1, 6-2 and promptly accepting Kramer's offer of $125,000. On this occasion, Kramer and his advisers finally realized that the top amateur stood little chance against a No. 1 pro such as Gonzales, and needed months of acclimatization to professional standards before starting on the head-to-head tour.

This meant a series of round-robin matches, which gave Rosewall a chance to continue to compete with the other top stars. Rosewall recalls a match against Hoad in Europe when he overheard Segura in the locker room coaching Hoad on how to beat him. When he realized he had been overheard by Rosewall, Segura sheepishly came over and coached Rosewall on how to beat Hoad. Rosewall beat Hoad fairly easily in their encounters, and significantly, in a round-robin at Forest Hills, he tied Gonzales 5-1 in victories; however, he lost first place as Pancho had beaten him in a close battle in their one match.

Meanwhile, in August that same year, Ken's mother, Vera, a rather pretty woman with dark hair, who had played an important role in inspiring him to reach the top of the tennis world, broke her hip playing tennis on a Sydney court. Ken returned to Sydney and visited her often during her recuperation.

Ken remembers his matches with the other players during the remainder of the year. 'I first played Jack Kramer in 1957. He hadn't really played competitively since 1953, when he beat Sedgman on the tour. You could see he had been very good. But even then he was having back trouble and took a lot of pills to relieve it. Then after our tour Gonzales was tired from playing in Europe, the Middle and Far East, and America and Australia, and in one of his moods decided he wanted to race cars. So Kramer worked himself into shape in South America and we had a tour of South Africa, Rhodesia and Kenya, with Kramer substituting for Pancho, me, Hoad and Segura. My wife came along. We flew in a rattle-trap two-engine chartered plane which had five seats plus one by the pilot. The promoter came with us. The lightest of the players had to sit up front with the pilot. It was usually me. We played twenty matches in twenty-one days, travelling in the morning, playing in the afternoon.

'I only lost to Kramer twice, but you could see what a great player he was. He couldn't move that well with his physical problems, but his anticipation was very good and he was a great competitor. His second serve was very good, with a lot of kick and spin. He could put it within a foot of where he wanted to. Also when Kramer sliced his forehand, usually on an approach shot as he came to net, he would add side spin to the ball—along with the slice—so that the ball moved away from one disconcertingly, flying out toward the side line. He was a master of this shot. That year I played from January 15th to December 21st.

'Kramer was a great competitor and always wanted to win, and this was how he beat Riggs, Gonzales and Segura, though Sedgman came the closest on their tour, say 56 to 44. Even when he filled in on the pro tour in 1957 and we were playing in Timbuctoo, a thousand miles from anywhere, a match that meant nothing in a place nobody'd heard of, he had that pride and wanted to win.

'Frank Sedgman had a very good all-round game. His only weakness, a minor one, was his second serve, which with its topspin bounced high, and occasionally he would hit it short, and I was good at hitting it cross-court. But he was very quick at coming in and getting to the return of serve.'

Ken said, 'The first year of travelling with me on tour nearly killed Wilma, and it took us a long time to recover from that. The loneliness of touring is always a problem. You write letters, but we've always tried to break up the trips. I try to be away no more than six or eight weeks, and if it's longer Wilma will often fly out to join me. The longest was four months in 1963, when Laver turned pro. Wilma then flew to California, where we took a vacation for two or three weeks. I've seen less of the two boys. Their grandparents—the Rosewalls and the McIvers—took care of them in the early days when Wilma joined me. Recently a good friend of Wilma's comes over and lives in the house.

'In 1957 we also played in the Middle East, Far East, including Singapore and Hong Kong, plus about twenty matches in Australia. Kramer left during the Asian part of it to return to the U.S., to promote the upcoming Hoad-Gonzales American tour, and Frank Sedgman replaced him. But Kramer seemed to worry Lew a lot when he played, though Lew played Segura and me much more. Sometimes among stars this happens, where one player's style bothers another. Though Lew won some matches off Jack, I'd say, if you go back to the records, that Kramer had a good record against Lew.'

By the end of the year, Rosewall and Hoad were tied for first place in wins on the pro tour with Kramer and Segura before Hoad began his tour against Gonzales. Rosewall had grossed over $100,000 for 1957.

Hoad in the Limelight

But Hoad was about to be launched on the highly publicized head-to-head tour against Pancho.

'Were you depressed after losing to Gonzales in the pro tour?'

'No. It was my first year as a pro. Kramer offered me the fill-in as No. 3 or 4 man, but I did not want that, as I wanted to have a chance to compete for the top and I knew I could play in pro tournaments.'

However, there were very few pro tournaments in those days outside the major three at London, Paris and in the U.S. And Rosewall knew the fate that had befallen Sedgman, who, after losing to Gonzales in 1954, had not only never been in the limelight again, but had been able to play only intermittently. At one point, Sedgman 'worked in his "own" gym—as a physical education instructor.' Rosewall said, 'I had three months at home with Wilma.'

Hoad started his furious encounters with Gonzales. Rosewall remained in Sydney. While Kramer was guiding his two antagonists through Australia, in a dispute between Kramer and Hopman, Kramer said, 'Rosewall should have been a net rusher all his life. He is one now and he is a better player. He has a better serve, too.' Meanwhile Hoad was starting to take a slight lead over Pancho, but then he hurt his back again. Then the pendulum swung the other way, and Gonzales went ahead.

The other players were surprised and amused at Hoad's behaviour in his close battle with Gonzales. After falling behind in number of wins, Gonzales caught up and then went ahead! There was a five-day vacation in New York. Hoad slept until 4 P.M. the first day. The second he went to three movies in a row. The third he mostly shopped and went to Toots Shor's in the evening. The fourth day, 'I relaxed,' he said. He made one tennis date and cancelled it. But finally his back gave out for good, and the head-to-head matches had to be cancelled. Hoad returned to Sydney to recuperate.

Rosewall was summoned by Kramer to join a round-robin tour.

4

The Peak

By the beginning of 1959 Rosewall's hard work on his game, persistence, regular living habits and dedication to his craft were beginning to pay off. A New York *Times* 'fact sheet', used by the sports department for background information, showed that 'in 1959 he won five of seven tournament matches against Gonzales'. And the newspaper clippings in the files of the *Sunday Times* state that Rosewall beat Gonzales in five of seven tournaments in 1959.

Ken says, 'In 1959 I won more matches than Gonzales over all the others, including him, but Gonzales was listed as No. 1 by the Kramer office, as the American tour that year was Gonzales, Hoad, Mal Anderson and Ashley Cooper. Hoad was more of a drawing card than me, which was why he was invited, and there were no records kept of the pros for the year except what the Kramer office put out.

'Ashley Cooper and Mal Anderson turned pro at the same time in 1959. They were then a step ahead of Neale Fraser and Roy Emerson. Ashley got married at the same time as he turned pro, and his wife, who went with him on the tours, didn't like the life. I had a much better record against him. He developed arm trouble, and the only time we played doubles together he was in considerable pain. He stopped in London to have it analysed, then went home to Brisbane.

'Ashley Cooper and Roy Emerson, who were the same age, toured the world as juniors in 1954, getting the competition against top foreign players young Australians need. Cooper was a fanatic on conditioning and worked hard. He had a solid game without flexibility—very good ground strokes and serve, a fair to medium volley unlike a sensational net game such as Laver and Hoad, but when he played a particular style he played solidly. He was at the peak of his game as an amateur from '57 till he turned pro at the beginning of '59 and had the most consistent game of the amateurs with the record to prove it. When he turned pro, other players exploited his lack of manoeuvrability at net and his low volley. He had a lot of physical problems with his back and did not really play much after '62. Now he's in the tennis-court construction business and also has an interest in a cattle property, has four daughters and is very happy.'

Although Rosewall could not, of course, play amateurs officially, he sometimes practised with them. He remembers, 'Neale Fraser had a very good first serve with a wonderful action, but his trouble was his backhand. Bob Mark, one of the bad boys of Australian tennis who was an exceptionally talented player but with a lazy attitude, and who now lives in Jo'burg and is almost as fat as a beer barrel, was on the Davis Cup team with Fraser in 1959 and did nothing but hit hard serves to Fraser's backhand in practice, and that was one of the reasons Fraser and Australia won the Cup from the U.S.

'Chuck McKinley [who won Wimbledon in 1963] was a very aggressive player, particularly on his forehand, and had one of the best lobs for a small man. He's done well in business through the contacts he made as a tennis star. He was a stocky, chunky man and moved very fast. I never played him.

'Everyone thinks the Grand Prix of tennis began recently, but we started it in 1959 with a tour of Europe for a Grand Prix of £1,000 with Sedgman, Trabert, Hoad and I competing. I beat everyone, but Trabert and Hoad sort of lost interest, and Sedgman beat Trabert nine times without a loss and so had one more victory than me. My record against Sedgman in the Grand Prix was five wins to four losses.'

The first Grand Prix also showed statistics in tennis, like other activities, can prove anything; Sedgman, because of his fantastic streak against Trabert, could be regarded as champion pro on the basis of the Grand Prix, though Rosewall was the better player by then than either he or Gonzales. Sedgman won the prize, but Rosewall was No. 1 over everyone on that particular tour. On a pro tour of that year Ken was described as a 'loner'.

On May 9, 1959, Ken and Wilma had their first child, a son named Brett, who was born in Sydney.

As the year came to the end, Kramer was starting to tire of being a promoter. He said he wanted to give up promoting because Ken remembers, 'Gonzales refused to go out of the U.S., except occasionally. Gonzales was suspended by Kramer for ten months for refusing to go to the French Championship in Paris, thus costing himself as much as $50,000.' In the September 1959 issue of *World Tennis* Gonzales was also reported to be in need of glasses. Perhaps the sight of Rosewall across the net, and to a lesser extent of Hoad, was blurring his vision.

This subtle shift in the domination of professional tennis from the Americans to the Australians may have prompted Kramer, nearing the end of his role as a promoter, to unburden himself of his views on Rosewall and Hoad. Life with Gonzales had undoubtedly not been easy, either, as he was paying Kramer back for not having been allowed to play in the head-to-head tours of the early fifties, after losing to Kramer in their 1949 head-to-head series, and for the tour that started in 1956 when Gonzales was paid $15,000 and Trabert $100,000.

Kramer said, 'When Hoad and Rosewall meet, it's always a grudge match, but I don't think the boys would be keen to have the public know. That's why I like to watch Hoad and Rosewall more than anyone else. They've really got it in for each other. Part of the reason is that Hoad gets all keyed up for the grudge match and shows it a little, but Rosewall conceals it and acts almost indifferent. This annoys Lew, who thinks Ken is putting on a "little Lord Fauntleroy" act.'

However, Rosewall and Hoad signed with Kramer for seven years. Nevertheless, within two years Kramer finally withdrew completely from promoting, to be replaced by a players' association. Trabert, who was playing less and less, acted first as Kramer's representative from a Paris office, and then became executive director of the players' group.

Though the best evidence seems to indicate that Rosewall was the outstanding player for 1959, slight confusion over statistics still seems to surround that year. Besides the New

York *Times,* the *Sunday Times* files state that Rosewall was
the dominant pro from 1959 to 1964. However, Mal Anderson,
in *World Tennis,* said that for 1959 Kramer established a point
system with 7 for first, 4 for second, 3 for third, 2 for fourth
and 1 for fifth and sixth over 14 tourneys, and Hoad was 1,
Gonzales 2, and Rosewall 3, Sedgman 4, Trabert 5, Anderson
6, Segura 7 and Cooper 8. Conflicting with Anderson's remarks
above, J.D.H. (Julius Heldman), in *World Tennis,* wrote that
Hoad never won a tour from Gonzales. These discrepancies
may be partly explained by the fact that Rosewall did not
participate in the American tour with Anderson-Hoad-
Gonzales-Cooper. Gonzales, of course, was still claiming he
was top banana as late as 1963. This uncertainty over who
really won what, and how much weight should be given to each
contest, and who did or did not play explains why the three
major pro championships—London, Paris and the U.S.—are
the only reliable measuring stick.

Paris and London

By the early part of 1960 Rosewall was described as the
'form horse' of a minor pro tournament in Australia, featuring
Rosewall, Hoad, Segura, Sedgman, Anderson and Olmedo,
though Hoad won this particular tourney, defeating Rosewall
in the finals 6-3, 10-8, 4-6, 15-13. At the two successive big pro
tournaments, the first starting September 18 in Paris, the
second September 24 in London, Rosewall was seeded first.

At Roland Garros Rosewall beat Kurt Nielsen, his old
nemesis in amateur days, in four sets in the first round. He
beat Anderson in three sets in the quarter-finals. He beat
Sedgman in four in the semi-finals. Hoad had been away from
tennis for a few months because of his bad back. Hoad's
handsome face had changed a lot after his spinal trouble and
three years of pro tennis, becoming heavier and older. Rosewall
beat Hoad 6-2, 2-6, 6-2, 6-1, in the final of the French
Championship.

Watching a film in 1975 of Rosewall playing Hoad in the
finals in Paris in 1960, I could see the strength and precision of
Ken's youth combined with the maturity of years of top
competition. On first viewing the five-minute BBC film, one

realizes how machinelike and yet how very good his play was. *He simply made no errors.* Of course, opinions on tennis players vary exceedingly. The editor of this book, Ned Chase, an intensive student and observer of tennis since the 1930's, says this film clip of the 1960 Paris final was 'a selected stretch that omits any Rosewall error'. However, I would reply that Rosewall did win this final; the editors of the BBC, though possibly mistaken, felt it was a film representative of the final; and most of the records of that period say that Rosewall was No. 1 in the world, including, of course, superiority over Hoad, a view also held by Jack Kramer, as will be shown later in this book.

Rosewall was fantastic in his length, the steady fast speed he gave to the ball, the furious pattern of his little legs, ankles, and shoes as he dashed like a marionette around the court. The accuracy was of course unsurpassed. Even the serve was swift and deadly in its placement. He could have played the top of today's players—Connors, Newcombe—equally and possibly better, even taking into account how the game improves from decade to decade. By inverse comparison this gives one an idea of how superior he was to the other players of the period.

This opinion of mine is a controversial one. Many would disagree. Chase, who greatly admires Rosewall's incomparable record, nonetheless replies, 'Not so. Gonzales and Sedgman were at least as impressive then.' To which I answer, 'Why then was Rosewall seeded No. 1 on the previously mentioned pro tour and why did he win the major pro championships?'

On the film even Hoad looked like a frustrated bear by comparison. There was also something mysterious about Rosewall's skill, it was so good. It had a touch of the unreal, the magical, the unworldly. If one watches old films of Sir Norman Brooke, for example, one realizes the players of that time would not have stood a chance against today's stars. But Chase says, 'That is true of Brooke, from a distant era, but Budge and Tilden at their top could play anyone, including the best of today's stars, and stay with them. Even when he was in his decline in the late 1940's, Budge was a match for Kramer, and Kramer was the dominant world champion in the early fifties and a link to the present generation of stars. And yet Rosewall fifteen years ago would, I think, have beaten Connors.'

One also notices a more boyish quality about the 1960 Rosewall than the 1975 one. He seemed almost embarrassed to have beaten Hoad, but still happy to have done it. It was a business, and he left the court quickly. Embarrassment after an important victory, regardless of his opponent, seems a typical Rosewall characteristic. The applause of the crowd was steady, loud and appreciative, admiring of the quality of the tennis, contrary to reports that the pros were too mechanical, businesslike and uninspired to be worth watching.

Observing Rosewall play was seeing a form of beauty, continuous action raised to a high art. Hoad was a handmaiden in this transformation, a very talented player, but Rosewall was the artist, and like all beauty it was his performance which gave the greatest satisfaction. One could admire the brute force which Hoad used to belt the ball, his determined power as he drove deep to come in, and yet the magician was too brilliant and hit it back with effortless ease past him.

Judgements on tennis players are often subjective, and my view of Rosewall is, of course, a personal one affected by my prejudices and opinions, a question of taste. Holding a contrary and equally valid opinion, Chase observes, 'This is just not fair. Hoad was physically the more impressive in the grace and overwhelming power of his shots, though his backhand was not the supreme shot Rosewall's is. Hoad was the visual paragon, Rosewall the brain.'

Another noticeable factor in the 1960 Rosewall was the superb delivery of his forehand, usually noted for being his weaker side. Stroke after stroke was hit with a crisp, steady powerful follow-through, the ball snapping off the racket and pinpointing to where he wanted it. There was an interesting difference between Rosewall's forehand in 1960 and the way he stroked his forehand as an amateur. Before turning pro he hit his forehand very slightly late, and in fact this same slight flaw often appears in his forehand today, but in 1960 Rosewall struck it perfectly flat and on time.

Hoad, a relatively graceful player, looked clumsy by comparison to Rosewall, and yet one could not help admiring the calm acceptance of defeat, as if he knew he was up against a superior force and was quietly going to go along with it, easily, pleasantly and normally. Chase, on the other hand, argues that Hoad, 'never clumsy' in his stroke execution, was 'brutally powerful, but never never awkward'.

Moving on to London for the Wembley tournament, Rosewall beat Peter Cawthorn 6-3, 6-2. Then he beat Trabert 6-4, 6-3. Rosewall remarks, 'I beat Trabert usually in the early 1960's, but he wasn't playing full-time, as he was also an administrator, running our tours in America and Europe from a Paris office.'

In the semi-finals Rosewall beat Olmedo 6-0, 6-0, 6-3. Olmedo had led the U.S. to a Davis Cup victory over Australia in 1958 and won the Australian and Wimbledon championships in 1959. Rosewall says, 'Alex Olmedo had a very good record before he turned pro, but he had a wristy forehand volley. His backhand was strictly defensive.'

In the finals Rosewall faced Segura. The *Times* described the match as follows: 'The opening two sets of the singles were full of magic. The smoke haze of a packed house hung eerily over the scene, given a yellow tinge by the battery of 60 arc lamps under the dome of the hall. This might have been some gigantic cabaret, or the performance of a symphony orchestra as the crowd was carried away by some of the rallies.' The spectators supported the underdog Segura, aged forty, but Rosewall's glorious backhand and exact lobbing outplayed and wore Pancho down. Even at the end Pancho, exhausted, was entertaining the crowd by pointing the racket like a rifle at shots passing by him. Rosewall defeated Segura 5-7, 8-6, 6-1, 6-3.

Ken remarks, 'Segura was a very good player at thirty-six when I first played him in 1957. He was much better in his mid-thirties than earlier, when he was in his twenties. His game was like mine. He was still winning a few pro tournaments in his early forties. He had a terrific two-handed forehand, which I tried to stay away from, as he could lob it, dink it, top-spin it, pass one, concealing his action right up to playing it. But his backhand was not that strong, and I would attack it, coming in on it.

'Our games were quite similar—good touch, few errors, quickness, similar lob and serve. We had no real weaknesses, and we could cover up our serves with our very good other shots. His only drawback was the backhand, but he was the other leading player who was the great exponent of the lob. Of course, he had a very unorthodox game with his two-handed style.'

These triumphs by Rosewall meant eight matches in less than two weeks, all but two of them the best of five-set affairs. Though Rosewall's victories were given considerable publicity in the British and French papers, ironically the only description of Rosewall in *World Tennis,* an American magazine, after these remarkable victories establishing him as the world's best, was that his play was 'accurate'.

Rosewall was liked by the other players, but he was not close to most of them. This relative isolation was not helped by the fact that he was beating them all regularly, though the No. 1 player on a team is not always a man apart. Still, domination does in a sense produce distance, and Gonzales was far better liked before and after he was the champion. As regards his feelings about Hoad, Rosewall said, 'Lew is happy-go-lucky, friendly and easy to get along with.' Julie Heldman said Hoad's casual, easygoing attitude made him popular: 'One player, contrasting Lew with another famous professional, said of the latter that he would dive in front of a truck for a nickel, whereas Lew would not cross the street for $100,000 if he weren't in the mood.' Was Rosewall or Gonzales the other famous pro?

An image of Rosewall during the pro years when he was No. 1 was of him lying alone on a bench in the locker room before a match, a towel over his eyes, avoiding the noise of talk and other players, resting quietly.

Despite his unique position, Ken was an active participant and supporter of the interests of the group as a whole, unlike Gonzales, becoming treasurer of the players' association, joining in business ventures with the other athletes.

Ken remembers, 'I bought a nice old hotel on an island off Melbourne with Sedgman and Hoad and several of the American players, though the Americans have sold out now. Then, with some partners, we own some land on the Gold Coast, which is being developed, we hope. It brings in some income from a gravel mining company to pay some of the costs and taxes. And with a group of tennis players I own a sixth of another block of land. John Newcombe, Tony Roche, Fred

Stolle, Owen Davidson and Roy Emerson are the other owners. It's gone up in value as it's a large acreage in the Gold Coast area outside of Birley Heads, and you can't find large blocks any more, and the region is expanding. We hope to start a sports complex there, perhaps a tennis village. It's only a mile from the beach.

'I wish I'd never been in the stock market. Many millions of investors have had similar experiences recently. I've had professional advice, but the recession has caused problems in most holdings on the stock market, of which I've had some.

'I always travel economy class, and over the years it's saved my family a lot of money. I read best-sellers, mysteries, watch the movies, sleep, play cards with the other tennis players, if there are any.'

Though professional tennis was gradually expanding in popularity and prize money, there were constant problems. One difficulty was obtaining publicity to boost attendance. A gimmick in one tournament was the sight of Eddie Alloo (a good German player of the second echelon) wearing a hood over his face, pretending to be a mystery pro.

Another difficulty was Hopman. Hopman said Rosewall was the only pro with a chance of winning the amateur title, though all the pros were not playing as well as they had as amateurs. Rosewall wrote in an article published during that period: 'Harry has been kind in many ways, but I find him hard to understand. None of the Aussies as amateurs or pros ever openly criticized Hopman or criticized his coaching ability. But after we turned professional, we dropped out of his life. Occasionally he would say in the papers that we were better players in the amateurs. When we played a pro tournament he never came over to say hello or shake hands. It was as though Mal Anderson, Ashley Cooper, Frank Sedgman, Mervyn Rose, Rex Hartwig, Lew Hoad and myself never existed.'

Today Rosewall remembers, 'We never had a chance to answer Hopman back, whereas he had his column in his newspaper. I think for Harry Hopman to say the pros were better players as amateurs is, to say the least, quite a long way from being accurate. I think his view stemmed from his very successful captaincy of the Davis Cup, when all the top Australian players at one time or another were under his control or management, and his feeling they could not be so good when they left him. But he was the only Australian tennis critic to hold this view. Of course, nowadays, with tennis exploding, young players have every incentive, and perhaps for the pros then there was slightly less incentive; but every pro in those days improved as a player from the competition and the feeling of being a good competitor and doing a good job for the pro game.'

Then there were the occasional hazards of unappreciative fans. In the final of a professional tournament in Tokyo in November 1960, Rosewall lost to Hoad in five exhausting sets under bright sun. Back in the locker room both players were recuperating when a middle-aged Australian sauntered in, saying, 'That was a great match. Too bad it wasn't for real.' Rosewall, his head and shoulders swathed in towels, said, 'If I was big and strong enough, I'd get off this bench now and . . .'

Meanwhile, furious battles on court continued to surface in different forms off court. Kramer sued Gonzales for skipping a tournament in Melbourne and banned him from one in Tuscaloosa and another in Cleveland, but Gonzales went ahead and played in Tuscaloosa anyway. Gonzales announced his 'retirement' after Tuscaloosa. According to Will Grimsley, 'In a limited tour in 1960, Gonzales lost fewer matches than ever before in two-night tournament stands against Rosewall, Segura and Olmedo.' Gonzales said that 50 percent of all points were won by the serve, but that Rosewall was an exception, winning only one point a game on his serve, the remainder by ground strokes and volleys.

Rosewall became treasurer of the first International Professional Tennis Players Association 'because he is so good at watching the dough', according to Trabert.

Hoad broke his foot playing Gonzales in Paris on March 4th, 1961. The local doctor said it wasn't broken, but it continued to bother him and three weeks later a new set of X-rays confirmed a London doctor's opinion that it was broken.

Rosewall was at the peak of his form. His old rivals were falling by the wayside. Gonzales, who was clearly ageing, had not been undisputed No. 1 since 1958 and had definitely ceded his crown to Rosewall at the beginning of 1960, if not earlier. Poor Segura, who had laboured so long in Pancho's shadow, was even older. Hoad had had recurrent back problems from his power game and slightly stiff upright posture on the court. Then he broke his foot.

In Paris on clay in September 1961, Rosewall whipped Haillet 6-1, 6-4, 6-3. He won over Cooper 6-2, 5-7, 4-6, 6-4, 6-2. Segura fell to Rosewall 4-6, 6-1, 6-4, 7-5.

Winning Over Gonzales

In the final against Gonzales Rosewall lost the first set 2-6. A great ageing player can often win the first and second before his legs give out. Gonzales was so angry that he often slammed the ball hard enough at net to bounce it into the stands. Besides his usual arguments with linesmen, he shouted 'please' 'with such venom' to the umpire, demanding that he wait for the linesman's call. Rosewall, for his part, aware of the implications of the match, talked to himself repeatedly, slapping himself on the thigh. The New York *Times* reporter, a trifle melodramatic in his report, after he had won the second set 6-4 and the third 6-3, described Rosewall's 'boyish' determination. At the intermission, Rosewall sipped tea and chatted with the other players in the locker room while the once-great Gonzales wisely brooded alone in the cool shade of the runway.

By the fourth set Gonzales was physically exhausted. His first serves started to hit the net, his second becoming shorter and shorter. Rosewall played brilliantly, slashing perfect placements from front- and backcourt like a machine with divine inspiration, as fast as lightning, as deadly for the opening as a cobra. The final score was 2-6, 6-4, 6-3, 8-6. The weather was very hot on the red clay courts before an almost sell-out crowd that supported Ken, and Pancho's temper and histrionics matched the heat, including glaring at Rosewall between points. The match lasted three and a half hours. The next day the New York *Times* reported in its headline and sub-headline, 'ROSEWALL CONQUERS GONZALES IN 4-SET TENNIS FINAL AT PARIS—Aussie Captures World Pro Title—American Fades After Strong Start.'

But in London the heat would not be a problem for Gonzales, the court inside at Wembley, English late summer weather

French Professional Championship—1961

Rosewall
Haillet
Rosewall
6-1, 6-4, 6-3

Cooper
Remy
Cooper
6-2, 6-3, 6-1

Rosewall 6-2,
5-7, 4-6, 6-4, 6-2

Segura
Davies
Segura
6-1, 6-4, 6-3

Ayala
Hoad
Ayala 6-3, 6-2,
4-6, 6-2

Segura 6-0, 10-8,
1-6, 6-3

Rosewall 4-6,
6-1, 6-4, 7-5

Gimeno
Olmedo
Gimeno 6-3,
3-6, 6-0, 6-2

Trabert
Nielsen
Trabert
13-11, 6-1, 6-1

Trabert 6-2,
4-6, 7-5, 10-8

MacKay
Buchholz
MacKay 6-3,
6-4, 1-6, 7-5

Gonzales
Anderson
Gonzales 6-2,
6-4, 4-6, 6-2

Gonzales 6-3,
6-4, 7-5

Gonzales
6-3, 6-0, 6-4

Rosewall 2-6, 6-4, 6-3, 8-6

cool as always in the evening. Though Rosewall had won both
these big tournaments the year before, proving his ranking as
No. 1, he had not met Gonzales, who had been eliminated by
other pros before the finals. London was Gonzales' last chance
or excuse to demonstrate the year before had been an accident.

Rosewall whipped Olmedo 6-3, 6-4. He beat Cooper 6-1, 6-4.
He destroyed Segura 6-4, 6-4, 6-3 in the semis. In the other
semi-finals big Pancho took on equally tough Hoad, who,
though not as tall as Gonzales, was very well muscled, like an
agile tank. There was no question of Gonzales physically
intimidating Hoad. He lost to Hoad in four sets. Rosewall
defeated Hoad 6-3, 3-6, 6-2, 6-3.

World Tennis magazine, in otherwise brief coverage of these
events, finally ran a photo of Rosewall, saying 'Ken Rosewall
now has a claim to the title of World's Best Professional.'
Gonzales was described as 'retiring', a state he had been in for
a year, though he was to continue in active play until the early
seventies. As for Segura, he would get a measure of revenge on
Rosewall indirectly many years later.

Rosewall bought two flats in Queensland for $20,000. A
sporting goods firm, which he had worked for, estimated his
worth at $290,000.

The extraordinary unwillingness of the vast majority of the
press to give Rosewall credit, or, to put it another way, their
persistent habit of underestimating him, appeared again in an
article in 1962 by Arthur Goldman, in *World Tennis,*
describing the Australian team's victory over the U.S. in the
Kramer Cup (an early equivalent of the Aetna Cup, now played
at Hartford), a sort of pro imitation of the Davis Cup.
Australia won 3-2. Hoad and Rosewall won their doubles. Each
won and lost a singles, but 'Lew Hoad was the star of the
final . . . he now assumes the title of world's No. 1 player. His
colleague, Ken Rosewall, may be more consistent over a tour,
but Hoad in a particular match has the beating of anyone.'
Rosewall's reticence and the press's superficial emphasis of
the sensational combined to keep him in relative obscurity.

The matches were held in Ellis Park, Johannesburg. They
were frequently interrupted by rain. Rosewall was the captain
of the Australian team. In the doubles, which were completed
before the first two singles due to the downpour, Rosewall and

Hoad defeated Trabert and Buchholz 7-5, 6-1, 11-9. MacKay then beat Hoad 5-7, 8-6, 3-6, 8-6, 6-2. Trabert beat Rosewall 1-6, 8-6, 6-3, 6-4. Rosewall beat MacKay 4-6, 6-3, 6-4, 6-4. With 17,000 people in the stands, Hoad won the fifth match with the score now tied 2-2, beating Trabert 6-4, 3-6, 6-3, 6-0.

Goldman obviously preferred Hoad's style of play, calling him a 'brilliant . . . modest fellow . . . built like a cruiser-weight, moves with the agility of a featherweight and hits the ball with the punch of a Marciano or Louis.'

The assertion in some tennis circles that because a particular player is brilliant occasionally he should be regarded as the best in the world is similar to arguing that Johnny Vander Meer was America's greatest pitcher of all time because he pitched successive no-hitters, or that Don Larsen was the supreme pitcher because of his perfect game in a world series, or that Johnny Miller, who broke a Masters record in golf with a 131 for two rounds in 1975, was the finest golfer of all time. Except for their moments of glory, Larsen and Vander Meer were middle-ranking pitchers, and Miller, though a very good golfer, is not yet considered one of golf's greats, like Ben Hogan, Bobby Jones and Jack Nicklaus. As it happens, Nicklaus won the Masters, in which Miller set a record, and similarly in their rivalry as pros, Rosewall would usually win the tournament, though Hoad would shine brightly on occasion. Except for a few weeks against Gonzales in their '58 head-to-head tour, Hoad was never ranked No. 1 pro in the world.

Early in 1962 *L'Equipe,* a sports paper in France, ranked Rosewall as No. 1, Gonzales 2, and Hoad 3. Rosewall's contract with Kramer had expired, as had Hoad's. Rosewall and the others continued their touring, gradually attracting more fans to tennis. Not everywhere was a sell-out. In Cloncurry, an Australian cowtown in West Queensland, in 1962, 80 people watched Rosewall and his fellow pros play a match when Rosewall was at his peak.

In the spring of 1962 I saw Rosewall play in exhibition matches in an indoor stadium in London. His tennis was so perfect as to be unbelievable. It is this quality of the unreal which has intrigued several observers of Rosewall over the years, explaining why his tennis is often described as 'magic.'

It may be related to the withdrawn side of his character. Interestingly, the term 'magic' is never used to describe Rosewall's play today. Nowadays he is more likely to be called 'The Little Master,' and his tennis termed 'glorious.' The reason for this change in terminology will be evident later on. But in 1962, the inhuman perfection showed itself in his long forehand and backhand drives ripping the length of the court exactly parallel to the side line, always hitting one or two feet before the baseline, a few inches from the doubles line. Their speed was uncanny, as fast as Connors' ground strokes of today, though Chase says that Vines hit harder than either Connors or Rosewall. These same qualities of unerring speed and accuracy applied to his volley and serve. Segura, his opponent that night, stood not a chance. Rosewall stood head and shoulders above the other players, one of whom was Hoad playing listlessly and sullenly.

Rosewall had now won the two big professional titles—the English and French—for two years running, in 1960 and 1961, a feat somewhat comparable to taking the Grand Slam for two successive years. He had not played in the U.S. pro championships in 1960 and 1961 due to the lack of support for pro tennis in America; promoters were unable to arrange enough matches for pros to make it financially feasible for Rosewall to come to the U.S.

Once again, in France in September 1962, Rosewall beat Molinari, Buchholz, Cooper and Gimeno in the finals, losing only one set to each of the last three opponents. Hoad, Trabert and Segura lost in earlier rounds.

Newcomers

Ken remembers, 'Andres Gimeno improved a lot after he turned pro in 1960—particularly his serve and volley. He was a very graceful player and likable, and the crowd liked his Spanishisms. He had an unorthodox forehand, hit rather loosely but it was effective, but he hit his backhand with the same grip as his forehand. So I would come in on his backhand, though he could be accurate with it. In fact the last time I played him on WCT in '71 in the Stockholm open tournament he won.' Gimeno has said, 'Rosewall's backhand is better than his forehand because he hits it more in front of him.'

Ken remembers, 'Butch Buchholz perhaps turned pro a little earlier than he should have, but Kramer was trying to promote the American tour. He had temperament problems. He hit very hard in streaks. I had little difficulty with him. Then he got discouraged, had arm trouble and gave up his hope of being No. 1.

The Peak

'Barry MacKay, who turned pro at the same time, was similar. He was six feet three inches and hit the ball violently—mainly serve and volley. He couldn't move very well, and if you hit a ball to the side of the côurt, he was like a truck or lorry and could only slam it back in the hope it would go in for a winner, and he'd keep going in the same direction. Trabert had a similar problem in that he was a solidly built man, but he developed a very good game with his knowledge of tennis and anticipation.'

In London, at the Wembley tournament in 1962, Mal Anderson, because of a shoulder injury, withdrew against Rosewall in the second set of the featured match. Rosewall had some trouble with Cooper, 6-1, 6-8, 8-6.

In the semi-finals Segura made a determined run at Rosewall's growing record of victories. Rosewall won the first set 6-3. He lost the second 4-6. Segura won the third set 6-3. Segura reached 5-4 and match point. Surprisingly, Segura hit his first serve to Rosewall's backhand. Gracefully, methodically, Rosewall struck it with speed and accuracy low toward the incoming Segura, while Ken himself startled Segura by following the lovely shot into the net so that he was able to put away Segura's return. Rosewall then proceeded to win 10 straight points.

In the fifth set Segura, gamely leaping and bounding around the court on his bandy legs, flashing his crowd-pleasing smile, took another shot at Rosewall's reputation. He led 3-1, then 4-2.

The tennis was a flurry of beautiful shots. In one rally they hit cross-court backhands so sharply angled that Segura's final winning shot was almost parallel to the net. But Rosewall was not to be played with. He hit a first serve wide to Segura's famed two-handed forehand, one of the best strokes in tennis. It landed just out. Then, contemptuously, Rosewall fired a second serve just as hard to the same spot, the ball skidding off the court surface an inch inside the line for an ace. Rosewall won the last four games for a 6-4 fifth set.

The finalist in the other half of the draw was his old friend and roommate from amateur days, Lew Hoad. Thus in the 1962 Wembley finals Rosewall and Hoad faced each other again. Rosewall overcame attacks of cramps in the third and fourth sets and was down 2-4 in the third set. The match lasted three and a quarter hours over 62 games. Rosewall beat Hoad as usual, 6-4, 5-7, 15-13, 7-5. For the third year in a row he had picked up the two major European championships.*

But there were hints of disasters ahead. Some tennis writers found the programme dull, preferring the amateur competition to the professional efficiency. Was Rosewall too good? A woman writer cattily observed, 'I saw nothing at Wembley which held me as much as the best contest at Junior Wimbledon.' The same lady decided Rosewall was not infallible.

Wilma said, 'I love touring with Ken, but now with a new home and two children it would be hard to tear myself away.' Glenn, their younger son, had been born in August 1961.

In the early sixties a journalist called 'Grandstander' wrote in an Australian newspaper that 'professional tennis is lingering in its death throes. . . . If ever a branch of sport has played itself into the gutter of public opinion, this is it.' This pseudonymous sportswriter advised Laver not to rescue Rosewall and the others, predicting what in retrospect was to prove 100 percent wrong: 'Sedgman, Hoad, Rosewall, and Co. backed professional tennis when it was a winner everywhere. It will never see those days again.' He called pro tennis a 'tired, sad, old vaudeville act.' Laver was advised to 'wise up.' Australian journalism called a spade a spade.

* It may be interesting to see what happened to some of the other stars in this tournament. In the quarters Buchholz defeated Gimeno 5-7, 6-3, 6-4 before losing to Hoad in the semis 12-10, 3-6, 5-7, 6-3, 6-2. Trabert was also eliminated by Hoad in the quarters 6-4, 4-6, 7-5, while MacKay lost to Segura 6-4, 5-7, 7-5 in the quarters.

Bud Collins, author of a book about Laver and ceaseless propagandist for Laver, as a commentator on U.S. television, called Rosewall 'not a colourful player' when describing what he thought was the near-death of pro tennis in 1962. 'Rosewall,' he conceded, was 'pre-eminent.' Laver conceded that Rosewall was probably the best player in the world in 1962.

One of the major changes in pro tennis between 1957, when Rosewall turned pro, and 1963 was that the fixed salary was discarded in favour of prize money on the basis of wins.

Laver as Rookie

Segura finally retired at the age of 42, but Laver signed on for $125,000 in January 1963. Would he be a threat to Rosewall? Rosewall remembers, 'Hoad and I, and several other pros including Trabert and Sedgman, guaranteed Rod $125,000 to turn pro. He had a difficult time as he had to play me one night and Hoad the next. This was in the days when Hoad was playing pretty good. We made the $125,000 quite easily.' Laver has since said that he would not have held Rosewall and Hoad to the commitment.

Rosewall beat Laver in the first match 6-4, 6-3, 8-6 on grass at Sydney's White City stadium. Hoad had polished him off the night before in his debut 6-8, 6-4, 6-3, 8-6, before 8,000, an almost capacity crowd. After a few weeks Laver had won 2, lost 11 to Rosewall, and lost all 8 to Hoad for a 2-19 record. Rosewall was the tour leader as usual.

Laver said that one of Rosewall's favourite shots was 'wrong-footing' his opponent on the volley. A left-hander, for example, would hit a cross-court forehand to him which he would volley with his backhand right back where it came from, often catching the opponent who had started to run to mid-court unable to turn around, or, if he did turn in time, causing him to hit an easy return which Rosewall then put away.

I said to Ken, 'Rod Laver said in his book that for seven years you were a friend and yet a deadly enemy.'

Rosewall replied, 'I'd have to agree with that.'

Rosewall, Hoad and Laver launched one of the longer tours

in tennis history, capitalizing on Laver's reputation as the winner of the Grand Slam.

Dave Anderson, now a columnist for the New York *Times,* in the June 1963 issue of *Sport* wrote, ' "Rosewall," says Jack Kramer, former promoter of the tour, "consistently proved to be the class of the field the past two years. As far back as 1959 he beat Gonzales in five of seven tournament matches. In our two big tournaments in Europe each year—the hard courts at Paris and the indoor at London—Rosewall has won both of them the past three years." As for Hoad, Rosewall has practically taken permanent possession of his Australian boyhood buddy. "I'd say," Rosewall estimates, "that I've beaten Lew twenty of twenty-five times over the past three years."

'Laver attests to Rosewall's reign. After his opening match with Hoad, Laver said, "Lew's the best I've ever played." But the next day, after losing to Rosewall, Rod said, "I thought Hoad was good, but Kenny is twice as good." ' Doubtless such remarks did not endear Laver to Hoad.

Laver, badly beaten by Rosewall, called Ken's serve 'excellent and he never misses on that forehand volley.' Laver became Rosewall's roommate.

Rosewall was changing. Though he was still the 'lone wolf,' he was more poised and confident. One reporter even described his replies to the press 'as smooth as his backhand.'

Rosewall now was under pressure from his wife to give up touring tennis. When he turned pro in 1957, he had said, 'I'll only tour for a year or two.' But he had got better and better. By 1963 he would say to Wilma, 'I'm going to do the U.S. tour.' Then, back home in Sydney, he would say, 'I'm off to play the European tour,' adding wistfully, 'I'd like to stay home with you and the boys.'

The other players would encourage him by saying, 'You're the best in the world. If you stop, you'll hurt all of us.' Despite Rosewall's relative lack of publicity in the press, tennis fans like to see him play.

Rosewall, Laver and Hoad flew to the U.S. and began a series of matches in New York for the U.S. part of Laver's first year as a pro in 1963. At Madison Square Garden the watchman yelled to Rosewall, 'Hold it. You can't come in here until I know who you are.'

'Rosewall. Ken Rosewall. I'm one of the tennis players.'

'All right. But you're awful small to be a tennis player.'

Rosewall became used to saying to guards at tennis tournaments, who doubted he should be entering the players' area, 'My name is Rosewall. I'm one of the tennis players.'

Rosewall defeated Laver as thoroughly as possible after the latter turned pro, taking 11 out of their first 13 matches. How did he do it? In the encounter at Madison Square Garden Rosewall used several techniques: He maintained his game at a constant high level, hitting carefully and accurately, so that on key points Laver often either overhit or stroked a volley so uncertainly that Rosewall passed him easily. Rosewall used deception in many shots. Neither his feet nor his body nor his racket gave the slightest indication where the ball was going. This concealment was particularly effective when Rosewall came to net for a volley. Laver, a fast reflexive player, frequently had to wait until the ball was actually hit before daring to make a move. Then on the key service game, when Rosewall had broken Laver for an 11-10 lead (it was a pro set and match, meaning the first to achieve a two-game lead after 9-all), Ken speeded his service up—faster than he had done despite the pressure of holding serve in the previous games—and defeated Laver.

For Rosewall, eating and sleeping habits on the pro tour were contrary to the regular ones he preferred. For example, Rosewall and the five other players drove in a car from St. Louis to Cleveland until just before dawn. After a couple of hours' sleep in a Cleveland hotel he was awakened by Jack March, the promoter of the local tourney, to go on a TV interview show at 9 A.M. Then he had to practise. He wrote a letter home. He searched for and found a fast laundry service. In the early evening he played his quarter-final match and an hour later his semi-final against Gimeno. Then he and Laver played a doubles against Don Budge and Al Doyle, the canny old pro who now dominates the fifty-five-year-old class. During the second doubles match, which Rosewall did not play in, Rosewall showered and changed into trousers and a sports shirt with jacket. At midnight he joined the other players, friends and entrepreneurs at the bar near the court. Laver and MacKay ordered a beer, Rosewall a ginger ale. Rosewall left the group to drive the former tour director, Myron McNamara, to the airport. At 2 A.M Rosewall rejoined all the other players, who were eating a late-night snack on the sixteenth-floor restaurant of the Manger Hotel. In a few minutes the restaurant closed and, as everyone was still keyed up from the evening's athletic excitement, MacKay, Laver and Rosewall went to a bar. In half an hour it closed. They all returned to the hotel. MacKay and Laver went up to their rooms. Rosewall granted an interview to a reporter who had flown out from New York several hours earlier. Rosewall talked alertly, wide-awake, until 5 A.M., when a hotel maid turned on a vacuum cleaner, the noise making conversation difficult. 'Shall we call it a day?' he said to the journalist. Late in the morning Rosewall ate breakfast, continued the interview, and at 3 P.M. drove the scribe to the airport before going out on the court to practise with MacKay.

MacKay said of Rosewall, 'Hoadie really loosens him up. He gets Muscles laughing in a couple of minutes. Ken basically wants to be one of the boys—and he's very well liked by all of us.'

The U.S. Professional Championship for 1963 was held that year at Forest Hills. Gonzales had been playing off and on during the past two years, but less than usual as he had taken a job as a pro at a lush resort in the Caribbean. He entered the tournament. Apparently he was nettled by the increasing number of articles saying that Rosewall was really pre-eminent, even in U.S. publications such as the New York *Times*. Before the matches began, Gonzales told New York columnist Gene Ward, 'Look up the records. I beat Rosewall 51 to 27 in our 1957 tour and 29 to 4 in that 1960 tour they say he won. In 1961, the last year I played in pro tournaments, I won 5 of the 8 I entered. Rosewall played in 6 and won 2.'*

* The parts of this quote for which I could find independent verification were a Jack Kramer programme for 1958, saying Gonzales beat Rosewall 50 to 26 in their 1957 tour, and the comment from Rosewall during one of our interviews that Gonzales won the 1960 tour in which Rosewall played and the 1961 tour when Rosewall did not play. From 1959 on, the ageing Gonzales rarely won the important pro tournaments similar to Forest Hills and Wimbledon, requiring the best-of-five sets, but could maintain his superiority in best-of-three set matches, the type used usually on

Meanwhile Gonzales' presence· was causing other com-
plications. One was that he refused to join the players'
association, which made him less than popular with the other
stars, who were hardly fond of him as it was. Laver said that
Gonzales was deliberately cool to Rosewall and himself in order
to set their nerves on edge. If he lost a match, he would brush
his hand against the winner rather than shake it. Before the
1963 U.S. Pro Rosewall said, 'This man comes out of
retirement and tries to break up our association.'

However, Gonzales was a drawing card and the promoters
had persuaded him to participate, hoping he would reach the
final. Ken remembers, 'Previously the promoter would make
the draw himself, and on this occasion the promoter placed
Gonzales versus Trabert in the first round. Trabert was the
tour director by then and had not been playing regularly. So
Gonzales had a good chance of winning, and he would then
probably have faced Laver in the semi-finals, as Rod would in
all likelihood have won his first-round match. As Laver was a
rookie pro, Gonzales would have had a chance of winning,
putting Pancho in the ·finals, which is what the promoters
wanted. However, the players, including Trabert and myself,
decided it would be fairer to everyone to draw names out of a
hat. Gonzales now faced Olmedo in the first round instead of
Trabert and, if he won, he would probably meet me in the
semis.'

Gonzales lost badly in the first round to Olmedo. After
Gonzales lost, Trabert chortled, 'I saw the match and enjoyed
it. He sure looked sorta through.'

the U.S. tours of those days. Laver has had the same experience in
the seventies. Unable to win a major tournament since 1969, Laver
has nevertheless done well in best-of-three set tournaments in the
1970's, particularly on the U.S. winter circuit. The indoor surface
was of course a Gonzales speciality, provided it was a three-set
match, unlike on grass and clay, where Rosewall was the stronger.
From 1959 on, Gonzales never won the best-of-five set Paris and
London tournaments, though he won the U.S. pro in 1959 and 1961,
in both of which Rosewall did not play, while Rosewall won London
in 1957, 1960-63, and Paris 1958, 1960-66 (every British pro
championship and the French pro championship from '63 to '66
were all indoors, while from '58 to '62 the French was on clay). The
newspaper clippings in the files of the *Sunday Times* state that
Rosewall was the dominant pro from 1959 to 1964.

One of the Greats

In this and other tournaments Rosewall's tennis was so superlative that some people were now for the first time comparing him to the greats of the past. The *World Tennis* reporter said, 'One group believes that not only is he reaching the peak of his game but that he could beat any of the great pros of history.' Another viewpoint, held by Gonzales, the deposed champ, and others agreed he was currently tops, but denied him a position among the greats, of whom Gonzales undoubtedly considered himself a member. Gonzales said, 'Anyone who makes Ken's confidence waver will become pro champ.' Gonzales delivered these views at Forest Hills just after he had lost in the first round to the cost of the promoters and the delight of Trabert and the other pros. Bobby Riggs was among the first group.

Rosewall then beat Laver 6-4, 6-2, 6-2 in the finals at Forest Hills in the U.S. Pro Championship in 1963. Rosewall and the other players were not paid, as the tournament went broke. However, having been paid appearance money beforehand, Gonzales received some money.

Jack Murphy, covering the Kramer Cup in Dublin in 1963, wrote for *World Tennis,* 'So good was Rosewall . . . that one could not help speculating how he would have fared against the greats of the past.' The semi-finals were South America v. Europe and Australia v. North America. This article referred to a 'devastating display by Ken Rosewall over Butch Buchholz. Flawless driving deep to the corners, neat compact volleying, all accomplished with the greatest of ease, made Buchholz look like a beginner, and one felt positively sorry for him as he was repeatedly caught moving the wrong way.' No score was given for Rosewall's win over Buchholz. In the finals, as South America defeated Europe in the other semi, Rosewall defeated Ayala 6-2, 6-1, 6-1; Laver defeated Olmedo 6-4, 0-6, 6-4, 6-3; Rosewall and Frank Sedgman defeated Ayala and Olmedo 6-3, 8-6, 7-5; Laver defeated Ayala 2-6, 6-2, 3-6, 6-4, 6-4; and Rosewall defeated Olmedo 7-5, 10-8, 6-4.

For the fourth year running Rosewall won both the French and British Professional Championships. There was also an

British Professional Championship—1963

```
Trabert
Nielsen
                Rosewall
Trabert
6-4, 6-4
                            Rosewall
                            6-2, 6-3
Anderson
MacKay
                Anderson
                6-3, 6-3
Olmedo                                      Rosewall won,
Sedgman                                     score not given
                Olmedo          Olmedo
                7-9, 6-3, 10-8  6-1, 6-2
                                                        Rosewall
                                                        6-4, 6-2, 4-6, 6-3
Buchholz
Haillet
                Buchholz
                7-5, 6-3
                            Buchholz
                            6-1, 6-4
Laver           Laver

                                            Hoad
                                            6-1, 6-3, 8-10, 7-9, 10-8
Gimeno
Davies
                Gimeno
                7-5, 6-2
                            Hoad
                            6-3, 2-6, 8-6
Hoad            Hoad
```

Italian Pro Championship for the first time. Rosewall beat Laver in that one 6-4, 6-3.

In Paris, playing indoors at Stade Pierre de Coubertin for the first time, instead of outdoors as previously on Roland Garros' red clay, Rosewall was allowed a bye in the first round, unlike any of the other pros. He proceeded to beat Anderson 6-2, 6-2, 6-2, Hoad 10-8, 6-2, 6-3 and Laver 6-8, 6-4, 5-7, 6-3, 6-4. In London he defeated Trabert 6-2, 6-3 and Olmedo. In the finals he took Hoad 6-4, 6-2, 4-6, 6-3.

Rosewall had won the Wembley, London, championship five times (1957, 1960-63), a record, one more than Laver would win in succeeding years.

Ken says, 'Comparing Laver to Hoad, I would say their first serves were about the same speed, perhaps Hoad's a little faster, but Rod hit his backhand and forehand always very fast while Hoad was not as consistently fast and sometimes hit softer ones. Hoad's service action changed later on due to his back trouble. He twisted his body less to protect his back, and I always thought it stemmed from when he and I would go to the gym in the early fifties and he'd do push-ups with a big metal wheel on his back. People would say to him, "Can you do this exercise or that, Lew?" and he'd say, "Okay." And he could do it.

'It was an old gym in Melbourne. As we were not often in Melbourne, we didn't often go there. A number of tennis players would be there when Lew and I went. Harry Hopman had a close relationship with the owner, Frank Finley. Frank Sedgman later bought it from Finley, but Stan Nichols was always the head trainer. We were not conditioned for those kind of exercises, such as lifting weights, and so at the end of a day we couldn't lift our arms above our shoulders we were so tired. But Lew never complained of being hurt after a day there. We never worried about injuries in those days, we were so young.

'In an entirely separate incident Lew was hurt and in pain when he was bitten by a poisonous spider while in training for three months in 1954 with the army. He was in bed for several days, but that did not affect his back.

'Lew unfortunately had a number of physical problems in the early pro days, and his back has prevented him from staying in condition for top tennis and competing. I can't really give any specific medical explanation for the back trouble.

'The tennis in the pro days may have been of a higher quality than today, as only the top players played each other. Still there were twelve or sixteen pros, and the level at the bottom was not the same as at the top. Against Luis Ayala I never had any difficulty, and at Wembley once I won fifteen straight games against him, but he practised a lot and was a good clay-court player. Nevertheless, the depth of players is better today, and there are no more easy first-round matches in a field of 128 at Wimbledon or Forest Hills.

'The pressures are different. Then there was the pressure of playing day after day in one city after another. Now there are often days of rest between tournament matches, but there is more money and pressure on winning each match.

'Some players are much better in practice. Ayala would practise his forehand volley and hit it straight or with top-spin, and then in a match he would go right back to his old habit. George Worthington was an excellent player in practice. He was known as the "Champion of Practice." As a great and popular friend of so many, it was very sad George died of cancer at an early age.'

Rosewall played an exhibition in a city street of St. Louis in 1964 with Laver, Gonzales and Buchholz in order to publicize a tournament, so low was the popularity of pro tennis according to Laver and Collins, though the increasing numbers of amateurs turning pro and the increasing amounts of prize money seem to belie this.

In the spring of 1964 Rosewall took a long vacation at home. His two sons played with cut-down rackets, just as their dad had. That summer of 1964, on an eight-tournament tour of the U.S. in as many cities, Rosewall earned $8,800, tops among the pros.

The first crack in Rosewall's throne came in September 1964 at Wembley, when Laver won over him in the final 7-5, 5-7, 4-6, 8-6, 8-6. But Rosewall had won in Paris over Laver 6-3, 7-5, 3-6, 6-3. Both courts were on indoor surfaces.

By that time, the mid-sixties, the promoter system had been replaced by a players' association, of which Rosewall was the

leading star and treasurer. Near the end of 1964 Rosewall and
Hoad, returning to Australia, offered Roy Emerson on behalf
of the players' association initially $75,000 to turn pro, then
$85,000.

Remaining No. 1

Despite Laver's triumph at Wembley, Rosewall continued
his domination of the tennis world, winning a European and
South African pro tour lasting 130 days, which ended in
November 1964. Butch Buchholz observed, 'Rosewall again
won the tour, edging out Rod Laver. This year, when Gonzales
was no longer No. 1, he was pleasant and friendly with
everyone. Perhaps there are two factors which have created
the change in Gorgo. First, he used to be against the Players'
Association; now he sees how it works and he feels that he is a
part of it. Secondly, our No. 1 player, Ken Rosewall, sets an
example for all of us by not asking for special favours or
appearance money which the champion might claim.'

Buchholz's observations on Rosewall in that period were
interesting, casting some light on his personality, the
challenge the champion was facing in fending off Laver, and
dispelling one canard that Ken was tight with money.

Still describing Rosewall as a loner, he pointed out that,
though it was not easy to become intimate with the star, Ken
was the essence of loyalty to those who were in need. If
Rosewall were to be asked for a loan, he would immediately
send it, even a sum as large as $2,000. The editor of the
magazine in which this assertion appeared challenged
Buchholz as a joke to cable Rosewall for $2,000, but Buchholz
refused to accept the dare. But then the press had long tried to
build up an image of Ken being parsimonious, when the truth
was that he was frugal in his personal living habits, preferring
to save his money for his family.*

---

* While I was in Australia writing this book, he was very generous to
  me, loaning me his car, a tape-recorder, tennis bag, constantly
  doing me small, thoughtful favours such as taking me to and from
  the airport, writing out for me a list of favourite restaurants, he and
  Wilma frequently giving me lunch or dinner, constantly plying me
  with tea, coffee and snacks.

Laver now was able to win some matches from Rosewall, though Ken still held an edge over him, and Rosewall's record over the other players was superior. Laver was now more successful than he had been against Rosewall's serve, returning it with angled topspins, slices, varying his shots, making it difficult for the champion to anticipate Laver's reply.

The long periods away from home were a constant source of loneliness for all the players. Buchholz maintained, 'Muscles takes it so much to heart that he breaks into a rash when he is away from Wilma.' Rosewall was very much admired by Buchholz. One of the causes for the appreciation was Rosewall's tireless work before and after playing as the treasurer of the association. He was in charge of the money. He wrote all the business letters. He calculated the constantly changing percentage of each player's share of the receipts.

Buchholz continued his praise. Rosewall's quiet manner meant that it took a long time to get to know him. Ken thought carefully before answering a question. He would become upset with himself when he lost, but he was always a good sport. When he won, he was humble. He never boasted about his triumphs. He never gossiped or belittled other players.

In the early part of 1965 Gonzales announced he was only playing pro tennis now 'to pay off alimony.'* That same year one of the first indications of the effect TV was to have on tennis and the pros was CBS televising a special series of matches involving Rosewall, Laver and the others, which was shown on seven Sundays in a row. Laver had a short, hot streak, winning four tournaments in a row in Australia in February, defeating Rosewall in two of the finals. Gonzales reunited with his beautiful wife and won a tournament, beating Rosewall in the final.

Rosewall was tired. He had won the preceding tour in Australia, but the rash had struck, inflaming his ankles while he was also in charge of all the business arrangements. In 1964 he had been away from home for eight months, in 1963 for ten months. In Melbourne, in a tournament final he lost to Laver,

---

* Pancho Gonzales remarried former beauty queen Madelyn Gonzales on Christmas Eve, 1970

his feet were so swollen they would only fit into sneakers. In New Zealand in 1964 he had had difficulty walking, dropping out of the singles, playing only in the doubles.

By the summer of 1965 Hoad's career seemed to have ended with an operation that removed half an inch of bone from the big toe of his right foot. Though Hoad was to play briefly in 1966 and 1967, it seems appropriate at this point in our story to bring down the curtain on Rosewall's old friend and rival, but before doing so I want to quote from a letter that Hoad recently sent me about Rosewall and to write of a current reminiscence of Rosewall's about Hoad.

Hoad said in his letter to me, 'My praise for Ken, first as a person and secondly as a tennis player, cannot be high enough.

'He is a great competitor, very fair against whom he plays. Has a great desire to win, and above all, does not complain when he happens to lose, which is not very often.

'Regarding my matches with him and against him, I always felt that if I played well I could win, but if I played badly, he would usually come out on top, because he was a little more consistent.

'Regarding the doubles, we had respect for each other and this is probably why we teamed so well together and had so many successes.'

Hoad and his wife, Jenny, now run a tennis camp near Fuengirola on the Costa del Sol in Spain.

About a year ago some Australians invited Hoad to fly out to Australia and play with Ken in a sentimental doubles match as part of a tournament in Sydney.

I said to Rosewall a few weeks later, 'Being out of practice, Hoad isn't much good these days, I would guess.'

With loyalty and warmth in his voice, referring to his friend of twenty-eight years, Ken replied, 'Well, we lost, but my flight from Tokyo was delayed a day, and I had to play more or less on arrival after a ten-hour flight, partnering Lew, and I was having trouble switching from metal to a wood racket. So I didn't play very well. But Lew's going to have some acu-puncture treatments for his back, and he should be able to play more often, if the treatment is successful.'

U.S. Pro on Grass

Although he lost to Gimeno in the semi-finals at Wembley, Rosewall held on precariously to his pro crown in 1965 by beating Laver 6-3, 6-2, 6-4 at Paris and winning the U.S. Pro tournament on grass in Boston over Laver in the final, 6-4, 6-3, 6-3.

Ken said, 'Quickness has helped me out of many tight spots. I remember playing Pancho Gonzales in the semi-finals of the U.S. professional championships at Boston in 1965. It was raining during much of the match and, even though we were both wearing spiked shoes, the footing was pretty bad. Gonzales had a lot of trouble with it and I beat him—largely because I was able to move better than he was.

'Unlike the others, Gonzales was usually very agile on his feet. His only flaw was the high forehand volley, but this is not to say you'd hit him a high one as he'd put it away, but if one hit there by accident he might make an error. Everyone said he didn't have ground strokes, but he was very accurate and would place the ball, thinking ahead to the next shot. He was a tremendous competitor with a lot of gamesmanship.

'I would not want to say I was a better player than Gonzales, and Gonzales would not agree either. That's one of my faults—to be too modest. I beat him pretty regularly in the sixties, but he won over me twice at Las Vegas in 1969 and 1970 on a fast surface.

'Because Gonzales placed his ground strokes, I knew he would not often go a winner on his return of my serve and I would come in to net, relying on my volley and anticipation.

'On Gonzales' first serve I would usually just try to get it back in and low. But if I met the ball right in the centre of the racket and my body was not off balance, swinging at it plus the speed of the serve would sometimes cause it to ricochet back, for a winning return or a forced error. But if I was off balance I'd just try to keep it in play. On the second serve I'd move in and chip it to either his forehand or backhand. He usually tried to serve wide to my forehand, and I'd hit it down the line sometimes or cross-court, but he was a great server and could serve at me or in any direction. If it was at me, I'd prefer to take it on the backhand, but sometimes it paid to receive it on the forehand.'

Santana was a famous amateur around 1965. He won the French in 1964, the U.S. in 1965, and Wimbledon in 1966. Ken remembers, 'Manolo Santana really put tennis on the map in Spain. He was a national hero. He's done very well going into business with partners since then. An exceptional player, he had a topspin backhand lob which many players can't do, and a lot of variation in his strokes. Like most European players, volley and serve were not his speciality, but he could do it, if necessary, as he did when beating Emerson in the 1965 Davis Cup. He was very popular with the crowds, saying 'olé' at appropriate occasions, his front teeth protruding so that he looked as if he was smiling. It was sad that Andres Gimeno, who was almost as good as Santana, was always in the shadow of professional tennis, which received less publicity than amateur tennis in those days, though now he's coach to their Davis Cup team and their leading juniors.

'Juan Gisbert was reluctant to play in the Davis Cup for Spain against Australia in 1965. It was a one-man team with Santana. I gave them some practice. I told Gisbert the Australians would beat him, but I said he had a chance as his game was so unorthodox their concentration might be thrown off.'

After resting at home and helping the Spaniards with their team in their Davis Cup contest against Australia, which Spain lost 4-1, Rosewall, Laver and Co. resumed their professional touring. A Johannesburg paper called Rosewall, who beat Laver in three sets there in October 1965, a 'cold, calculated "killer" of the courts.'

But a British sportswriter, a woman, never a fan of pro tennis, noticed that Rosewall was missing the perfect shot one out of ten times instead of never failing to make it. She noticed too his head drooping, racket dropping, 'as the old impassive master with everything at his fingertips would never do.'

Laver Emerges

Nevertheless, just before the end of 1965, Laver finally caught up and apparently won his first tour over Rosewall. As with most of the other professional records prior to open tennis in 1968, the statistics for this tour are very uncertain. Those results that were printed in the rear pages of *World Tennis* for the last months of 1965 and the early ones of 1966 showed Laver winning more tournaments than Rosewall and beating Rosewall more often than Rosewall beat him. However, the pro tournaments and occasional head-to-head exhibitions, which were printed, were obviously only a minority of the total number of pro tourneys and matches played. The only other evidence for this period is a letter in *World Tennis* of April 1966 from Paul Lippman, of San Francisco, which confuses matters even more. Lippman quoted a reporter's question at a press conference during a pro tourney in Sydney, which occurred some time after the Australian National Championship, an amateur event in January: 'Now that the play of Laver and Rosewall is so even, who do you professionals regard as the world champion?' But the answer was not given in the letter which was mainly devoted to criticizing press coverage of tennis in Australia. Lippman said that he had been for ten years a sportswriter for the San Francisco *Examiner*.

Rosewall's seven-year reign was over—the finest and probably the longest in tennis history, in which Rosewall had overcome every great player, including Laver, Hoad, Gonzales, Kramer, who was past his peak, and every other outstanding player such as Sedgman and Segura; beyond a shadow of doubt he would have beaten the few leading players who remained amateurs such as Santana, Fraser, Emerson and Chuck McKinley.

Nevertheless, age, as it must to all athletes, had caught up with him at the end of his thirty-first year.

Laver has never been one of my favourite players, though he has many admirers. His habit of slamming the ball as hard as he could always struck me as a less attractive approach to tennis than either Rosewall's artistry or Gonzales' shrewd placement of volleys and ground shots and power serve.

But Laver had worked and practised hard, and now he seemed to be on top, aided in his triumph over Rosewall by time. Rosewall would have to play him day in and day out—plus other young stars coming up—over the years to come. When tested over major championships, consisting of the best-of-five set matches, no tennis champion, once deposed, had ever regained the title of No. 1.

5

Decline

'Were you discouraged by Laver's dominance from 1965 to 1969?' I asked Rosewall during one of our many conversations recently in Australia.

'No, I never expected to be No. 1. I was always in the shadow—first with Gonzales, then Laver.'

'Laver says in his book that you and he resented how you were better players than Gonzales, but that Gonzales got most of the publicity and was regarded by the American public and much of the rest of the world as the tennis champion.'

'Rod and I did much more than Gonzales to establish the pro game. He was very difficult sometimes with sponsors, promoters and organizations and would not cooperate.'

However, Rosewall and Laver were making progress in their attempt to establish professional tennis as a popular sport. For Rosewall, this was some compensation for Laver's new ascendancy. Fortunately several Hollywood stars were keen tennis players. Rosewall remembers, 'Chuck Heston and James Franciscus were very helpful in pro days from 1964 on, appearing in exhibitions countless number of times.' Among Rosewall's personal memorabilia is a friendly telegram from Charlton Heston congratulating Rosewall on a win over Newcombe in 1968 at Wembley.

In one of the ironies so typical of Rosewall's life, Rosewall, who had seen Laver sweep the South African pro tour near the end of '65, was finally given credit for his now-past dominance and contribution to pro tennis by *World Tennis*, which placed him on the cover of their February 1966 issue inaugurating a new format. Somewhat belatedly they wrote, 'Like Bobby

Riggs, he never received the recognition that his great game warranted. The "Big Boys" took precedence, although Ken played the Big Game (despite his size) and thoroughly dominated the pro ranks. If it were not for "Muscles," there would be no pro game today since he more than any other player has given so selflessly to the organization and running of professional tournament tennis.'

In an article in *Sport Business* in July 1966, Kramer wrote under the title, 'The Professional Season at Longwood': 'The fellow who has to be listed No. 1 in the game at the moment is Ken Rosewall.' But Kramer was no longer so active in promoting and was probably unaware of how Laver had finally surpassed Rosewall.

Though Laver was now No. 1, Rosewall remained No. 2. A big tournament at Forest Hills in June resulted in Rosewall narrowly losing to the 'Rocket' in the finals 31-29, using the Van Alen Scoring System. But Wilma was with him to comfort him.

In September 1966, Laver crushed Rosewall in the finals of Wembley 6-2, 6-2, 6-3, but Rosewall demonstrated how especially skilful he was in France for some reason, beating Laver in the final on an indoor surface in the Stade Pierre de Coubertin for his seventh consecutive victory, a record similar to Tilden's famous run at Forest Hills in the twenties.

Laver, having married an American woman, bought a house in southern California, the first of the great Aussie stars to emigrate to the U.S., which initiated or coincided with the start of the decline of Australian tennis. By the time Laver led Emerson and Hopman across the Pacific, Australian youngsters and fans had lost interest in the game, and, conversely, Americans had become rabid for tennis, though the remaining Australian stars such as Rosewall, Newcombe and Roche continued to play very well. Another factor, probably more important, was the growing spread of colour TV in the U.S. Tennis, with its simple rules, attractive hues of costumes, court, balls and racket, played by lithe, tanned young athletes, was ideal for home viewing, involving only two players and an easily seen ball on a relatively small surface. The efforts of Rosewall, and to a lesser extent Laver and the others, coinciding with this sociological and technical development, were starting to pay off.

Ken remembers playing Dennis Ralston for the first time during this period: 'I didn't play Dennis Ralston until about the end of 1966, when he turned pro. He had a good all-round game, but he had trouble with his serve, a hitch in his action. His first serve was flat, and the second one with slight spin. Sometimes he would double-fault a lot, if he lost confidence and rhythm on his service action.'

Laver's ascendancy over Rosewall from 1966 to 1969 may not have been as great as the press and popular opinion have decided. A 1967 article in the Boston *Globe* by Bud Collins, normally a fervent Laver admirer and supporter, said, 'Rosewall has irritated Laver considerably more than the pterygicin [an eye infection Laver had]. Although Laver is the current champion, the 5′ 6″ Muscles Rosewall refuses to recognize the Rocket's ascendancy. They are 3-3 in their rivalry this season and Laver has only a slight lead (11-9) over four years of tournament play on the American circuit. . . . "I just can't rattle Muscles," Laver sighed. The rest melt before the Rocket's burst of shot-making. . . .' The article then went on to describe a typical match where Laver had triple-match point on Rosewall: Collins quoted Laver as saying, 'Muscles went out of his mind and hit three great shots to get to deuce. . . .' Rosewall won the match, having been down 4-6, 3-5, 0-40 on Laver's serve.

Laver said, 'Rosewall is the player we all have the most trouble with.' Laver called Rosewall 'the doomsday stroking machine,' although this description was probably Bud Collins' invention. Laver said Rosewall's forehand was flat, lacked topspin.

Ken remembers some of the other new stars of the period: 'I didn't play Roy Emerson much until he turned pro in 1967, though I knew him from when he was eleven years old. He was on our Davis Cup teams in 1954 to 1967, but Hoad and I were ahead of him, then Fraser and Laver. He developed late, but won every major championship twice. He was a fanatic on conditioning, always doing exercises or running. His agility was excellent, but, like Ralston, his trouble was his serves, which he hit with a kind of cartwheel motion, but he was quick enough so he could get to the return. He was always changing his service style.'

The last time I saw Emerson play at the beginning of 1975, he was using a very curious new serve, consisting of a backswing like the upward flip of a dolphin and a frontal action like an angry housewife swinging a mop at a neighbour. It was in a doubles match at the Philadelphia indoor tournament. Laver and Emerson were playing Tanner and Pasarell. Emerson lost his serve and the doubles match then, too.

Ken said, 'I first met Fred Stolle when he was a banker and a good district player. He would be the first to admit his game has faults. I'd play his forehand; he didn't bring his head close enough to the ball, or bend his knees sufficiently on it. Perhaps his game lacked imagination, too. He's one of my oldest friends—very honest, and he knows tennis very well.'

I said, 'I saw Stolle play Okker, who's very clever, and Stolle always seemed to hit the ball just where you expected.'

'That might be true, though Stolle won over Okker several times. Okker's an outstanding player with a natural action on his ground strokes—very quick.'

The All-England Club, sited at Wimbledon, sponsored its first professional tournament in August 1967, aided by BBC colour television. First prize was $8,400. Despite a thrilling match between Hoad and Gonzales, both semi-retired (which Lew won 3-6, 11-9, 8-6, Gonzales angrily hitting a ball out of the stadium after he lost, then throwing his racket on the court before shaking hands with Hoad), the tournament resulted in the expected final of Rosewall and Laver. Laver, inspired as usual by his old nemesis and current victim, tore through Rosewall with a barrage of first serves and deadly spinners to all sides of Rosewall's court. His steady progress in the first set was delayed only by being 0-40 down on his serve, being a service break up at 2-1. He came back to take the game for 3-1 and soon won the set 6-2. The second set was Laver's at 6-2.

However, Laver's terrific pace and onslaught slowed in the third set and the ageing little master struck back to achieve a 5-2 lead. Rosewall had three set points on Laver, all of which Ken lost, and Laver evened the score to 5-all and finally wore his opponent down with a service break, to win 12-10.

The tournament drew capacity crowds in the semi-finals and finals, providing a tempting suggestion to Wimbledon that it consider open tennis. Tennis-experts and fans applauded the

brilliance of the Rosewall-Laver match, but Laver had
continued his edge over Rosewall.

Laver had been beating his opponents, three and four wins to
every loss, including the Wembley show. Rosewall was also
starting to lose occasionally to lesser opponents such as
Gimeno (No. 3 in the world) and Barthes.

I said, 'In Grace Lichtenstein's book on the Virginia Slims
tour she quotes Rosemary Casals describing the 1968 tour
with the men: "In France, in 1968, we sometimes had to share
the dressing room with the fellows. There were cobwebs, the
water didn't come out of the showers, there were johns you
didn't believe. We slept two hours a night for thirty days,
travelling six hours by car and three hours by plane all in the
same day. I'll never forget the time we played on asphalt that
had just been poured that day. The balls got black!" Do you
have similar experiences?'

Rosewall said, 'Rosie Casals had it for six months. We went
through it for twelve years. It's not true we shared the same
locker room. The tour really didn't work out very well for the
women and didn't draw good crowds. They went off on their
own matches sometimes. But there was room for better
promotion.'

'Rosie Casals says, "Losses stay with you forever." Do you
agree?'

'No. Not if you play well even if you lose. Rosie Casals
should have some twinges of conscience for some of the
matches she should have won.'

In a key match in early 1968, ballyhooed by the press to
settle a long 'feud' and the position of No. 1 woman player in
the U.S., Billie Jean King, that apostle of women's lib, or lob,
one of the most unpopular women ever to play in England and
subsequently the most popular in America, lost to Nancy
Richey in a very close match at Madison Square Garden in
three sets after leading match point, 5-3, the second set.
Afterwards she sought Rosewall's advice and consolation. He
said, 'Forget about it. You're always going to have a few
matches like that.'

After years of arguments and bans of the pros by the
national and international lawn tennis associations, 'open'
tennis finally arrived in early 1968. The increasing number of

top amateurs turning pro, the growing crowds and TV coverage of professional tennis, the disappointment by amateur officials at seeing their national championships reduced to second-rate affairs, and the hard-working efforts by Rosewall and the other pro supporters had achieved this major event in the development of tennis from a social outing of the upper classes, who had invented it a hundred years ago, to an international sport of the people. However, those who think the democratization of tennis is a recent development would be well advised to read John Kieran's article, "The Ruler of the Scene," published in 1941, about Maurice E. McLoughlin, who was famous before World War I: 'McLoughlin brought tennis down to the common ground. It was no longer a game for the Four Hundred—not the way Red McLoughlin played it. He made it a game for the millions, for the young fellows at the small clubs about the country and the youngsters just starting out on the courts in the public parks.'

Regardless of Laver's domination over him, Rosewall felt a flicker of pride in himself as the world's first professional-amateur tournament, called an 'open', started at Bourne-mouth, in 1968. The weather was deplorable. The results were mildly shocking in the early rounds. The pros, sup-posedly so superior to the illegally paid amateurs, suffered several blows to their collective pride and pocket-books. As the days progressed, the knowledge of the waning professional reputation seeped into Rosewall's consciousness. For Pancho Gonzales, the old lion once king of the tennis 'jungle' and presumably still a terror to any amateur, a mere babe in the woods, was defeated by Mark Cox in five sets, though winning the first set 6-0. Roy Emerson, another seasoned warrior, fell to Cox in three sets in the next round. Meanwhile, Rosewall, ignoring his fellow pros' shortcomings, dispatched with professional ease all the amateurs in his path, and then disposed of the No. 3 professional player in the world, the elegant, tall Andres Gimeno, with the beautiful smooth forehand. Laver, similarly stirred by this amateur affront to expert standards, finally stopped the impudent Cox with an awesome display of power tennis. But Rosewall still had to play his new 'boss', Laver.

Bournemouth stepped in again with grey clouds and

increasing drizzle. But this time Ken launched a determined attack on Laver, mainly from the baseline. Rosewall ignored the bitter cold and overcame the rain. Laver had been over-confident, winning the first set 6-3. Laver, curiously off his game after teaching Cox a lesson, having lost the second set 6-2, was down 0-3 in the third set. The referee stopped the match when conditions became impossible. The next morning the weather had cleared. The red clay was damp and wet, yet playable. Laver, rested from a night's sleep, intended to start the day off right by announcing firmly to the world and the press that he was ruler not only of the pros but also the amateurs, and anyone else who cared to play tennis for that matter. Rosewall volleyed at devastating angles; his first and second serves stayed deep, driving Laver back; his backhand struck with rapier passes the onrushing Laver. Laver struggled. Occasionally, he pulled off a brilliant volley. He attempted to get his backhand under control, which Rosewall mercilessly played. By noon, Rosewall had won the third set 6-0, and the fourth 6-3. For a day or a week at least, Rosewall had dethroned the pretender, who had so long usurped his crown, and was again No. 1 in the world—at the beginning of a bright new day for professional tennis.

With the intermixture of pros and amateurs, Rosewall met an English player who had the fastest serve ever recorded in the history of tennis, 154 m.p.h., a record which still stands, though Colin Dibley has come close to it. This was Mike Sangster, who once reached the semi-finals of Wimbledon. Ken says of him: 'Mike Sangster had a terrific serve. It seems all he could do was serve, and I'm told he would play a whole match with his warmup jacket on. Maybe he was trying to use gamesmanship, pretending he was so good he didn't have to take it off.'

Bobby Riggs and the French

I said, 'I read the following story in Bobby Riggs's book: Do you remember staying with Bobby Riggs for two weeks before you won the French Championship in 1968, playing with Jack Dreyfus of the Dreyfus Fund in a doubles against Riggs and

Tony Vincent? You lost the majority of seven sets on which Dreyfus bet $500 a set and then played Riggs in singles giving Riggs the alleys; and Dreyfus won $500 off Riggs betting on you; and then in another set you gave Riggs the alleys plus two games and Dreyfus won another $500 betting on you; and then in a third set you gave Riggs the alleys, two games and 15-love, and Dreyfus lost $500 to Riggs, betting on you.'

Ken replied, 'Bobby Riggs exaggerated in his book. In the doubles there was some handicap arrangement. I don't like to bet.

'He bet me double or nothing. Finally, I was ahead about $1,000, and I had still beaten him at 0-4, minus 30 for me, plus 30 for Riggs, alleys for Riggs. He then gave me only one serve, and won his $1,000 back, which was fine with me. I was not aware what Dreyfus bet when I played Bobby in singles. We played on clay all week in two former engine repair yards just across from the midtown tunnel in Queens. Bobby played so much better at the end of the week. It couldn't have hurt because I won the French Open immediately afterwards.

'Nowadays Riggs makes $5,000 every time he does something silly on some show.'

In the first French Open Championship in 1968 Rosewall fell behind, having split the first two sets, 5-1 in the third against an amateur of medium-to-low ranking, the tall Herb Fitzgibbon, looking like the Princeton grad he was, with his square, even shoulders tapering down to long legs. However, professionalism reasserted itself, or better, world class skill over a player at a lower level, as Rosewall threw his ground strokes into the attack, kicking up the white powder off the baselines with chalk, and pulled out the match. Princeton might have a higher educational level than Rockdale elementary school, but not in the Stade Roland Garros. Another tall man had been felled by Rosewall's axe.

In the final he confronted Laver. This tournament, or at least its professional equivalent, had been virtually Rosewall's private fiefdom, but in 1967 Laver had finally usurped it. Interestingly, for those who claim Rosewall was only outstanding on clay or a slow surface, the French Professional had been played indoors on fast wood from 1963 on, and Rosewall had won it in 1963, 1964, 1965, and 1966, besides of course winning it in 1958 and 1960-62 when it was outdoors on red clay in Roland Garros. The indoor arena had been in the Stade Pierre de Coubertin, a small intimate stadium holding 4,000 spectators, lit by overhead skylight. But now, with the advent of open pro-am tennis, the French pro tournament ceased to exist, having served its purpose, and attention reverted once again to Roland Garros.

In the final against Rod Laver, Rosewall played impeccable tennis before adoring French fans, who with Gallic wisdom had always recognized him as the great player he was, and he won 6-3, 6-1, 2-6, 6-2. Instead of the youngest, he was now the oldest—an extraordinary, legendary feat for a man of thirty-four on what is recognized as the most gruelling, exhausting test in tennis. Sensibly, not wanting to push his luck too far, Rosewall, now forty, does not play in the French tournament. In addition, he says, 'The field and the length of the event is limited, and early rounds are only best-of-three sets.'

Surprising Pasarell

The great match of Wimbledon's first open tournament was to come. R.E. Storer, the editor of *Tennis*, U.S.A., the official publication of the USLTA, made one of the most astute analyses of Rosewall's game among the piles of reportage written about him over twenty-five years: 'His game is built around superlative ground strokes, delivered with pinpoint accuracy, and incredible ability to cover court and the areas around it, a diabolical perception of his opponent's weaknesses, and an unwavering concentration. He is · truly a connoisseur's player.' The match of Rosewall v. Pasarell lasted five sets, was interrupted by rain twice and brought the crowd to its feet for an ovation at the end. Pasarell was a big hitter with powerful long swings of the racket. Pasarell flailed a topspin lob that tore over Rosewall's head, dipping viciously to the rear of the court. Rosewall dashed furiously back, barely reaching it only a step from the backstop net, while Pasarell triumphantly moved to the net, but Ken managed to flick up a lob so surprising Pasarell that he belted an overhead into the bottom of the net. Storer said of Rosewall, 'He still covers the court like a rabbit.' Rosewall had won the match, but lost a subsequent one, failing to reach the finals. Laver won the tournament over Tony Roche 6-3, 6-4, 6-2. The general gloom about Rosewall's future as an active tennis player was portrayed by Herbert Warren Wind, a *New Yorker* writer, in a well-written, sympathetic account of the 1968 Forest Hills tourney, its first open. Free from the raucous sensationalism of the daily press, unencumbered by the daily deadline pressure on most reporters, Wind analysed the prevailing wind as to Rosewall's future. He said Rosewall was 'a discernible shade past his tennis peak.' He was no longer fast enough on a fast surface like grass. Wind, incidentally—unlike some less astute, chauvinistic commentators of the tennis scene such as Julius Heldman, who failed to list Rosewall among the top ten players of all time in an article, 'Styles of the Great,' published in Will Grimsley's *Tennis,* including people on his list such as Ashe, Riggs and Alice Marble—recognized that 'the best player in the world from 1960 to 1965 was Rosewall.'

Wind had noticed Rosewall's career in the past. He had admired his ability to win with a baseline game, coming to net only when it was tactically prudent. He saw him achieve an even par with Gonzales, and then, as Gonzales slipped into semi-retirement, surpass him. He observed Rosewall become a net player by necessity after turning pro. Rosewall told him, 'I felt I had to try to play that way, because under the conditions, it was the easiest and most certain way to victory. Indoors, the percentages for making good passing shots are very low.' He had extolled Rosewall's 'incredible speed and agility' going into the net after his serve to volley the return. This was of course remarkable because Rosewall's first serve was slightly less fast than the other top players'. His quickness and decisiveness on the final volley compensated for a serve sufficiently takable to enable the opponent on occasion to make a good return. Wind also detected that, after turning pro, Rosewall had 'beefed up' his serve.

Wind, too, made some very interesting remarks on Rosewall at his peak in 1963. First of all, wrote Wind, 'He was so far superior to all his opponents, Laver included, that none of his matches was ever remotely close.' Then Wind made a fascinating discovery. He had been perplexed as to why

Rosewall was always in position for the ball when 'men of comparable agility weren't.' I would disagree that there were men of equal agility,* but Wind unveiled a Rosewall secret: At the grass-court tournament of pros in Forest Hills in 1963, he placed his hand in front of his eyes so that he could only see Rosewall and his half of the court.· He noticed that after Rosewall made a shot, he took twice as many steps getting into position for the next one as the typical player. Wind said fifteen was average, but Rosewall took about thirty. There were, he described precisely, 'a series of quarter- and half-steps.' The moment Ken hit the ball he began to get into the best place to receive it—that section of the court providing the location with the highest defensive percentage. Usually this was the middle. When the other player committed himself, 'he went on adjusting with a succession of tiny side-steps.' Rosewall had usually guessed where the ball was going anyway, but by the time his dance was complete, he was perfectly ready to meet the ball, his weight and feet properly balanced, the sphere the correct distance from his body, the racket meeting it square in the middle at the right height and forward trajectory to drive it with perfect timing and fluidity to the opponent's court.†

This matter of being perfectly in position was also noticed by Gonzales in recent years: 'The reason Rosewall has lasted so long and avoided injuries is that he's always perfectly in position for the ball.'

Wind did not want to say 'how Rosewall at his peak would have fared against Kramer, Gonzales and Laver at their peaks,' and he concluded his lament for Rosewall's sad future by saying 'Rosewall stands as the most attractive player of the

---

* The period in question spans Rosewall's past twenty-five-year career; however, Chase says, 'Fred Perry and Bobby Riggs, whom I saw play at their peaks, were very fast; Rigs in particular could get to almost any ball, and so, too, could Gonzales.'

†Rosewall's invention of running with a series of short steps is now being indirectly recognized by other players, albeit through the advice of track star Henry Hines, who has been helping Ashe, Tanner, Smith, Lutz, Gorman and Pasarell with their running on court. In *Tennis*, May 1975, Pasarell is quoted as saying, 'Hines showed me how two or three little steps were faster than the one big stride I was accustomed to taking.'

postwar era,' but 'he is now starting down the far side of the slope.'

As if to prove his point, at Forest Hills in 1968 Rosewall lost to Okker in the semis, 8-6, 6-4, 6-8, 6-1. Wind detected that what really did Rosewall in was being up against 'a young Rosewall.' This sharp insight was to be remembered some years later when Rosewall met another young version of himself. Okker's speed and quickness in returning in 'rat-tat-tat' fashion shots Rosewall normally would have won with, 'may more than anything else have convinced Rosewall of the impossibility of his task.' In this tournament, in which he was the last pro to fall before Ashe, who, still an amateur, made his career's first great tournament triumph, Rosewall tried 'to work Tom as hard as he could, but Okker's stamina was his equal that day.'

In an exclusive interview he granted me at the Philadelphia tournament in January 1975, Tom Okker said, 'The first time I played [Rosewall] was in the semi-finals at Forest Hills in 1968. I asked Dick Savitt how to play him and he said to hit out against his serve, that it was useless to chip against him because he was too quick on the volley. His serve is much better and faster than one thinks, and with its low trajectory is not easy to hit.' Okker is a bit reserved on first meeting and has deep brown eyes which are enigmatic. I could not tell if he was mocking me, deeply serious about my questions or worried about me.

Subsequently, Rosewall gained an edge over Okker in their encounters, and he says, 'Tom Okker is a very clever player and very talented and quick. His problem is he gets nervous in a big match, though he wins lots of matches and tournaments. He says he always loses in Holland. He keeps twirling his racket. His forehand is very unorthodox and hit with a lot of wrist and topspin. You cannot defend against his forehand when at net but just go to the middle and hope. I don't think even Tom knows where he's going to hit it. His only weakness, perhaps, is the forehand volley, which he hits up with the wrist set back too much. He has a very good serve for such a relatively small man.

'The best thing with Okker's topspin forehand is to hit through it. Otherwise, if you just meet it, it'll bounce high off the racket and go too high, and you hit through it with a low trajectory at net if you're volleying it because otherwise the spin will carry it deep past the baseline. It's virtually a ping-pong stroke, very unorthodox, hit off balance and out of position, but very effective.'

Problems With New Players

Laver did better against the amateurs in 1968, while Rosewall was being beaten by a number of them such as Roche, Newcombe and Ashe. But Laver had played them as an amateur, whereas Rosewall had not. Newcombe said, 'Some of us had played Laver as an amateur. So we knew about him. But Muscles was new to us. It must have been tough on him. All of us were out to get him, and he had to learn how to play each of us one by one.' It might be argued that Rosewall was new to the amateurs as well as vice versa, and therefore just as difficult for them. However, the newcomer in tennis does have a slight advantage over the established player. He will know more about the seasoned star than vice versa. Two recent examples were when unknown Jeff Borowiak won his first WCT tournament, and then never another, and when Cliff Richey reached the finals of his first WCT tournament, rarely doing as well again.

Rosewall was earning around $50,000 in winnings in 1968, though doubtless the heavy expenses of flying, hotel bills, taxis and restaurant food were comsuming much of this. Rosewall was careful about money. 'I come from an ordinary hard-working middle-class family. I was taught to be thrifty.' As a result, his fellow players made a joke of pretending he did not like to pick up cheques. Rosewall sent his money home to his family.

Ken says, 'When I first turned pro with Jack Kramer, he paid some of the expenses. The team, when touring America, travelled by car, and he paid for the car and gas and oil. The players drove it. Later on, in the early pro days, we got no expenses, which usually meant no travel expenses, and you had to pay for them out of what you won. Nowadays some tournaments will give hospitality to the players due to the courtesy of the people in the area where the tournament is being played. There are very few tournaments on the circuit which have any form of paid expenses over and above the prize money.'

In the finals of the 1969 French tournament, Rosewall lost in three sets to Laver. Someone asked Rosewall after his loss, 'Are you still the same weight as in 1953 when you won here?'

'I'm a bit heavier in the pocket.'

Despite his shyness, Rosewall can be quite witty on occasion, particularly when his hearer gains his confidence or, as happened in a victory speech after one tournament, where listeners were amused by how clever and charming his talk was.

Fred Stolle says, 'Rosewall is never off. The pressure is on you every second because you know when you hit a bad shot he'll make you pay for it without fail.

'He's got you crazy serving because his return is so good. You know if you miss the first serve you might as well forget the point, because Muscles will murder the second ball. You're pressing so hard to serve well on the first ball that you usually miss it, and you're at the mercy of what he'll do to the second. I'd rather play Laver any day.'

A low point of Rosewall's career came at Wimbledon in 1969, when he lost in the third round to Bob Lutz in four sets. He even allowed himself to be distracted more than Lutz by an adjacent crowd's cheers over the score on the electronic board describing the Centre-Court match between Ashe and Graham Stilwell, one of the better English players. Rosewall was on court No. 3.

At Forest Hills David Gray, in *World Tennis*, said Ashe had trouble with Rosewall's cleverly placed serve, while Rosewall could not return sufficiently Ashe's fast ones in the first set. Then Ashe began to lash Rosewall's serve back, 'and Rosewall wilted. It was a beautiful wilt, but he suddenly stopped taking part in the match.' Was this the prelude to a Rosewall disaster-fiasco in a tournament years later?

Rosewall lost in the quarter-finals to Ashe, 8-6, 6-3, 6-4.

Rosewall was dropped to fifth in the world by Lance Tingay, never a Rosewall admirer, in his annual rankings. A *Daily-Express* sports reporter listed Rosewall as tied for fifth with Ashe. So forgotten was Rosewall—to some degreee—that

Adrian Quist, a famous old Australian star, called Laver 'the best tennis player Australia has produced,' ranking him with Budge, Kramer and Gonzales.

A *World Tennis* reporter listed Rosewall as No. 5. In 1969 Rosewall lost all six matches to Laver. For the whole year he won only two minor tournaments—the pro-only tournament at Wembley, which had lost its importance with open tennis, and one at Bristol.

6

Comeback

Early in 1970 Rosewall said, 'I wish I was ten years younger. There's never been so much money in tennis before.' Though he was far from being No. 1 and increasingly in the shadow of Laver and a few of the younger stars like Newcombe and Roche, there was the compensation of winning $39,250 in a week by losing in a $10,000 match to Laver for a runner-up prize of $4,250, and winning two $10,000 matches over Stolle and Okker and a $15,000 one over Emerson—all in the U.S.

At the final of the Dunlop Open in Sydney, March 1970, Mr. Rosewall was in the stands watching his son play Laver. Ken remembers, 'He had a fainting spell, which proved to be a mild one, caused by excitement and from sitting in a cramped position for the three-hour match. Now he does not see me play very much.'

Mr. Rosewall says, 'I wish I'd worked more on his serve. But Ken had a good overhead smash, and I thought the serve would come naturally.'

Wimbledon, 1970

At the age of thirty-five, the end of Rosewall's playing career seemed to many to be nearing. An observer at Wimbledon in 1970 was the well-known American writer, John McPhee, who had previously written an unusual book about Arthur Ashe and Clark Graebner, attempting in part to analyse their games on the basis of their life-styles and political opinions. Now he was covering the major tournament for a pictorial essay, titled conventionally enough, 'Wimbledon', but in passing his eye rested on Rosewall in an initial round, and he wrote felicitously, 'Rosewall is the most graceful tennis player now playing the game and gracefully he sutures Addison two, four and zero.' As Rosewall progressed through the early rounds of the 1970 Wimbledon, five years away from his peak, excitement gathered little by little. He beat Roche in the quarters, staying back on half of his first serves. Roche avoided Rosewall's backhand too studiously, enabling Ken to hit easier forehand drives than usual. He was like a lizard in his speed around the court, anticipating Roche's best shots. Ken says, 'That was one of the best matches I've ever played. Tony was about to prove he was the best, or the second or third best player in the world. We all know he's had a lot of physical problems since then, but he's still a wonderful player. In that match he figured that as a left-hander it would be more profitable to have his shots spinning into my body on my forehand than to hit them to my backhand, where I had good placement and very good control. Of course, in a match of that length it's not possible to hit every shot to one side, and I had to play a lot of good backhands.'

Meanwhile Roger Taylor encountered Rod Laver and upset him, the sensation of the tournament to that point, and it is interesting to note that Laver has not won a single major championship since then. Rosewall comments, 'The reason Laver lost to Taylor at Wimbledon in 1970, and Taylor is not anywhere near as good a player, may have been because he was nervous about protecting his record. After a top player has won a big tournament several times in a row, he begins to feel the law of averages is against him, and tightens up, protecting the record, and is not loose.'

Rosewall met Taylor in the semi-finals. Taylor, the son of a coal miner, is a tough-looking, handsome man with dark hair and a perennial look of anger at the world.

Taylor, wanting to escape Roche's error of emphasizing Rosewall's forehand, hit often to Rosewall's backhand, and for his pains he was frequently passed. Rosewall remembers, 'Roger Taylor's flaw is his backhand, which is defensive—as a lot of left-handers used to be, though when I played him in the WCT round of eight in Dallas in 1973, his backhand was the best I've ever seen it. His big, swinging left-handed serve is effective against left-handers as it bounces high and away from their backhands, which is why Laver has had trouble with him.

'In a WCT tournament in 1973 Taylor was involved in a final against Ashe, had match point against Ashe and hit a volley which was one foot in; the lineswoman, who was behind Ashe, must have watched Ashe and, when Ashe didn't hit it and let it bounce, assumed it was out. It was shocking. I was watching with Stolle before our doubles. Then Taylor lost the set and the next set, but you have to put up with these things. But it would have thrown anyone.'

The excitement about Rosewall finally reached its peak when he entered the last round to play for the championship against the tall, twenty-six-year-old John Newcombe, the then emerging Australian champion, who looks like the sort of man who would eat one alive and laugh cheerfully as he did so. Newcombe has a rather large nose and pronounced thrust to his shoulders to add to the piratical impression. He also likes to tell jokes. Newcombe also has the classic big game—smashing serve, powerful forehand with topspin—which he employed frequently then by running around his backhand. The evening before Rosewall and Stolle had played in a long doubles match, but Rosewall had beaten Newcombe the three times they had played earlier in the year.

However, Hoad and Drobny, those old, now-retired warriors, one-time victors over Rosewall at Wimbledon, and Jack Kramer, told the world on television that Rosewall would win. It certainly seemed to be his last chance.

Rosewall was the sentimental favourite, and the crowd roared its encouragement. In the finals Newcombe, too, learned from Roche's mistake. The serve wide to the forehand in the deuce count leaves too much court open for the defender to pass the incoming server. So Newcombe most often served the ball to Rosewall's backhand in the deuce count. Making a major effort, Rosewall won the first set. The crowd cheered as wildly as the British ever do, stirred by memories of Drobny's great victory sixteen years earlier over Rosewall. The little champ at the close of his active tennis life was at last going to receive his reward—Wimbledon.

Nevertheless, while Rosewall had several break points

against Newcombe in the second and third sets, he lost both. Newcombe was throwing up a number of lobs against Rosewall's net play. Rosewall sat on his chair between changeovers, his chin on his hand, looking confused and lost. Gloom hung around the boyish figure as he desperately tried to figure a way out of his predicament. He looked 'old and weary'. Only the tremendous support of the crowd drove him to fight on.

Then occurred another Rosewall comeback. He cut and slashed with the volley, dancing to the net, flicking shot after shot past Newcombe. Suddenly the fourth set was his. Ken remembers, 'I recall being down 3-1 in the fourth set. I guess I was the sentimental favourite. The crowd was more for me than against John, as I had never won and had been so close on previous occasions, and John had won once before. Somehow, through the support of the crowd and maybe having lost the two previous sets reasonably comfortably, it was a question for me of going for broke, and I played very well. John perhaps became a little nervous so close to the championship.'

But in the fifth set Newcombe wore Rosewall down with some more lobs. Newcombe, bothered by the crowd's partisanship, succeeded in overcoming it. His shirt hung outside his shorts, his hair was matted with sweat. He roared back, winning game after game. He reached and muffed match point. At the second match point, Newcombe hit a hard first serve to Ken's backhand, which Rosewall lifted fairly high down the line; Newcombe, racing over, stroked a forehand volley cross-court which Rosewall, dashing towards it, could not reach.

Afterwards the newspapers described Rosewall in the match as 'a dying man'. Another journal said that for Rosewall it was 'heart-rending'. Even Newcombe, sitting beside Rosewall in the postmatch press conference, added to the atmosphere of farewell to Ken by telling him, 'You're going to Newport, Wales, next week, aren't you? Good, you can win that.'

Rosewall said of his Wimbledon miss, 'If I had not played in the doubles, I'm not saying I would have won, but maybe I could have stood the pace a little better. Maybe I put too much pressure on myself there.

'At Wimbledon, in the final against Newcombe, I had a little bad luck. The day before, the Centre Court was dry as was the outside court I practised on before the match. Why, I don't know, but the tarpaulin cover was left on the Centre Court until just before we played, producing a different surface—heavy and slick. I won the first set 7-5, but the effort burned me out more. My game, where I have to break service and often play the return of serve after it has bounced on the court, depends on the court more, whereas for a big server it makes less difference because he wins more points on his first serve, which is additionally helped by a poor surface.'

Over the remaining summer months a change was starting to kindle in Rosewall. The memory of his loss at Wimbledon and the valedictory attitude of the world towards him made Rosewall realize his great talent had not been recognized and that certain alterations in his approach to life and tennis were necessary. He was gradually coming out of himself, becoming slightly more open with the press and those around him. He was learning to concentrate more on the key matches, saving his energy, conserving his strength, going for winners to prevent a match from tiring him out. His style on the court became both more relaxed and yet more aggressive.

Forest Hills 1970

When Forest Hills began at the end of August, Ken was seeded third behind Laver (1) and Newcombe (2). He was very accurate in beating Pilic in the round of 16. Pilic had done well earlier, defeating Gonzales. Laver was eliminated in five sets by Ralston, showing too much caution throughout the match, on one point before he finally won it, hitting four overhands. Laver had overcompensated for his wildness against Taylor at Wimbledon.

Like Newcombe and Roche, Stan Smith was a new young star who had risen to the top in tennis. He had first made a name for himself by winning the U.S. doubles championship with Bob Lutz in 1968, then the U.S. singles in 1969, and the Australian doubles championship in 1970 again with Lutz. Rosewall outfoxed Stan Smith in the quarter-finals by watching him carefully. When Smith leaned slightly towards the alley, waiting to receive Rosewall's serve in the ad court,

Rosewall would hit it straight at him. Manoeuvrability has never been Smith's strong point. Smith would step back, preparing to swing his backhand, but the ball would curve into his body, thus forcing 'big Stan' into an ungainly error or weak return. Smith lost all three sets, winning only six games. So much for six-foot-four-inch Stan, who had, by the way, entered the match brimming with confidence, having knocked off Roy Emerson. *World Tennis* described Rosewall's quick victory over Smith in the quarters as 'a soft-shoe shuffle'. Ken said, 'Against Smith at Forest Hills I jammed him with my serve so that he couldn't hit his backhand with enough distance from his body and consequent topspin. The uncertain bounce on grass helped.'

Then came Rosewall's semi-final match with Newcombe, his conqueror at Wimbledon two months before, the young, tall athlete who had destroyed his last apparent opportunity to win the biggest prize of all. As play began, Newcombe looked overconfident. There then ensued one of the most brilliant and devastating displays of perfect tennis that I have ever seen. Rosewall, inspired by determination to compensate for his earlier Wimbledon defeat, dedicated to establishing himself now or never, hit the ball with such unerring accuracy and speed, never letting down at any moment, that it was interesting to see Newcombe's face suddenly darken, first with anger and then frustration, as the shots flew by him beyond reach so acutely angled that they forced him from side to side, back and forth, driving him to defeat. Sometimes Rosewall served soft balls that floated more than normal. He gave Newcombe a lesson in the return of serve as well as assorted other strokes. Rosewall's backhand, forehand, lob, volley and serve were individual studies in the highest art, driven by the determination of an older star to overcome his opponent's youth. To compare Rosewall's play that afternoon with his peak in the early- and mid-sixties is impossible, for whereas the one was the result of effortless control, the latter was a hard fight to overcome age, producing a triumph of spirit over time as deadly as it was deliberate.

Rosewall had one lucky break in his semi-final revenge on Newcombe. Down 15-40 on his serve, 5-4, second set, he mis-hit his second serve, which might have been a double fault but instead spun awry, aceing Newcombe. *World Tennis* called Rosewall's tennis 'mind-boggling. . . . There were moments when one felt one had never seen anyone, anywhere, play better.' Rosewall reached Newcombe's widest-angled shots. A British newspaper told its readers that Rosewall made only seven errors during the match. It was revenge for Wimbledon.

When we were discussing the match together once down in Australia, I said, 'You played brilliant tennis in beating Newcombe two months later at Forest Hills. Did you learn to concentrate more and develop authority in key situations?' Ken replied, 'John was a little overconfident, and he may not have been as match sharp as he had been coaching at his tennis ranch, but still he had four or five matches to get back into form. One reason I played better was I knew the season was over and I was going home to Wilma and the kids right after the tournament.'

In the other half of the draw Tony Roche was advancing successfully. In the quarter-finals he had won over Brian Fairlie of New Zealand 6-3, 7-5, 7-6, while Cliff Richey defeated Ralston, Laver's conqueror, 7-6, 6-3, 6-4. Roche then overcame Richey, who was having his best year ever, surprisingly easily, 6-2, 7-6, 6-1. Roche was expected to win the finals by most observers. Consistently underrated, though the records showed him second only to Laver, Rosewall's age and careful game were not judged to be strong enough by those mysterious processes which make up public opinion. In fact, most tennis fans and writers, if asked, would have said Roche was Laver's heir and already second best. After their matches of the day before Roche was bound to be fresher.

In an interview he gave me some years later, Tony Roche said, 'I don't serve to Rosewall normally as a left-hander usually does to a right-hander. My serve would usually go to the backhand, but with Rosewall I hit to the forehand, and I like to return serve to his forehand volley as that's his weakness, while his backhand volley is deadly.'

Rosewall said, 'My plan against Roche was to aim for his topspin forehand and either cut if off with volleys or hit ground strokes and serves to it. I warmed up with my friend, Ray Ruffels, who is a left-hander like Roche.'

The stadium was filled. The videotape of the match, which I

watched several years later in a CBS studio in New York, shows that it was a day of bright sunshine, a typically hot late summer day for New York. The grass looked quite parched and brown in some places. Rosewall would use his favourite racket, the wooden Slazenger, reputed to have a cracked frame. Ken says, 'The racket was not cracked, but it was an old one of mine, and well used, and I had four or five strings replaced in the centre as they were a little too tight.'

Tony Roche was once a member of a pro touring group in the early part of 1968 known as the 'Handsome Eight'. However, beauty was not his speciality. His chest was like a barrel, his face a kind of squashed pancake, his physique marked by bent, powerful sloping shoulders, so that he resembled both a tank and a duck on the tennis court. At the same time there was a likeable quality to his face, notable for its lack of guile and rugged features. He did not look as though he would hurt a fly, except under extreme provocation.

Both men were slightly tired from the pressure of their semi-final matches the day before. The tennis was not as sharp as it could be, often a feature of championship contests in tennis, where the pressure to get there in the first place and the frequent scheduling without a day's rest meant the players were fatigued. Tournament officials, of course, want to end the tournament within its scheduled period, without incurring extra expense or irritating the ticket-buying public.

Roche had little trouble with Rosewall's service in the first set, winning 6-2. In his inimitable style Rosewall trudged between serves from one side of his end of the court to the other, trying to figure out what to do. Patiently he would take up his position before serving. He would inhale deeply. Then he would gaze at Roche.

Rosewall said, 'The first set went badly, but in the second my shots became sharper. I was getting more used to the left-handed spin.' By the second set Rosewall's serve was becoming more accurate against Roche's weaker forehand, so Roche started to return Rosewall's serves shoulder high and Rosewall volleyed them away easily. Roche tried to swing his service around the court, looking for a weak spot in Rosewall's return of service. Roche could not get low enough to the ball on Rosewall's deep serves, which also had a low trajectory, so that Roche could not come over the ball with his topspin stroke. Ken won the second set 6-4.

The extraordinary quality about Rosewall's play in the middle of the match was how cleverly and sensibly he paced himself, rising to the important occasion with superb shots, thinking all along how to win over Roche. In the third set he was down three set points, but managed to raise his game to a peak and won the set 7-6. In the fourth set, immediately following the tie-breaker, he turned on again his great championship skill, hitting a lovely surprise forehand. His serve was a marvel to watch—similar only in the technique to the work of a great baseball pitcher. He never seemed to hit the same serve twice in a row to Roche. He would hit a few hard ones to either corner. He hit an ace several feet up from the ad corner by the alley line. He hit down the middle to Roche. He served slightly to his left and slightly to his right. He served some soft spinning ones and many medium-paced ones.

Between points he took his time, neither being laggardly nor rushing it, sometimes relaxing totally so that his feet almost dragged along and his head drooped slightly to one side. Once he signalled politely, 'Wait a minute,' until he was ready. He was acutely aware that in order to go to the extreme of physical effort, as he had to during a point, it made sense at his age to relax as much as possible, between moments of play.

After he had won the third set, Rosewall maintained a high level of concentration. Roche, on the other hand, hurried the first two points of the fourth set, losing both of them, the second one a terrible smash into the net of a blooping Rosewall return of Roche's serve. With the score 5-2 in his favour, needing only one more service to win to become champion, Rosewall relaxed on Roche's serve, letting him win it. In all the other games he ran as hard as he could for everything, wearing Roche down.

Roche, however, despite his impressive equipment of faster first serve, his big topspin forehand and his powerful volleys decisively angled to the side, played with little imagination. Most of the time he seemed just to hit the ball back, making the standard shots and volleys. Between points he was planted on his feet, staring intensely at the court and Rosewall, summoning up his concentration but without really taking a broader view of his situation. After Rosewall won the third set tie-breaker, something seemed to go out of Roche. There was an air of defeat about him, though he tried on every point.

On match point Rosewall just served an easy first serve slightly to Roche's forehand, surprising him so that Rosewall swiftly volleyed away the return. Dropping his racket, he raised both arms high in victory showing the relative frailty of his ribs under the white sports shirt. Then he shook hands with Roche, put his arm around him and a few moments later gave him some comforting pats.

Both men sat on the benches drinking soft refreshments. Rosewall was very cool for the first few minutes as if unwinding from the effort. Poor Roche sat glumly, motionless, looking as if he was going to cry over his lost chance, his face burning with humiliation and anger and rage. But a few minutes later he had mastered himself, his sportsmanship coming back so that he was even able to make a joke about Rosewall to the crowd: 'It just goes to show you, you should never do Muscles a favour. I took his laundry out for him last night.' Rosewall said to the crowd over the microphone, 'I've been preparing my speech during those long times between wins.'

The press and Rosewall were still having trouble communicating. After the match a reporter asked, 'Will you play Wimbledon next year?'

'Well I don't know why not.'

'How did you beat Tony Roche?'

'Well, I played my regular game. I hit a few serves and a few volleys.'

Rosewall said to me recently, 'I had some difficulty when open tennis began, as I had not played any of the amateurs or registered players, whereas Laver knew many of them, having been an amateur in 1963. I was an amateur in 1956. I studied them, and this may have been a reason for my come-back starting with the Wimbledon final in 1970 and Forest Hills later that year. Also there was more pressure on the pros while the amateurs had nothing to lose.

'One of the ways I beat Tony Roche was that I stood three feet from the centre of the baseline when serving to the ad court. This meant my serve was able to go over a lower part of the net than if I was at dead centre, and it pushed him wider. It gave me with my short height less chance of hitting the net. Also, his forehand is hit with a lot of topspin and comes a little high sometimes, and you can spring in there and take it on a high volley. This applied to serving into the deuce court, too.'

Rosewall was starting to achieve recognition. *The New Yorker* critic said of Rosewall at Forest Hills in 1970, 'The ball blew off his racket in a low, flat trajectory, the way breakfast cereal used to be fired from guns.' He went on, 'A hoard of tennis lovers admired him as the supreme artist among the postwar players.' Grimsley compared Rosewall's tennis technique to 'the artistry of a volin maestro.' His strokes were like a 'sabre slash.' Rosewall's win at Forest Hills caused *World Tennis* to put him on the cover underneath a headline, 'Learning to play Tennis After the Age of. Fifty.' Laver described Rosewall as 'rejuvenated' after winning Forest Hills in 1970, predicting he would be 'tough' into his forties.

The tie-breaker had been introduced for the first time at Forest Hills in 1970. Rosewall had done well, winning three out of four, unlike Ashe, who lost all of his, but afterwards Ken said, 'It's nerve-racking.' Rosewall was the oldest player to win Forest Hills since Tilden won it in 1929. Rosewall was thirty-five, Tilden thirty-six.

Rosewall had made the first major step of his comeback. He was discovering how to wed his talents to wise guidance from his brain, turning age into sagacity, controlling his game and his temperament for the utmost effect. At that time, a new player coming up was Ilie Nastase. Ken says of him, 'I only played Nastase once, in 1970 and won. His serve and volley have greatly improved since then. Gonzales is right when he says he must stop playing around and concentrate or people will lose interest in him. Perhaps he started to believe what the newspapers had written about him. It's all right for a top player to joke sometimes but it's not amusing when a minor one tries to and is losing at the same time. Nastase's game, with his very fast reactions, has no weaknesses, except possibly his second serve, which he hits with a lot of topspin, and this makes it fall short sometimes; but he's so quick that he can compensate when coming to net. The topspin makes it jump high and you can come down on it and hit it cross-court.

This is one advantage the lower trajectory my serve has, which is deeper and comes in low to the opponent.

'When Nastase is standing way over in deep by the side-lines in the ad court, receiving my serve, I don't try for a shot to his backhand, nor do I hit it fairly short and quick for the Tee as he's too quick and would get into it; but I serve it deep down the line and take my chances, coming into net as I can get a volley to either side, and if he hits a passing shot either side, striking the lines, there's nothing you can do about it anyway.'

Rosewall won $140,455 in 1970. A leading tennis magazine still failed to recognize his achievements for the year, listing Newcombe No. 1 as the Wimbledon winner, but the more important Martini and Rossi Award for the year's top player, voted by a more astute international panel of tennis journalists, was given to Rosewall. Unappreciated was the fact that his record against the other twenty top stars, from the start of open tennis in 1968 through 1970, was second only to Laver's. Rosewall had 66 wins to 30 losses, and, except for Laver, he had an edge in matches over all the remaining eighteen. (However, his one match with Okker was a loss. Newcombe, much more highly touted, had a 131-114 record. Stan Smith was 23-41; Ashe 72-56; Roche 118-100 and Emerson 151-103.)

At the same time the Australian Championship began. Rosewall was seeded second behind Laver. Rod's reputation in Australia was affected by the discovery of a newspaper that he had reserved a seat on a plane out of Australia prior to his defeat in a doubles match.* He had already lost in the singles, probably reducing the tournament's attendance.

Aussie Champ Again

Rosewall faced Arthur Ashe in the finals of the open. Ashe was described as the 'American Negro' by the Australian press. Rosewall had wisely returned to Sydney three weeks

---

* In fairness to Laver it should be pointed out that players often make airline reservations before a tournament is concluded so that if the player loses, he will be able to get a seat on the next flight; if the player wins, he cancels that reservation and makes another for the day immediately following his next match, and so on.

before the tournament to rest and practise on grass, unlike many of the other WCT players who flew in just before opening hostilities. Rosewall had won over Dick Crealy in the second round 7-5, 7-5, 7-5; Ismail el Shafei 6-0, 6-2, 7-5; Roy Emerson 6-4, 6-4, 6-3; and Tom Okker, in the semis, 6-2, 7-6, 6-4. The latter match was held Saturday afternoon, giving him Saturday evening for recuperation. Ashe played his semi-finals Saturday night and Rosewall beat him the next afternoon 6-1, 7-5, 6-3.

Though Rosewall, the better and more experienced player, would probably have won anyway, as Ashe admitted afterwards, the White City officials had proved as bright as their counterparts at Forest Hills and Dallas in scheduling in such a way as to favour one player over another. Newcombe beat Kodes in the finals of Forest Hills in 1973, having had a .relatively easy win over Rosewall in the semis, while Kodes had overcome Smith in five exhausting sets the day before. Rosewall similarly suffered in WCT 1973, losing in five sets to Ashe after playing five sets against Taylor less than twenty-four hours earlier. Riessen had been eliminated from the WCT finals in 1972, having led Laver two sets to love, then losing the next three *after beating Drysdale the night before in five sets,* while Laver had had forty-eight hours' rest. Tournament directors put forward arguments of attendance and expense for their unfair scheduling.

Ken remembers, 'Ashe, a mediocre player on clay, is always dangerous on grass. The American tennis ball is lighter and faster than the heavier Australian or European. In the Australian Championship in 1971 I beat Ashe on grass at White City here. He beat me at Forest Hills in 1969. Ashe doesn't like clay courts. He doesn't hit his forehand volley that well. And he doesn't vary his game sufficiently, always hitting all out, though occasionally I've seen him be careful on clay. Newcombe is right in saying that Ashe's second serve is shorter than his own, which is the best in the game, and it bounces high with topspin; a player like Laver can roll his wrist and racket over it and put away the return of serve. Laver won sixteen straight matches over Ashe. Ashe was under a lot of pressure for political reasons, as the only member of his race.'

'How do you play Rosewall?' I asked Arthur Ashe in an interview he gave me in January 1975.

'Badly . . . he beats the shit out of me. He beats everyone except Connors. I try to get my first serve in and change it around from forehand, backhand, down the middle, particularly altering the pace and spin, using a slice wide to his forehand, and then volley it cross-court as he has an awful lot of court to cover.

'The best way to play Rosewall is down the middle because if you give him an angle, he's so good on his ground strokes—the same with Laver and Connors—that wide angle will get you out of position and he'll pass you.

'Rosewall is like God, motherhood and apple pie. You can't argue with that.'

Rosewall had won the Australian and South African opens without losing a set, but he gave up a chance for the Grand Slam by not playing in the French in order to rest, much to the annoyance of the Gallic officials, who were equally upset at Laver's refusal. The French, with its long five-set matches on red clay, is a gruelling affair.

An Epic Contest

Just why Rosewall involved himself in an epic match against Richey at Wimbledon in 1971 in the quarter-finals is hard to say; Richey was the inferior player, though the previous year he had been the top player in the Grand Prix. Rosewall suffers from hay fever at Wimbledon due to the profusion of flowers. In 1971 he tried cortisone. The day before, Ken had a presentiment: 'He's young and he can run all day.'

To counter Richey's youth, Rosewall made him move all over the court—back and forth, side to side, with delicate dropshots and perfectly placed lobs. Richey attacked with hard first serves and forehands which slipped past Rosewall at net.

Near the end of the fourth set word of this tense drama had spread to the fans watching the matches on the outside court. Many congregated in front of the electric scoreboard. They began to cheer whenever Rosewall won a point. This action was a few seconds after the point had been played so that the delayed applause coming into the centre court produced an eerie effect.

Richey, though younger, appeared to be using more energy. His shirt was soaking wet. The crowd, solidly behind Rosewall, began to support Richey, too, as the match progressed. Richey, never known for a cheerful, relaxed demeanour on the court, behaved well, even accepting foot-fault calls without arguing. In the fifth set, Rosewall was behind on his serve 15-40 on three successive games, a familiar Rosewall drawback, but each time he won the game. Richey's comment to Rosewall at the net when he had just lost, 6-8,5-7,6-4,9-7,7-5, was 'Congratulations, iron man!'

When the match was over, the applause lasted so long that it continued until both men had disappeared from the court walking under the Royal Box. In view of this gruelling four-hour quarter-final against Richey, it is interesting to note that when Rosewall next played the same opponent in Forest Hills, in 1973, he dispatched him in three sets. Despite a day of rest, the ordeal against Richey had drained Rosewall and he was finished for that year's Wimbledon. In the semi-finals he lost to Newcombe in three quick sets.

The Queen honoured Rosewall with an M.B.E. Following the ceremony in Government House in Sydney, Rosewall remarked wistfully, with his usual modesty, that it seemed unfair that he, a young athlete, should receive such an honour compared to the elderly women similarly rewarded after lifetimes of dedication and work for charities.

During the U.S. Professional Championship in Boston, still a prestigious contest though no longer with the same significance as in the pre-open days, what aspect of Rosewall's character was it that Bud Collins discovered when he said other players at the tournament had dubbed him 'Saint Kenny'? Rosewall beat Ashe 6-3.6-4. In the semi-finals the temperature was 118°F. in an enclosed, open-air arena on a hard sunlight-reflecting surface and Rosewall saved his strength. His opponent, Marty Riessen, has a reputation for becoming nervous in big matches to such an extent that reportedly he will stay awake all night beforehand so that he will be sleepy and relaxed on the court, with the result that he usually loses. Riessen, a full ten years younger, melted in the heat and lost 3-6, 6-1, 6-4, 6-3. Ken says of Riessen, 'Marty Riessen lacks confidence in himself though he was never expected to become a top star and has developed his game into a good one.'

Married to a slim, beautiful girl with a childlike gentle walk, Marty Riessen is a tall, thin, handsome chap, an ex-basketball star, with a neat brown moustache and a stylish haircut. In a conversation with me in January 1975, Riessen said, 'I was always amused by Ken after late night matches when you have to unwind. Most of the guys go somewhere and have a beer, but Ken would take two beers out of the locker in the locker room and go back to his room to watch T.V. and go to bed. With all his wealth he was like Jack Benny. No one knew him well, but everyone liked him and for me he was—is—an idol. I love to watch him play. I always tried to rush him on my serve and on his. I figured I had to play percentage tennis against him. You couldn't afford to make errors, which was why he was so good. I think most of the players admired his game over the other great champions. I hit my serve three-quarters speed on the first serve to get it in rather than risk a second serve and come to net. On his serve I attacked too. I didn't want to let him get set for a shot. His backhand lob is particularly dangerous and gave me a lot of trouble. I couldn't cover the lines at net. If you came in too close, he would lob you, and he liked to hit the lob cross-court because it gave more court for it to land in. If you were too much over to one side he lobbed to the other. It wasn't an attcking lob, but it was perfectly placed.'

I watched the final of the 1971 U.S. Pro Championship in Boston on television. Ken faced Cliff Drysdale, a tall, good-looking South African with curly hair and a disgruntled determined expression. Drysdale had been harassed—justly or not— during the week by demonstrators protesting apartheid. But what fascinated me was how Rosewall reacted to the cauldron in which he was centre stage. The heat must have been simply unbelievable. Drysdale did not wear a hat. Ken wore a floppy Australian hat covering his head, ears and neck. Around his throat was tied a handkerchief. He moved very deliberately. With effortless grace he stroked the ball from side to side. Between points he rested, so cool he could have been at a garden party, the coolest person in the stadium.

In the intense heat of the Longwood Cricket Club Stadium, measured at 120°F. courtside, Rosewall threw up lob after lob, exhausting the much younger Drysdale, who had had a hard five-set victory over Newcombe the day before. Even Drysdale's famed backhand collapsed. The score was 6-4, 6-3, 6-0.

After the tournament people remarked on Rosewall's longevity in the heat compared to his more youthful rival's exhaustion. Once again he said he was lucky because Riessen and Drysdale had had hard matches the day before. 'Yes,' someone said, 'but at thirty-six don't you ever get tired?'

'Oh, well yes. I suppose so, but I seem to be able to keep going okay,' he replied, grinning.

Ken remembers, 'Cliff Drysdale's strength was his ground strokes, giving him a good return of serve, but he would strike the volley softly, not hard, and it paid me to hit the ball well nearer him when he was at net rather than go for a good passing shot, which has a higher element of risk, because he would return it so that I could get to it and hit a winner.'

Forest Hills officials in 1971 were particularly incensed at Rosewall for skipping the tournament in one of the perennial feuds between tennis factions. He was the defending champion. Several other stars did not play either. But at the time both Ken's sons were ill.

After Rosewall won the U.S. professional tournament in Boston in 1971, Ray Ruffels, a minor Australian star, observed, 'He just isn't interested some weeks. He seems to know that he has to give his mind time off between efforts.' As Ruffels had noted, and as Rosewall had done in particular on that very hot afternoon, Rosewall was learning to pace himself. Laver, his great rival, though he hadn't won a major tournament since 1969—except for the freak series of $10,000 matches which supplied a week's rest in between—was gaining all the headlines. Rosewall's comeback had gone almost unnoticed, even though in a year he had reached the finals at Wimbledon, won Forest Hills, won the Australian and won the U.S. Pro. As far as the public was concerned though, Laver was still the champ.

7

Laver

On the 1971 WCT tour Rosewall had the reputation among the younger players of being approachable for advice: I am having a problem with this shot, Ken. What should I do?' He was always happy to help. This was in contrast to an increasing reluctance among the older stars to help the newcomers, because of the vicious competition engendered by the WCT point system which gave points for every match leading to the big final in Dallas.

It had been a long hard year for Rosewall. The major tournament was only about two weeks away. Although he had made considerable progress in his comeback, winning Forest Hills in September 1970 and the Australian in January 1971, except for the U.S. Pro in Augest the year had not lived fully up to his expectations. He felt he needed some relaxation, a total break from tennis day in and day out travelling from one match and city to another in the WCT contest, which Rod seemed to be dominating anyway. So one night in Barcelona Ken used his sports jacket as a muleta, and to the entertainment of his friends the small, lithe figure made a series of passes at an imaginary bull, performing a graceful Australian version of the 'veronica'. Not relaxed enough, a week later he was in Alexandre's discotheque at 3 A.M. in Stockholm.

Dark Horse

Rosewall had come in second in the WCT standings, though winning four tournaments, and Laver first. Two of the minor players, Australians Phil Dent and Bill Bowry, for their own amusement and the entertainment of the others, pretended to be 'your friendly bookies' and issued a 'form guide', photocopied to show the odds on each of the eight 'horses' (WCT culminates in a tournament featuring the eight stars with the most points). This little joke was interesting as it demonstrated, at least in the case of Dent and Bowrey, the attitude among the players toward Rosewall and Laver. Laver, the public's idol, was described as 'champion since 1960.' Even though Rosewall had won more WCT tournaments than Laver, he was given odds of 7/2 behind Laver, 5/4, Okker, 3/1, Ashe, 5/2, and Newcombe, 2/1. Bowrey and Dent said their sheet had been typed by 'friendly Lucy.'

Though the final was to be held in Dallas the quarter- and semi-finals were played in Houston. In the first round, which was the same as the quarter-finals, Ken's accurate play combined with widely angled shots forced Newcombe into numerous errors. Ken won 7-5, 6-2, 5-7, 6-3. In the semi-finals he passed Okker with ease when Tom came to the net. When Rosewall was at net, Rosewall volleyed through Okker's famous topspin forehand and flicked back Tom's topspin lob with a lob of his own, then coming to net himself, driving Okker to the baseline and winning 6-3, 6-3, 6-1. He then faced Laver.

The $50,000 Final

This was the first WCT final, and though not exactly Wimbledon yet, there were four days of promotional appearances such as banquets and radio-TV interviews, television cameras at the match, Lamar Hunt's Texas efficiency and lavish hospitality, and $50,000 to the winner, plus assorted goodies such as a small car and jewellery. Rosewall was listed as a 12-to-1 long shot by Las Vegas. Representing three Texas values—fame, courage and sex— Charlton Heston, astronaut Neil Armstrong and Miss Texas were also present. Laver had won eight of his last nine matches against Rosewall.

Laver wore an incredible gold-amber tennis outfit, while Rosewall wore pale blue. Laver from the time of the toss of the racket had looked confident. The fast Sportface surface favoured Laver's style.

Laver was foot-faulted twice on his first serve in the first game—a rare event—his right foot moving onto the line an instant before his racket struck the ball. From then on he was unnerved, serving well inconsistently. Later during the match Laver received a new foot-fault judge—thanks to the decision of referee Tony Trabert—who never called another.

However the Sportface helped Rosewall a little too. Rosewall, by tossing the ball more to the right, was attaining more spin on his serve than Laver. His spin service jumped more than usual, making Laver lunge wider on his forehand and cramping him on his backhand. Ken remembers, 'At Dallas in 1971 I might have sliced the ball a little more by tossing the ball slightly more to the right to increase the side spin against Laver on the carpet, though his left-handed spin benefited too.

'The Sportface type of surface is only used by World Team Tennis now, as it's going out of favour, whereas WCT in 1975 used the Supreme court type of surface being developed currently, which plays much slower and makes for longer rallies and an all-court game. All synthetic surfaces seem to exaggerate the spin, but the Sportface did particularly so—at least on side spin, though the topspin jumped less than on some other surfaces. So Rod's serve which has a lot more spin than mine, was helped by it, but the side spin, caused by my slicing it or coming round the ball, was increased and helped me to get the ball into his backhand, if I intended serving to that shot.'

Laver tried ineffectively to chop his returns back. Rosewall's backhand cross-court passing shots were so sharply angled that they hit eight to ten feet from the net. Rosewall won the first set 6-4.

Then Laver unleashed one of his attacks for the second set, winning 6-1.

In the third set Rosewall moved like a cat, his feet dancing furiously in a succession of brilliant bursts of speed, flicking himself back and forth, racing like the wind, dashing off the court with his back to it to fire a backhand past an amazed Laver. Rosewall, as was his wont, gave his fans mild heart failure by facing 5 ad points against him with the score 3-all on his serve, all of which he won.

They entered the tie-breaker. Laver had won the two tie-breakers he had played against Rosewall earlier in the year in minor WCT tournaments. One of them was the final of the Redwood Bank International in San Francisco, which Laver had won 6-4,6-4,7-6.

A Bad Spot

Rosewall had served the ball several times so that it hit a bad spot on the court, about the size of a cereal bowl in width. Laver had hit the ball on the wood of his racket, losing points.

In one of our discussions in Australia a few years later, Rosewall told me, 'I didn't aim for it.' In a magazine article Rosewall's old friend, John Barrett, a leonine, friendly Englishman, had observed, 'It was uncanny the way Ken was hitting that patch. One couldn't help wondering.'

I said, 'John Barrett said you had an uncanny ability to hit those areas.'

Ken replied, 'I don't want to take my old friend John Barrett's story away from him that I aimed for the soft spots in the Dallas court in 1971, but I had noticed in practice the court was a carpet laid over concrete that had some slight depressions in it. I assume Rod knew, too, as he practised as much as me on the court. In fact, I was hit in the eye by the ball hitting one of those spots.'

When the ball ricocheted off Rosewall's racket after a few points of the third-set tie-breaker, striking him in the eye, forcing him to bend over in pain, touching his face, Laver jumped the net to come to his aid. On the WCT film the announcer said, 'Rod doesn't want it to be a "freak" victory.'

As the two rivals—temporary enemies—stood near the net, Rosewall rubbing his eye, trying to get vision, Rosewall said, 'I might have to default.'

Laver said, 'It will cost you $30,000.'

Rosewall said, 'Better than losing the eye.'

Trabert said, 'The eye is watering.'

Suddenly Rosewall hurled a towel to the side, 'I'm all right.'

Play had been delayed three minutes.

Then Rosewall won three points in a row on backhand volleys, anticipating on each shot where Laver would put the ball. Taking a 4-1 lead, Rosewall won the tie-breaker, 7-3, when Laver missed a volley on the last point.

The fourth set swung in Rosewall's favour when Laver netted three balls and double-faulted, losing his first service game. He double-faulted twice, losing his second service game. But again the tide swung in Laver's direction, as he broke Rosewall's service twice.

At 5-6, Laver's favour, in the fourth set, Rosewall demonstrated the courage and imagination of a great champion. 'I continued to move to net on my own serve,' Rosewall remembers. 'This tactic kept pressure on Laver.'

They were now in the second tie-breaker. All Laver had to do was win it and win the next set and the victory was his as usual. If Rosewall won the tie-breaker, Rosewall had won the match. Rosewall remembers, 'Rod would be favoured to win the fifth set.' For a top star Laver did not have a good record in tie-breakers.

Rod Overhits an Overhead

The key shot was to occur when the score was 4-3 in the tie-breaker in favour of Rosewall. A Rosewall speciality is the attacking lob. As his opponent charges toward the net he lifts the ball at the last second, flicking it over his opponent's head, in effect wrong-footing him. Rosewall's high lob landed near the baseline. Laver was back in plenty of time to let it bounce so that he could rifle it away. But there was something loose and overconfident about the way he whirled his racket overhead, and the ball shot the length of the court, down the middle, to land a fraction out.

Ken remembers, 'In the 1971 final of WCT there was a very high ceiling and I lobbed Rod a lot. Rod would sometimes miss a high lob. He would let it bounce. He hit a key one out in the tie-breaker of the WCT '71 final.'

And Rosewall's backhand came through. Laver, to give him credit, went down swinging, smashing the last ball for an all-out winner out of the court. Now that Rosewall had won the seventh point, score 7-4, he hurled his racket high into the TV lights, an uncharacteristic Rosewall gesture.

Despite the bitter enmity—in a tennis sense—of a few seconds earlier, Rosewall put his arm on Laver's back twice and Laver did likewise to Rosewall. Neil Armstrong, presenting the award, said, 'Ken, you have given lots of encouragement to us who are in the well over thirty club.' Rosewall replied with that shy, cute smile, 'I am enjoying this opportunity to speak to you as I may never have it again.' At the press conference Rosewall said, 'Rod's had a pretty good run against me, and I think it is about time he lost.'

'Richard Evans, who described the match for *World Tennis*, rather shrewdly observed, 'When Muscles wins the big match his innate shyness disappears. After he was presented with his trophy, he burst into a witty loose oration that was totally un-Rosewall and totally delightful.'

I watched the match some years later on a WCT film, seeing how small Rosewall looked compared to the 'champion', seeing Rosewall's incredibly graceful shots, the tension of the tie-breaker and final points which he overcame, and listening to his voice narrate happily after the match what had happened as the slow-motion camera showed him leaping into action against Laver and the odds. Among the statistics of this famous match, it is interesting to note that Laver served ten double faults and was foot-faulted four times.

Soon after his WCT '71 victory, Rosewall said, 'The younger guys in the game cannot realize what Tony Trabert and Rod and a few of the pros who no longer are playing put into pro tennis to keep it alive. It hasn't always been like this, and it has been hard work getting there.'

Ken said to me recently, 'In the WCT '71 finals we had four or five days of publicity appearances. Rod had played very well on the tour and in the quarters and semis, but I think he was more nervous than me, tired from the TV and radio shows.'

Surprise in Dallas

Despite his victory over Laver, most tennis people regarded it as a lucky break for Rosewall and a temporary lapse for Laver. Due to a scheduling change the next WCT final would be held six months from then in May 1972.

Rosewall was more popular with Australians, as he had stayed there, than Laver and Emerson, who emigrated to the U.S. According to one sports columnist, Rosewall had his followers among other small players, too, though I am inclined to doubt this, sensing that similarities in small size can induce dislike as well as kindred feeling. Rosewall also had his special following among aficionados of tennis, though now his popularity was spreading among all fans. Dick Crealy, a craggy-faced young Aussie with a pleasant grin and awkward style, compared Rosewall and Laver: 'With Laver you will make your best shot and he will knock it for a winner and do it with contempt. With Rosewall you think you are playing well, but he seems to anticipate everything you do. And he never misses. He doesn't maul you the way Laver does. He just breaks your heart.'

Wilma remarked at the time, 'I have been waiting for Ken to retire for fifteen years now. My lady golfer and tennis friends tell me, "Oh, you must be used to Ken being away." But you *never* get used to it. Not if you care. They say, "Well, it won't be long now." ' Mrs. Rosewall glanced humorously up at the ceiling and then looked at her husband.

Rosewall said, 'It is not often a man is lucky enough to do what he loves for so many years. I owe that to Wilma. She has been strong enough to take care of things in my absence. But the time is coming when I may have to put on the brakes,when maybe I won't be able to justify being on tour so long. The boys are getting older, and it is hard to concentrate on your game when you get news from home. We will just have to play it by ear.'

'Play it by ear,' Wilma said. 'That is your favourite expression, love.'

A Sentimental Final

The day of the finals of the Australian Championship in January 1972, traffic was jammed for a mile around. There had been an exciting build-up to the last day, for a number of older Australian stars had performed well in the tournament, defeating younger men, who were supposed to overcome them easily. For example, Frank Sedgman, forty-four, conquered

Robert Casey and Owen Davidson before finally bowing out to John Cooper, twenty-five. Mervyn Rose, then forty-one, had defeated a very promising youngster, Paul Kronk, 7-5, 6-3, 6-1. The Australian Davis Cup captain, Neale Fraser, had eliminated one of the members of his own team, the twelfth seed, Geoff Masters, 7-5, 7-5, 6-2. Barry Phillips-Moore, thirty-four, had conquered John Alexander, twenty. After the first day's results the Australian newspapers called it 'Father's Day.'

But the pièce de résistance was the progress to the finals of two more 'old-timers'—Mal Anderson, thirty-six, who eliminated Fraser, then John Newcombe in an exciting five-set match interrupted by cold winds, rain, lightning, thunder and hail, and Metreveli in the semis—and Rosewall, thirty-seven, who beat Dick Crealy in the quarters and Allan Stone in the semis. Thus the older Australian fans, who had been flocking to the stadium for the previous rounds, were delighted with the match-up of Rosewall v. Anderson for the championship.

Rosewall's car broke down. The taxi he took with Wilma and the boys got caught in the traffic. Rosewall approached a policeman, who said, 'It is no good going to the tennis, mate, you can't get in.' Discovering who he was, the officer escorted him on his motorbike through the crowds.

The nostalgic crowd was the largest ever in history of an Australian tournament—13,000. People had queued from early morning. The stadium's aisles were filled. The only bigger crowds in Australian tennis history were at the Davis Cup challenge rounds of 1953 and 1954. At Melbourne's Kooyong Stadium in 1953 there were 18,500 with extra seating, and 25,000 at Sydney in 1954. On each occasion Rosewall had played.

Rosewall played with finesse. Shot after shot whizzed by or at Anderson so low they were level with 'my shoelaces,' observed Mal. There were Rosewall's dazzling backhands—rapier thrusts down the line and across the court. Rosewall won over Anderson 7-6, 6-3, 7-5. Rosewall became the oldest ever to win the title, as well as the youngest, and tied Jack Crawford in wins at 4 each, though Roy Emerson during the years when Rosewall was a pro and Emerson an amateur, won the title six times, five of which were while Laver was a pro, too. Thus one of Rosewall's most extraordinary victories was his winning of the Australian Championship in January 1972. Ironically, the day before the final the ILTF had prohibited all WCT players, of whom Rosewall was one, from participating in tournaments sponsored by the National Lawn Tennis Associations, such as the Australian championships.

Ken remembers, 'Mal Anderson was a very fine person and player. His trouble is that he is a perfectionist. He has to make the perfect shot each time with perfect style and put it perfectly on the line, instead of aiming for some safety to give himself a margin of error. In the Pacific Southwest in 1974 he had two match points on Connors, who made a fantastic backhand save while out of the court, which Anderson, instead of volleying safely, hit two inches beyond the line on the other side of the court.'

'That makes one sick,' I said.

In January 1972, Don Mordecai, a WCT official in Dallas, begged Rosewall on the trans-Pacific phone to play in the Richmond tournament: 'But you've *got* to be there. Your picture is on the programme cover.'

'I can't make it, Don. Wilma's not that well.'

Rosewall said later, 'If I have to make a choice, Wilma and the kiddies come first.'

Ken remembers, 'I did miss this tournament because of family problems and Wilma was not well. One of the problems of being a professional sportsman is that it can be very upsetting to the wife and children when one has to pack up and go away. It was just one of those things where I just was not able to be away.'

Rosewall frequently sends Wilma roses while on tour.

The second WCT tour began, and at the first tournament, a big one, in Philadelphia, Rosewall insisted on watching over a stricken ballboy, attracting a reprimand from the umpire, who declared, 'Let's *play*, Mr. Rosewall.' Characteristically he refused to criticize the official afterwards: 'I just wanted to see how the little fellow was.'

Ken says today, 'I suppose the ballboy was suffering from exhaustion, though they were changed frequently during the matches, and the couple who run the tournament are very experienced over many years and do a wonderful job. The umpire was a little bit severe. The boy had fainted and was flat out in a position more or less on the court, and yet the umpire wanted to play. I was kind of concerned as to how the boy was. So we waited until the boy had been taken care of.'

Rosewall is rarely affected by line calls which go against him—at least his game rarely suffered, no matter how much he felt the injustice of the call and its importance in the match. One exception, and a muted one at that, was in 1972 at Philadelphia. Rosewall met Laver in the finals of the Philadelphia tournament. Rosewall won the first set 6-4. Laver was ahead, 0-1, Rosewall serving. Rosewall led 30-0, then fell behind to 30-40. After a brief rally, Laver hit a deep top-spin backhand. Most of the crowd thought it was out. Rosewall agreed. The linesman called, 'In.' The umpire, surprised himself, asked the official to repeat his call. The man did not change it. Rosewall shrugged his shoulders with resignation, his game was slightly off after that and Laver, encouraged, went into one of his wild hitting streaks, serving and volleying with that blinding speed which is a Laver speciality. He won the next three sets 6-2, 6-2, 6-2.

Laver said in the postmatch discussion, 'I thought it was a little long, but you have to take the calls as they come. They can go against me sometimes.'

Rosewall said, 'My concentration was affected for a moment. I thought it was out, but the man there thought it was in. This isn't an easy court to call in. It did not upset me too much, but it seemed to make a real change in the way that Rod played.'

Laver said, 'Whenever I play Rosewall I reckon I need two breaks of service in each set because he returns the ball so well and puts so much pressure on me. I never lay off on my service because I know I will lose mine sooner or later. He is more consistent than any of the other players.'

After his loss to Laver in the Philadelphia tourney, Rosewall rode silently out to the airport in a car with a friend. The friend was driving. It was one of many, many losses to Laver in the last six years. He was 10,000 miles from home. In the coat pocket of his raincoat was a letter to his beloved Wilma. It was raining. The windshield wipers cleaned the windows for a clearer view of drab Philadelphia. He noticed a junkyard of cars. Next week he might have to play Laver again. Suddenly he looked as if he was going to scream.

'What do you do,' I said, 'about bad calls in your favour? Do you accept them and say nothing or do you deliberately throw a couple of points to your opponent?'

'I try to go halfway in between these two approaches. I question the linesman once, asking him, "Are you sure that was a correct call?" '

The Loose Tape

'The only injury I've ever had was in the CBS Classic at Hilton Head in 1972. On clay courts, like the ones at Hilton Head, the lines are shown by laying strips of tape on the surface, which are held in place with nails. In the first set of the final against John Newcombe, playing for $10,000, the score 5-4, my right foot sliding into the ball hit the head of a nail that had come up, and I went over, spraining the ankle. What I said had to be edited out of the TV tape by Bud Collins, who was doing the commentary. I was referring to such conditions on the court being allowed. It was painful every time I stepped hard on it and I knew if I defaulted it would swell up immediately. I calculated the risk of my seriously hurting the ankle by playing on was not that great. I had to go for winners on every shot, playing each ball very well, hitting hard. I don't know if John Newcombe became over-confident, knowing the shape I was in, or felt sorry for me, as he should have run me, hitting the ball short sometimes so that I would have to run forward as well as sideways. But he didn't, and he must have cursed himself afterwards for letting the opportunity go by. But I hit my shots very well and won in two sets, 7-5, 6-3. I hobbled off the court, and the ankle immediately blew up.' Rosewall demonstrated with his hands a shape the size of a grapefruit or melon. 'I didn't play for a week. My wife and I were able to take a week off. Luckily the tournament I missed wasn't one that counted for points on the WCT tour, and the next three or four months I played with an ankle brace for safety, even in the famous 1972 WCT final.'

'That must have taken courage to go on during the CBS match,' I said.

'Oh, yeah, well.'

Rosewall's manner was like that of a serious schoolboy at times. He also conveyed an impression of quiet authority. Rosewall avoided business managers for years. 'Maybe I am wrong, but I feel that I can work things out myself.' However, he eventually employed an agent.

He was a constant source of discussion among the younger players. Jeff Borowiak, who is a well-educated Californian collegiate star, said to Rosewall, 'Did you realize there is a balance to your game also found in Bach?' Rosewall listened politely. 'You both have symmetry, perfect control. You are not showy like one of the romantic composers, like Liszt, but your game builds to a peak—to a whirlwind of perfection like Bach, in other words.'

Rosewall said, 'Thank you, Jeff. I don't know too much about music.'

Borowiak persisted with his analysis of other players until Rosewall, provoked, as if he had been linked romantically with Bach, said, 'I am not sure what he is getting at.'

Newcombe said, 'We never see Muscles after dark. It's marvellous how he lasts so long.'

In 1972 Rosewall said, 'Sometimes I feel like I am twenty-one again.' Another time, also in 1972, he said, 'This year may be my final fling—my swan song.'

As the tour progressed, Ken won several tournaments. One that I watched on TV was against Richey. Rosewall recalls it: 'Cliff Richey, a very good scrambler, has not lived up to his promise since 1970, when he won the Grand Prix. He doesn't like the backhand when he has to hit behind him, as he cannot slice well and hits it either flat or with topspin. In Charlotte, in a final of WCT in 1972 when I was playing very well on the tour, only a few weeks before the WCT final, I met Richey, who had just joined WCT, leaving the USLTA indoor circuit. He reached the final in his first tournament, where I met him. It was on clay, which is a Richey speciality. He and his family used to rally for hours on the clay courts in Texas, where they are from.'

I said, 'His father was in the stands.'

'And probably his wife and his sister,' Ken added with a grin. 'They are a close-knit family. I lost the first set and was losing the second. It was the best of three sets. We were rallying from the baseline, and I realized I was playing his game and he was going to wear me out. More often nowadays I like to force the issue so that my opponent has to try and pass me, and the rally is cut short. I started coming to the net. I played Richey's second serve and came up to net.'

'I noticed you started winning, and Richey's face grew grey with frustration. Why didn't he change tactics?' I asked.

'I don't know. He should have tried to lob me. He doesn't lob very often, though he will sometimes hit a forehand top-spin lob.'

'It must have been discouraging for him with you playing so well just before your famous victory in Dallas,' I said.

'I guess so,' he said with a grin. 'Richey perspires more than any other player. He's not a natural player. He has to work hard on every shot, and to someone watching Richey on the court his style must seem very tiring. A lot of tennis players don't like to meet him in a match, as they know they'll have to work hard to beat him. He's a tough competitor.'

Ken continued, 'In 1972 we played ten tournaments on WCT in twelve weeks. They have it easy now. In 1974 they played two out of every three weeks and in 1975 each group has a minimum of only seven tournaments.'

Rosewall added, 'The WCT tour took something out of a player. Stan Smith played excellent tennis in 1973, and he's never been as sharp since. John Newcombe was in very good form in winning the 1974 tour, but he's lost an edge since then.'

I said, 'How do you feel about Bud Collins, constantly publicizing your rival, Rod Laver, on supposedly impartial TV broadcasts, in magazine articles and newspapers? That's a hot one,' I added.

Rosewall laughed. 'I've had some sparring matches with Bud. Of course, he's known Rod much longer than me, going back to amateur tournaments in Boston. I've got my own back once or twice. I said he was bald. He said to me. "How did it go? Are you still using black shoe polish on your hair?" I replied, "At least I have some to use it on." I told him once I'd run more miles than his tongue had wagged.' Rosewall added, his face tightening, 'But I think Bud's been fair enough to me . . . Bud and I are friends.'

I said, 'Bud Collins has written that you are not a colourful player, but I think, though on the surface you give the impression of being poised and quiet with a controlled style, you are inwardly a very emotional player and that is why you draw such crowds.'

'That must be why Bud Collins says I'm not "a colourful player," ' Rosewall said dryly.

'How much did the other players practise on the 1972 tour?'

'Brian Fairlie and Harold Solomon, though they did not join WCT until 1974, practised more than any of the other players. Rod Laver was a great one for practising. I really can't remember anyone who did not practise enough, though some players, realizing they were not up to the level of the others, practised less. On the winter circuit, where there's often only one surface and practice time is limited with four men on a court, it is important to practise seriously and not waste one's time.'

Prior to the 1972 WCT final Rosewall won the U.S. in 1970, the Australian in 1971, WCT in 1971, and the Australian in 1972. He had not entered the French in 1971 or Forest Hills in 1971 and did not win Wimbledon in 1971. Thus of the five important championships, since and including Forest Hills in 1970, which Rosewall had entered before WCT '72, he had won four.

The finals began in Dallas on Wednesday, May 10th. In the quarters, Rosewall beat Bob Lutz 6-1, 3-6, 6-3, 4-6 and 6-1; in the semis, Ashe 6-4, 6-2, 7-6. Laver overcame John Newcombe 6-4, 6-4, 6-4 and Marty Riessen 4-6, 4-6, 6-1, 6-2, 6-0.

For the first time the last match was to be televised on prime time at 3 P.M. on NBC-TV nationwide. The contest was expected to end by 5 P.M. when other shows would go on the air.

Before the match Laver and Rosewall walked through the tunnel into the SMU indoor stadium. Though they exchanged a few words, Laver was several feet ahead of Rosewall.

During the pre-game ceremonies, as they stood side by side yet miles apart for the playing of the Australian and American national anthems, Laver's expression could only be described as confident, as if he were saying to himself, 'I'm going to get you, you little bastard, this time.' But there was another aspect of Laver that was quiet and naïve. Both men exuded tension. Rosewall looked innocent and determined.

Remembering that match, Rosewall says today, 'I would say that both Rod and I have the same stature and maybe personality. I think maybe we're both naïve. I mean, we're not really flamboyant, although the way Rod's game is on the court, it could be the term used, but you could put it that we're not big talkers like a lot of other sports people and other tennis people who've gotten around to the stage of being known as big talkers.'

This time for the WCT final, Rosewall wore white shorts and an orange shirt, while Laver switched to pale blue, the colour Rosewall had worn six months earlier. The colour of the court was deep green, and at one end stood the trophy, a great silvery-gold glitter, which had once rested in the basement of Ken's home. The trophy had originally been used by the pros during the professional days and had been used as the cup for the Kramer Cup (a professional team competition in the early 1960's), and Rosewall had kept it in his home and had then given it to WCT. The college auditorium, containing 7,800 spectators, was of course packed with a mixture of local Texans and Dallas society, international sportswriters, tennis businessmen, tennis stars such as Riessen and Drysdale, the referee, Tony Trabert, show business celebrities such as Rod Steiger and James Franciscus, Rod Laver's wife, Mary, and assorted Texas beauties who acted as courtside hostesses. One had to admire the efficiency and hard work of the Texans in the World Championship Tennis organization who in two years had developed WCT into this shimmering final, reflecting the energy, love, dedication and discipline of life outside the arena. And now these two Australians, who had become part of the Lone Star and American dreams, would enact a drama for their entertainment and the rest of us.

Ken remembers, 'The carpet was a new one and thus slower than other carpets we'd played on during the tour that had been worn down and were faster.'

Rod Blazes Away

Laver had warmed up for an hour in the morning while Ken had restricted himself to twenty minutes. The moment the match began, Laver came out with all guns blazing, in a racing fury of shots blasted at all corners in an awesome display of controlled power tennis. He was like a battleship which suddenly opens up with all guns and keeps it up incessantly. One rally typified the exchanges. Rosewall stroked a deep perfect lob which landed exactly in the corner of the deuce side of the court. Laver sped back, whirled completely around and unleashed a backhand shot at fantastic speed down the line. Rosewall, who had come up to net, looked at it. Rosewall was playing competently, wondering how long Laver could maintain such a pace.

Ken said, 'Rod got off to a 4-0 lead and I just wanted to get back into the match. I played consistently throughout the match, whereas his play went up and down more than once. With a service break, I drew up to 4-5, and he had a tight game serving to win the set. The second set his play fell off.'

The second set produced one of the strangest turnarounds I have ever seen. Rosewall danced into magnificence, winning game after game. Suddenly the score was 6-0. It had been a long time since Laver had lost a love set.

The tennis was absolutely beautiful, scores of perfectly placed shots, rifled at all angles, on and on they went.

'I lobbed him very often in the '72 final period. He did not know when at net if the lob was coming, and so he had to hesitate a little more rather than getting set to volley away my passing shot.

'When you lob over Laver's right shoulder, you know he will hit his overhead probably away from his body and cross-court. It's his favourite overhead.

'The extra light required for colour TV made the court especially hot. . . . My shirt soon became wet through. . . . After a while my body became dehydrated and I could feel the back side of my shirt had dried. . . . I was saving my strength between points.'

Rosewall Wins the Third

Rosewall continued his devastating technique, taking the third set 6-3. The crowd now started supporting Laver, preferring the underdog, though the feeling was that Laver should win, counting on his advantage of age and supposedly stronger offensive weaponry. The contest had now gone over two hours and the match coverage on TV forced the elimination of one programme after another. The TV audience was growing, gripped by the spectacle developing before them.

Jean Drysdale, wife of Cliff, who was watching the match, said, 'To Laver it must seem as if Kenny has developed a diabolical plan to drive him mad.'

The fourth set saw Laver catching up with Rosewall. In the middle of it one point began with a deep Laver serve to Rosewall's forehand. There followed a series of brilliant ground strokes from side to side. Running forward, Rosewall dashed from side to side at the net. Laver threw up an excellent lob. Rosewall ran back. Laver came to net. The two men were like fish in an emerald-green sea darting back and forth in a dance of death. Rosewall tossed up another lob, came to net as Laver retreated and volleyed a succession of Laver top-spinned ground strokes. Laver stroked another good lob which landed deep near the baseline on the right side of Rosewall's court. Running back, Rosewall hit an overhead down the ad court line at an angle, surprising Laver, who had come to the middle of his baseline and was himself tired. Ken said, 'He would have got a less perfect shot. I was becoming tired and knew I had to go for a winner.'

Jean Drysdale said, 'It was rare and strange.'

A Letdown

Laver tied the score at 6-all and entered the tie-breaker. The match had already lasted three hours and fifteen minutes. Ken remembers, 'The way I was feeling was not real good. In a situation like that you have to kick yourself several times because my confidence was down, which I did. Rod had hit four backhand smashes for winners and come back from 0-2 in the tie-breaker to win 7-2, and entering the fifth set he must have had a wave of confidence.

'At the start of the fifth set my legs felt as if they were filled with lead. Yet during the rallies, though they pained me, I didn't really notice it.'

In the second game of the fifth set, Rosewall ran way off the

"The photo was taken at the rear of our house in Rockdale, Sydney. I was eight and a half years old, and I had just bought my first racket with a long handle," remembers Ken.

Photo courtesy of Ken Rosewall

Ken was sixteen years old when this photo was taken near the Kooyong stadium in Melbourne. His father, Robert, gave him the technique to become a champion, and his mother, Vera, gave him the inspiration and encouragement.

Photo courtesy of Ken Rosewall

Ken points out today that Harry Hopman's contribution to his development was questionable, but at the time, September, 1952, when they had just returned from their first sensational trip to America, Hopman was regarded by most of the tennis world as the discoverer of the two famous "twins," Lew Hoad and Ken Rosewall.

Photo courtesy of Ken Rosewall

Hopman kisses Ken's bride, Wilma, as the groom looks on.

Photo courtesy of Ken Rosewall

The 1973 Australian Davis Cup team, which beat the United States 5–0, was one of the greatest. Neale Fraser, face slightly obscured by the cup, was captain. Left to right were Colin Dibley, who hits the world's fastest serve of about 150 mph; Rod Laver; Rosewall; John Newcombe; and Geoff Masters (Mal Anderson is not shown). Though he was a major reason for bringing the team to the peak of its brilliance, Rosewall did not play, perhaps explaining his slightly sad smile.

Photo: Eiichi Kawatei

The Rosewall high forehand volley is one of the outstanding shots of tennis.

Photo: Eiichi Kawatei

Ken, Brett, Wilma and Glenn Rosewall at a tennis ranch in Arizona. Their support has been an important reason for the success of his subsequent career. Ken can throw a ball twice as far with his left hand as with his right, and the two boys play left-handed.

Photo: Eiichi Kawatei

Most experts regard the Rosewall backhand as the best in the world.

Photo: Eiichi Kawatei

This photo is a study in how to hit a perfect low forehand drive—racket back, knees bent, eyes on the ball.

Photo: Le-Roye Productions Ltd.

Though he was always confident of his ability, this photo shows Ken, seventeen years old, a few moments after his first major triumph, which established his name throughout the tennis world—the defeat in five sets of twenty-nine-year-old Vic Seixas, the no. 1 seed at Forest Hills.

Photo: Le-Roye Productions Ltd.

court to reach and hit a blazing backhand. It won the game and broke Laver's serve. 'To my surprise I got off to a good lead 3-1 and 4-2.'

I was watching the game on TV. When Laver climbed up to 4-all, I became convinced Rosewall would lose. Dragging himself along between the points of the game from one side of the court to the other, his head hanging loosely on one shoulder, his racket trailing behind him, his legs wobbling from one step to the next, it seemed just a matter of time before the end.

Near Exhaustion

Many people in the audience thought Rosewall was going to collapse from exhaustion. Even some professional tennis individuals felt he was about to crumble. In the rally his face looked taut and drawn with fatigue and concentration. Every tendon and muscle in his neck stood out. His hair, normally smoothly oiled in place, was becoming awry. His mouth in the middle of the point was half open in a grimace reminiscent only of great tiredness. Between the points he waited for the ballboy to throw him the ball. Then he dropped it, watching it roll away.

It was partly a fight for the money, and it was partly a fight for the entertainment of the crowd. But what was eerie and strange was that it was also a fight for survival. Laver was the hunter and Rosewall the hunted. Laver, with his big reputation and power game, the killer, and Rosewall, the victim, defensive.

Rosewall was groggy, like a boxer back on his feet after several knockdowns in the latter stages of the match. Laver's face was white from the effort.

Rosewall held on, and at 5-4 in his favour he had a match point on Laver; but 'the Rocket' aced him. 'Now, quite suddenly, I felt exhausted,' said Rosewall.

The Tie-Breaker

They held their serves. Rosewall remembers, 'At 40-30 on Rod's serve 5-6, I hit a good lob but made an error in not following it in.' Laver smashed away another lob and they entered the tie-breaker.

The match had now lasted three hours and forty-five minutes, the audience on TV had grown to 23 million and the time was 6.45 on that Sunday night. They had begun play at 3 P.M.

'How were you able to think between points in the tie-breaker at the end? You looked so tired,' I said.

'I may not have been as tired as I looked. It had been a long hard tour. It was gruelling. All the players were fatigued, including Rod. And before the final match between Laver and me there were the special appearances on TV, radio and a ball to promote the tournament.'

'Your legs kind of loped along between points and your head hung on your shoulders. Some people have compared you to Jim Brown, the famous Cleveland fullback, who rested between points. But you really did feel that tired?'

'Yeah. I wasn't putting it on or trying to stall between points. I was thinking what to do after each point, and I may have looked that way because I was thinking, "If I had only hit this shot better earlier in the match, I would be out of here." A major incentive was the knowledge I was going home. A key turning point was Rod serving a double fault at 3-2 in the tie-breaker.

'At 5-4 in Rod's favour, Rod about to serve in the ad court, I wondered if he would go for the big ace. He had served an ace down the line to save match point when the score was 4-5 in games. Or would he try to get his first serve into my backhand? I thought he would do the latter, and I decided to hit a cross-court backhand, which is to his forehand volley where there's a weakness if he has any.'

The score was 5-4 in favour of Laver, Laver to serve into the ad court. Many people have speculated as to why Laver chose to serve the way he did at this point. Rosewall's backhand was known to be his strongest shot, but Laver had become a star defying the odds, liking to break his opponent's best weapon. Laver went into his motion, flicking the racket up to the level of the wrist of the hand holding the ball. The tension in the hall was unbearable. He hit a first serve deep to Rosewall's backhand, which Rosewall hit straight through with an open racket face, undercutting it with his perfect stroke, hitting the ball cross-court as Laver ran forward, barely reaching the ball with his forehand to lift it up and volley it too high in the air, landing it beyond the baseline.

A Perfect Backhand

Ken remembers, 'The famous shot in the WCT '72 final, the score 5-4 in the fifth-set tie-breaker against me on a Laver serve to my backhand, was a perfect cross-court backhand hit low to his forehand volley. It's a difficult volley to make, and he lifted it out of the court.'

The score was now 5-all. At stake was $50,000, the loser to receive only $20,000. With inflation, the value of this sum today would be $60,000. Throughout the four-month tour there had been the Texas motif of going for broke, rolling for high odds, culminating in a shootout at high noon, and much of the publicity of these matches has been built around this gun-shooting theme. In fact, the WCT film of their first finals six months earlier is titled 'Showdown at The Big D', 'D' standing for Dallas. Rosewall and Laver were the victims of this enterprise, the participants and the winners.

Ken continues his reminiscences of the match: 'Rod had not been serving that well in the final. We were now in the deuce court. He could have hit a fast flat one to my forehand, but there was more risk as to whether it would be in or not; or he could have hit a slower topspin, but there was the danger I might come down on him with my forehand and hit it cross-court or down the line. Therefore he would go for the percentage shot, which was his favourite, down the centre-court line. This was what I thought he would do. The score stood at 5-all in the deuce court. The slice served down the line comes in lower, too. During the set I had decided to try hitting some backhands from the deuce court down the line harder than I normally stroke them, and they had worked. I hit three or four like that. I made up my mind to do it again.'

Laver then hit a powerful first serve down the middle. Rosewall stepped over and swung his backhand for a fantastic rifle shot to Laver's left—right down the line—which Laver, running in, could only watch as it flew by him. 'It went very fast and Rod could not reach it.'

After Rosewall flashed his second backhand, Jean Drysdale remarked, 'Hearts in the crowd are bleeding for Laver and cheering for Rosewall at the same time.'

The score was now 6-5. That year WCT was playing a 12-point tie-breaking system, but the winner had to either reach 7 points with a minimum 2-point lead over his opponent, or reach a number higher than 7 with a minimum of 2-point surplus. It was now Rosewall's turn to serve.

A Cunning Serve

'On my serve to the ad court I wanted to get it in and did not wish to risk serving straight down the centre-court line, as it might be out by an inch or two. I had usually been serving to his backhand, but sometimes I hit to his forehand to keep him honest. So I served about 3 or 4 feet to my right of the centre line. He may have even thought it was coming to his forehand. Also, he may have guessed it was going to be wide to his backhand, and thus he was awkward on his backhand; but I did not intend to surprise him with a backhand close to his body rather than wide, because when he hits a backhand near his body he likes to roll his wrist over the backhand on the return of serve, and it's usually very hard to get back.'

After a let first serve, Rosewall cleverly hit a deep one to Laver's backhand, the ingenuity being that it was placed about three feet inside the centre line instead of near it, as most serves to this area are when done by professionals. As Laver had crouched slightly, bending his shoulders, swinging his racket, his face looked slightly discouraged, but it still wore the confident look that he had displayed through most of the match. He still thought he was going to win. He still imagined, 'I'll get the little bastard.' The ball came in deep and hard to him, and without moving his body entirely, Laver lashed it back, the ball striking just below the top of the net in a direct line in front of him.

Joy of Winning

Rosewall ran to the net, slamming his second ball onto the court with joy. A number of women in the stands dried their eyes. Poor Laver's face went through a variety of emotions. One photo of him shaking hands with Ken at the net could only be classified under 'if looks could kill'. Another showed him to be in a state of shock.

At the presentation ceremonies, Rosewall gracefully passed Laver. They both avoided contact. During the speeches, Laver's face had a humble, contented look. The overconfidence was gone. Mike Davies, his voice rumbling with emotion, said, 'It's the greatest tennis match I've ever seen. There should have been two winners. The audience here and the tennis world are the real winners.' Near to tears, twice Rosewall brushed his thumb past his eye. Holding the cup, he said, 'We're just about all out of time . . . and I'm out of breath. I'm sorry there weren't two winners.' Rosewall smiled that shy, joyous smile. His face suddenly looked aged, the lines noticeable, but his expression and everything about him was filled with delirious happiness.

Rosewall was so dazed by his win over Laver that he forgot his $50,000 cheque, leaving it on a chair in the locker room. That night he had dinner with some friends and the next morning flew home.

And it was the mongoose that had killed the cobra. Some of the feelings underneath this match may be discerned from Laver's comment about Rosewall in his book, 'For seven years he was a friend but also a deadly enemy.'

Several years later Wilma told me, 'Mrs. Laver refused to see any more of Rod's matches after the WCT '72 final.' Marty Riessen said to me, 'You realize just how very good Rosewall is when he can raise his game in two premier events at Dallas in the WCT '71 and '72 finals and beat Laver. Laver had been beating him in the minor tournaments. By all rights, he should have beaten Rosewall badly.'

Sports Illustrated, after Rosewall's great victory over Laver, finally listed Rosewall's name first in the headlines: 'With Ken Rosewall and Rod Laver just dazzling, the WCT Championship was a coming out party to remember.' The sports magazine conceded, 'Now Rosewall has given everybody reason to pause and contemplate who really is the world's finest player in the big ones.'

Laver's biographer, Bud Collins, wrote, 'Rosewall's 4-6, 6-0, 6-3, 6-7, 7-6 victory over Laver in the grand finals seemed to establish the pro game once and for all for the American public, who had been unaware of pro tennis only a few years before.' On TV 23 million people had seen the WCT '72 final.

The *Time* account caught the drama of the match, comparing Rosewall's feat to Willie Mays hitting two game-winning home runs off Mickey Lolich in the World Series, to George Blanda outplaying Roger Staubach in back-to-back Superbowls and to Sammy Snead beating Jack Nicklaus in successive playoffs. It was beginning to dawn on *Time*, as on the rest of the press, that Rosewall was one of the all-time greats. Already familiar with its guile, *Time* even recognized the power of Rosewall's backhand—the press had always seen his feathery touch, but had never spotted just how damn hard he hit the ball. *Time* also spotted another Rosewall trademark—the hanging of his head between points to save his energy for the actual play. In this they found him similar to Jimmy Brown, the great Cleveland fullback, now movie star.

Of this habit, which could better be described as a look of total discouragement, Tony Trabert says, 'Muscles starts moping around and the ladies all want to mother him. Meanwhile he's cutting you to ribbons.' Some months later, Rosewall or a ghost writer wrote that when Laver netted the final point, Rosewall felt 'the utmost relief', which seemed to be stretching understatement to its limits.

Looking back on the match in 1975, Rosewall said, 'I played Laver about the same all through my career from 1963, when he turned pro, to the WCT finals in '71 and '72 and the present day. His only weakness is the low volley to his forehand. I found it was best to vary my game against him, and this is what Gonzales discovered, too, in the early seventies. Usually, if one hits a deep shot and comes in behind it, it's more difficult for the opponent to get it back. This is what every tennis book teaches. But Laver is so quick with that wrist action that it's almost better not to volley deep. So I would hit it to mid-court and angle to the side, particularly on the forehand side. He can move from side to side very well, but he doesn't seem to like to come forward as much. But you have to vary all the time against him, so that he doesn't get grooved. The same is true on my serve. I've never had much trouble against left-handers, as I can slice my serve to the backhand in the number one (deuce) court and down the centre line to the number two (ad) court. I'd serve to him to the forehand and backhand. Sometimes serving towards his body works. I'd vary the speed between fast and medium but never a soft one against Laver as my serve is not all that fast.'

8

Forest Hills at Forty

Rosewall's great victory over Laver, truly one of the most remarkable events in the history of tennis, was the culmination of a unique comeback in the annals of the sport. C. M. Jones, editor of the magazine *Lawn Tennis*, in an article in the 1973 WCT magazine classified it as one of the three greatest tennis matches in history, the other two being Gonzales v. Sedgman at Wembley, England, 1956, and Crawford v. Vines, Wimbledon, 1933. Once having been No. 1, no other player had ever regained the title, going back through the list of the greats—Gonzales, Kramer,* Budge, Cochet and Tilden. Tilden had come the closest to recapturing his crown by briefly taking Forest Hills at the age of thirty-six and Wimbledon at thirty-seven. But Rosewall was the world's top player from September 1970 through May 1972, winning the Australian twice, Forest Hills once and WCT twice. In fact, for the four years, 1970 to 1973, he was in my opinion co-No. 1 with Nastase, Newcombe, Laver and Smith, all of whom fluctuated up and down near the top. And comparing Rosewall's and Tilden's comebacks over a four-year spread, it is clear that over the longer period Cochet dominated Tilden, while in 1929 and 1930, the years of Tilden's revival, Tilden and Cochet had a major championship each both years (Tilden: Wimbledon, 1930, U.S., 1929; Cochet: Wimbledon, 1929, French, 1930) so that Tilden equalled Cochet but did not surpass him; whereas Rosewall over his two-year period led the field. By any reasonable standard, Rosewall was thus the first

---

* Chase points out, 'Kramer retired undefeated.'

player to make this accomplishment of regaining the title of undisputed No. 1.

Forest Hills

World Championship Tennis launched its 1973 season, and Rosewall was seeded first in his group. For the first time the players had been split into two sections. At the Cologne WCT tournament, Lew Hoad, in town on a business trip, observed Rosewall play Barthes. At a set each, Barthes was leading 5-4. Rosewall trudged back to the baseline to receive serve, his head dropping, racket trailing. A guest said, 'How tired he looks!'

Hoad exclaimed, 'Tired? He's looked that way since he was eleven.' Ken remembers that year's WCT tour: 'One of the players in my group was Mark Cox. Cox's only flaw is he always hits the ball hard and does not vary his style, and some players, like Laver, love this type of approach. For me, however, I try to be consistent and place them well and he starts to make errors. Cox has a great deal of ability, but I think he has always never expected to get to the top, and this attitude may have held him back. He's one of the fairest players in the game—a sportsman. In about the third tournament of the 1973 WCT tour, he played Taylor, with whom he's had a long rivalry as they are the two leading English players of about the same age. At match point for Cox or some key point, Cox received a strange decision in his favour so I think he gave the next point to Taylor. Taylor went on to win the match in a third-set tie-breaker. It was best of three. At the end of the tour, the top eight players are selected for the $50,000 final in Dallas on the basis of points accumulated over the tour. Taylor and Cox were tied for eighth place. Taylor was chosen because he had won over Cox in their only meeting.'

The year 1973 was to be a curious one for Rosewall. After his great victory in the '72 WCT final, he seemed to be less interested in the minor tournaments he appeared in, saving himself for the key ones. Age was clearly a factor, too, in that he played less than any previous year, earning only $54,400 in singles' prize money, compared to $130,590 the year before. At

CAREER RECORDS FOR LEADING MEN PROS

	ASHE	BORG	CONNORS	DRYSDALE	GORMAN	KODES	LAVER	LUTZ	METREVELI	NASTASE
ASHE	*	2-4	0-2	10-3	6-1	5-3	2-17	19-4	2-0	2-3
BORG	4-2	*	1-0		1-1	1-2	1-2		0-1	1-2
CONNORS	2-0	0-1	*		0-3	1-0			1-1	2-11
DRYSDALE	3-10			*	4-2	2-1	3-13	6-3		·3-2
GORMAN	1-6	1-1	3-0	2-4	*	5-1	2-2	1-6	1-0	2-17
KODES	3-5	2-1	0-1	1-2	1-5	*	2-4	3-4	4-7	7-12
LAVER	17-2	2-1		13-3	2-2	4-2	*	9-4	2-0	2-1
LUTZ	4-19			3-6	6-1	4-3	4-9	*	0-1	1-0
METREVELI	0-2	1-0	1-1		0-1	7-4	0-2	1-0	*	2-2
NASTASE	3-2	2-1	11-2	2-3	17-2	12-7	1-2	0-1	2-2	*
NEWCOMBE	12-6	1-0	1-0	8-6	6-0	5-2	5-12	5-2	3-2	1-3
OKKER	8-17		2-3	13-8	4-3	7-2	3-18	6-3	4-2	9-6
ORANTES	0-4	3-2	1-5	2-3	1-2	2-3	0-1	1-0	1-1	3-9
PILIC	2-9	1-1		6-12	1-3	2-2	2-7	1-2	1-0	2-6
RICHEY	5-16	0-1	0-2	4-0	0-3	5-0	5-6	8-2	1-2	4-6
RIESSEN	9-19		0-1	6-7	0-5	4-3	7-6	9-1	1-3	2-4
ROCHE	4-4	1-0		6-9	2-0	3-1	9-11	1-1	3-0	2-2
ROSEWALL	12-6	0-1	1-0	10-4	3-2	3-1	6-19	3-2	1-0	3-0
SMITH	8-8	1-0	3-4	6-1	12-2	7-6	7-9	18-2	5-0	7-6
TAYLOR	3-10	1-0	1-1	6-8		3-2	3-12	5-4	2-5	1-9

Statistics through WCT Final, May 12, 1974. Figures
do not include professional matches prior to 1968.

NEWCOMBE	OKKER	ORANTES	PILIC	RICHEY	RIESSEN	ROCHE	ROSEWALL	SMITH	TAYLOR	TOTAL W-L VS TOP PLAYERS
6-12	17-8	4-0	9-2	16-5	19-9	4-4	6-12	8-8	10-3	147-100
0-1		2-3	1-1	1-0		0-1	1-0	0-1	0-1	14-18
0-1	3-2	5-1		2-0	1-0		0-1	4-3	1-1	22-25
6-8	8-13	3-2	12-6	0-4	7-6	9-6	4-10	1-6	8-6	79-98
0-6	3-4	2-1	3-1	3-0	5-0	0-2	2-3	2-12		38-66
2-5	2-7	3-2	2-2	0-5	3-4	1-3	1-3	6-7	2-3	45-80
12-5	18-3	1-0	7-2	6-5	6-7	11-9	19-6	9-7	12-3	152-62
2-5	3-6	0-1	2-1	2-8	1-9	1-1	2-3	2-18	4-5	41-96
2-3	2-4	1-1	0-1	2-1	3-1	0-3	0-1	0-5	5-2	27-34
3-1	6-9	9-3	6-2	6-4	4-2	2-2	0-3	6-7	9-1	101-56
*	14-12	2-1	14-9	7-2	20-12	28-12	8-9	9-4	20-4	169-98
12-14	*	4-1	10-5	4-4	13-6	10-6	4-4	4-2	15-10	131-114
1-2	1-4	*	0-1	1-4	1-0	1-2	1-0	1-4	2-0	23-47
9-14	5 10	1-0	*	2-6	3-6	3-10	0-7	0-5	6-3	47-103
2-7	4-4	4-1	6-2	*	8-7	4-7	1-5	4-15	6-4	71-90
12-20	6-13	0-1	6-3	7-8	*	6-12	6-16	4-3	13-1	98-126
12-28	6-10	2-1	10-3	7-4	12-6	*	5-6	6-2	11-4	102-92
9-8	4-4	0-1	7-0	5-1	16-6	6-5	*	3-2	13-1	105-63
4-9	2-4	4-1	5-0	15-4	3-4	2-6	2-3	*	1-3	111-72
4-20	10-15	0-2	3-6	4-6	1-13	4-11	1-13	3-1	*	55-138

World Tennis

Hartford, Connecticut, in 1973 he led the Australian team in beating the Americans in the World Cup, defeating Stan Smith, the upcoming star player of the other WCT section who was gaining an edge over Laver.

Stan Smith said, 'What keeps that old guy going?'

Rosewall answered, 'Well, I think it might be psychological: A little guy trying to beat big guys. I felt pushed to do that all my life and it is my life. I'm not ready to quit.'

Age cost him his third WCT final by having to play Ashe less than twenty-four hours after a gruelling three-hour fifteen-minute victory over Taylor.

Ken said, 'After Rod's loss to Stan Smith in the '73 WCT semi-final, which was close in the first three sets but not the fourth, Rod looked shell-shocked.'

But Rosewall led his half of the WCT players. After reaching only the quarters or semis of most of the tournaments, he suddenly leaped forth and took three in a row.

Rosewall came over to England in June 1973 for the ill-fated Wimbledon tournament which resulted in a strike by most of the male pro stars, but Nastase, Kodes, Borg, Metreveli, Taylor and Connors played. The immediate cause of the strike was the suspension by the International Lawn Tennis Federation of Nikki Pilic, a well-known Yugoslavian star whose national tennis association had accused of refusing to play Davis Cup for Yugoslavia after he had supposedly said he would. Pilic denied this. The Association of Tennis Players, of which Pilic was a member, demanded his reinstatement, and when this was turned down by the Yugoslavians and the ILTF the ATP players, with a few exceptions such as Nastase and Taylor, went on strike. Rosewall was among the strikers.

But underneath the immediate causes of the controversy were several major factors. On one side was the growing power of American tennis, supported by increasing TV money, commercial sponsors of tournaments such as Virginia Slims and the growing millions of Americans playing tennis. Allied with this syndrome were the majority of professional players, who liked the greater financial rewards and demanded an equal say in the control of the game. For the players, it was a democratic uprising. On the other side was the largely European-ruled International Lawn Tennis Federation, which, through its national associations, had previously dominated the game. The associations were usually led by amateur officials stemming mainly from the country-club world of tennis—men who, though they devoted much of their spare time to tennis, worked in other occupations such as business or the law if they were not independently wealthy. Ironically, the old tennis establishment—what might be called the country-club world of tennis—was supported by the associations from the Communist countries, who wanted their players to be obedient to the national tennis bodies and play in the Davis Cup, a contest between national teams involving international prestige, which was why Nastase from Rumania, Metreveli from Russia and Kodes from Czechoslovakia ignored the strike. Wimbledon was to be the crucible for these elements, and interestingly enough it was American financial strength and stress on equal opportunity which eventually won, as the following year Wimbledon dramatically enlarged the prize money and the Association of Tennis Players, of which Rosewall was a leading member, became as powerful, if not more so, than the ILTF.

But the boycott aroused strong passions among the tennis public throughout the world, particularly in England and the British Commonwealth. One of the hazards of being a celebrity is receiving abusive letters. On returning to a tournament in Melbourne, Ken was disturbed to get one from 'E. Blyth' saying how 'very disgusted and terribly ashamed' he and 'thousands of Australians' were with Rosewall and the other pros over the Wimbledon controversy. The letter was interesting too, for the personal asides, such as comparing him unfavourably to Hoad, telling him 'It's time you retired as you've had plenty from tennis without giving any of it back.' A parting shot was the hope that the Czechs would beat Rosewall and the other Australian stars in the Davis Cup.

Because of the absence of Rosewall and most of the other good players, Wimbledon recruited a number of minor-league personalities. Ken remembers, 'Bob McKinley's serve and volley were not up to Wimbledon or Forest Hills standards.' Jan Kodes won the tournament in a weakened field. Ken says of him, 'Jan Kodes, a clay-court player, has improved a lot on grass and indoors. He's not very popular with other players.

The Europeans on the circuit stick together. He has long, fluent ground strokes with a lot of pace. If you're at the net and hit wide to him, he likes to go down the line with his backhand and forehand, and when he's at the net he often hits his forehand volley straight to the baseline. The two last times I played him, I beat him on clay and lost to him indoors.'

Rosewall gave up not a set in beating five opponents at the 1973 Forest Hills to reach the semi-finals. He ended his late summer tour by winning the Osaka and Japan opens, defeating Newcombe in the latter. (By the end of 1973 Rosewall's lifetime record against Newcombe was nine wins and seven losses.) When a big tournament or the climax of the pro tour was nearing, he would leap out to reach either the semis or finals or win it.

During the year, Ken met many of the younger players now coming into prominence for the first time. He says of them: 'The most intelligent way to play Bjorn Borg is to emphasize shots to his volley, which is not so secure yet. I certainly would not try to play him conservatively as softer safe shots he will murder with that big, swinging forehand. Instead, I would keep up the pace with well-hit shots, but nor would I make them faster than I usually do.'

I said, 'Do you think Borg's heavy topspin style with the great twist of his body on shots may lead to injuries for him?'

'That might be.'

Ken went on, 'I only played Borg once and I was out of match practice, but his volley is not that good. I would hit some soft-angled shots to bring him in. Also, his backhand is not as good as his forehand. His second serve has a lot of topspin and rises high, and so one can come down on it and hit cross-court, and sometimes it does not have enough depth.

'Buster Mottram has a nervous temperament. He doesn't play in a lot of tournaments which is surprising for a young player who should be getting all the play he can. He would be wise not to play in the WTT, with its one-set matches and the uncertainty of playing on any night.

'Phil Dent does have a great deal of ability. He has developed as an adult rather than as a junior, and his style is very graceful.

'Dick Stockton's backhand needs improvement. He's been practising it.

'Roscoe Tanner's action on serve is very fast. I stand three or four feet behind the baseline instead of one or two receiving it. But he has to improve his volley.

'Vilas is obviously better on clay, and already has improved his serve since I beat him in a Canadian tournament in 1973. Vilas' volley needs improvement, and his forehand ground stroke has such a heavy top spin that it comes over the net high and can be cut off. He needs more control on the forehand volley and forehand ground stroke, particularly on grass where the ball is lower, but on clay it's less of a problem for him. In the Masters tournament in Melbourne in December 1974, which he won, he showed improvement on a fast grass court. He has the ability to improve even further.

'A lot of European players like Vilas, who though South American was trained on clay, too, like to lift the ball on the volley and push it deep rather than volley it firmly like Hoad, Sedgman, and Laver.

'Metreveli's game reached a certain level and stayed there, and now he's at an age where I don't think he'll move into the top. He and Kodes, another Communist-country player, played a lot, knew each others' games inside out. On the WCT '73 circuit in the 'B' group every time Metreveli met Kodes he became nervous and lost, and the same thing happened in the '73 Wimbledon final. Metreveli is certainly the best Russian player, but perhaps his game is a bit wooden.

'John Alexander has depended too much on his big serve and has to work hard on his ground strokes before he will reach the top, particularly his forehand which he used to hit straight and now tries to whip over it exclusively. He is not that agile either. John Alexander needs to work on his game a lot more to become a top player.

'Orantes, whose upset win over Jimmy Connors for the 1975 U.S. Open title was the sensation of the scene, has a very good game with no real weaknesses. Although he is strong physically, he does not seem to like to hit hard. Like other top European players, he prefers clay and has developed his ground strokes more than his serve. But his serve is well placed. His volley is quite good, and he can play serve and volley. In fact, he beat Tony Roche in a long five-setter on grass at Wimbledon in 1974. I only played him once, in, I think, the quarter-finals of a WCT tournament in '71 in Barcelona, which was on clay and is his hometown, and I won the first set and was leading in the third with two match points, but he won and subsequently won the tournament. He's an exceptional player and, as a left-handed player, has great control of his shots, particularly on his forehand.'

In the fall of 1973 occurred the Bobby Riggs-Billie Jean King extravaganza. Ken observed, 'The Billie Jean King-Riggs match was poor tennis, though a lot of amateurs like to play with soft shots, dink stuff. Bobby Riggs was terribly out of shape, but he did a brilliant job of promoting it. And he has done very well for Bobby Riggs financially since then, which was good for Bobby Riggs and good to introduce so many people to the game.'

Rosewall's feelings about Billie Jean King can be inferred from his comments on her behaviour in the playoffs of World Team Tennis in 1974 as 'typical Billie Jean King.' Rosewall was the player-coach of the Pittsburgh WTT team. Billie Jean, accompanied by her male players, disrupted the singles between Rosewall and Buster Mottram, whom Rosewall had earlier in the season reprimanded for heckling one of the Pittsburgh players during a match. Billie Jean threatened an official protest over a line call dispute. However, Rosewall won the set, delivering afterwards his dry comment on an American superstar.

In the autumn of '73 some excitment developed over the Davis Cup because the Australian tennis authorities had been able to persuade Rosewall, Newcombe and Laver to play for the team that year. Ken remembers, 'Esso was the sponsor, and travel and other expenses were paid, and some additional money given to each player, but certainly nothing to retire on.

'Well, uh, I hope I can make the team,' Rosewall said at the time. He had just beaten Newcombe in the Japanese final. However, his modesty on this occasion was not Rosewall downgrading himself, but based on an awareness that Fraser was the team captain.

But before the Aussies met the U.S. in Cleveland, they beat Czechoslovakia. A relatively unknown Czech player, Jiri

Hrebec, played very well, defeating Newcombe and losing to Laver in five sets. Ken says, 'Hrebec has a bad attitude. After doing well in the Davis Cup against Australia, he said to himself, 'I've done fine against Laver and Newcombe, as well as I'll ever do. I might as well quit.' I've heard he's thrown matches. Sometimes the European temperament is suspect. It would certainly benefit his game if he worked harder. I suppose he had nothing to lose when he faced Laver and Newcombe, and everything he touched went in. In practice he was nowhere near as good, and we did not know which of the Czech players was going to be No. 2 after Kodes. In fact, we were a little surprised when Hrebec was chosen, but he certainly lived up to the selection, and even today he might be capable of an outstanding performance.'

Rosewall had an outstanding record in best-of-five set matches in the seventies, whereas Laver had a mediocre one, having failed to win a Big Four tournament, WCT final or Masters since '69. Laver's sole claim over Rosewall was a narrow victory, winning two out of three sets, in a minor tournament a month earlier, which was not the same as competing against Rosewall in a best-of-five set match, where Rosewall clearly had the edge over Laver and which was the format for the Davis Cup. Rosewall had beaten Laver in their two previous best-of-five set matches—the WCT finals of '71. and '72. Fraser's reason for not selecting Rosewall was that he 'liked the power game.' Rosewall spent two weeks in Cleveland giving Laver and Newcombe practice, though in a key match he had an edge over both of them, as was shown by their head-to-head records in best-of-five set matches during major championships around that period.[*]

Ken remembers, 'In 1973 Colin Dibley did the same thing for Laver and Newcombe, hitting serves to them, as Bob Mark had for Fraser in '58, and I played good points against them to sharpen their ground strokes and volleys, as Anderson, Masters and Dibley could not press them as I could. It was an unusual situation—the first time the Davis Cup had been

---

[*] Rosewall lost to Newcombe, Wimbledon, '70, beat him U.S., '70, lost to him Wimbledon '71, beat him WCT '71, lost to him U.S., '73, beat him Wimbledon, '74, beat him U.S. '74. Rosewall beat Laver WCT final '71, beat him WCT final '72.

played indoors and the very poor type of stadium compared to the other great stadiums in America, and it was without any great television coverage. I was very happy to be with the winning team. I think I was the one that helped to get both Laver and Newcombe into such great form for those particular singles matches, as well as for their doubles. Mal Anderson was not physically well at the time. Colin Dibley could really only help with his thundering service, and Geoff Masters was not playing well or strong enough to force either Rod or John in singles matches. So I would think I was the one who helped to get the boys into great shape and great form.'

At one point in the matches a section of the crowd began to chant 'We Want Rosewall,' which Fraser ignored. The result of Fraser's favouring Laver over Rosewall was that Laver only barely won his match over Tom Gorman, not a top-ranking player, requiring five sets. The irony of the 1973 Davis Cup was that neither nation used its best player—Connors and Rosewall. For Australia Fraser of course chose Laver over Rosewall, while the USLTA insisted on retaining Ralston as the U.S. coach. Ralston barred Connors because he would not play in early-round Davis Cup matches.

Over the winter of 1973-74 Rosewall rested. He became player-coach of the Pittsburgh team in the new World Team Tennis League.

World Team Tennis is a new sports league, employing new concepts. Scoring is simplified, eliminating 'love, 15, 30, 40, and deuce' in favour of '1, 2, 3, 4.' The fourth point wins the game. A match consists of two singles contests, one between men, the other between women, one men's doubles contest, one women's doubles and one mixed doubles. Each contest is limited to one set. The games are added together so that the team winning the most games wins the match. Teams represent cities such as New York or Boston and play each other over a regular schedule in the spring and summer. The most controversial part of WTT is the league's policy of encouraging spectators to comment during play, as is the custom in American football or baseball or international soccer. 'Comment' can include shouts, yells, cheers, etc.

Ken remarks, 'I may be too old to adapt to the approach of World Team Tennis. Some players did not like the unkind remarks made by some very stupid people in the stands. The girls particularly found it very hard to concentrate through the personal remarks shouted at them. Evonne Goolagong, who was on our team, was near to tears on several occasions, and the volatile Bob Hewitt, who played for the Minnesota Buckskins, was brought to boiling point on numerous occasions. His team went bankrupt shortly before the end of the season, and their supporters were among the most vociferous in the league. If Bob was playing well, he was a hero—"Hewitt can do it! Hewitt can do it!" they would chant. If he started to play badly, they would yell, "Hewitt blew it! Hewitt blew it!"

'There has been a lot of criticism of the scoring system and the travelling. The problem of transforming what is after all an individual sport into a team context is something which has not yet been satisfactorily solved. They expected to draw the regular tennis fan and new ones from other sports, but traditional tennis lovers tell me after seeing matches that they would not come again and put up with all the carryings-on. Our Pittsburgh team was happy, but some players were not paid on the other teams and owners complained of the poor attendance. They have now had three presidents of the league in a year. I found the coaching, with its responsibilities, travelling and playing, tiring, and I won't do it again.'

While I was in Australia in December 1974, Ken's wife, Wilma, said to me, 'I know I shouldn't say this, but we didn't like team tennis. The shouting just didn't seem right. It wasn't tournament tennis.'

Ken said, 'The shouting was rude.'

Wilma said, 'It didn't seem like tennis to me.'

Rosewall continued on the subject of the team tennis: 'In the last eight matches I noticed the fans began to pay more attention to how we played.

'One of the WTT players was Clark Graebner. He was known as "superboy" when he first came out to Australia in '67 or '68 because of his dark curly hair, horn-rimmed glasses and Clark Kent look. Even then he would be looking at the crowd after hitting a good shot before the point was over or after stroking a winner. Some people have said he lacks courage when behind in a match, though this may not be true, and could not fight his way back, though he did better in the one-set WTT matches. He had a very powerful serve and, though his ground strokes were not so good, you did not always know where he was going to hit them.'

I said, 'In Grace Lichtenstein's book, *You've Come a Long Way*, she says he came into the stands with a new girl friend while his wife, Carole, was playing a match and her game completely collapsed.'

'They were living apart but were together on the Cleveland WTT team, saying that they would make it a team effort; but she was traded to us at Pittsburgh, and since we then had four women players she went to New York, where she played against us several times and won some matches. She is a very attractive personality and an intelligent commentator on TV. She had an unusual style as a player but knew the game and was a good woman player. But now, with two children, she can't give that much time to tournament tennis.'

Pittsburgh, Ken's team, had a 30-wins, 14-losses record for the season, reaching the semi-finals of the playoffs. In the singles he won 237 games and lost 216. Shortly after the WTT season for 1974 ended, I asked him how he had done, as I had been in Italy for the summer and had not been able to follow Pittsburgh's progress. We were sitting alone in the quiet dining room of the Westchester Country Club, and Rosewall was eating breakfast a few hours before playing a match at Forest Hills. 'I didn't play very well,' he said.

Wimbledon At Forty

Fortunately, World Team Tennis was suspended for three weeks in June 1974 so that Rosewall and other players could participate in Wimbledon. He told Bud Collins soon after arriving, 'At Wimbledon . . . ah, yes, I still get keyed up, nervous before a match. Why? What am I trying to prove? After all these tries. But yet I come here to win it—not just to play. It takes luck and stamina, but yes—I always think one year I'll be champion. I believe in miracles.' In his first match he won easily over Barry Phillips-Moore. The next morning—it was a Tuesday—Rosewall remarked to me over the phone ' . . . If I'm still in the tournament by Friday.' I started watching him halfway through the second set of his second-round match, which was against Vijay Amritraj. He had won the first set 6-2. He looked alternately sharp and groggy. He lost the second set on two beautiful passing shots by Amritraj. Amritraj was murderous, nervous and determined. It was only the second round. Rosewall's serve was harder and deeper than one suspected.

On Friday I met him for the first time at breakfast in the coffee shop of a London hotel where he was staying with Wilma, Brett and Glenn. He was still in the tournament. His manner was quiet but confident. His appearance was elegant in a casual, sporting way. He wore light beige chinos, a sort of mauve-pink coloured shirt open at the neck, and a green sweater tossed over his shoulders, the arms tied in front. It looked like a cashmere. His face was moderately tanned and lined.

He said, 'When I first played Gonzales, I lost, as he was used to indoor courts. The indoor surface was right for the power game. But Gonzales was very good on any surface—indoor or outside. He was big and quick.

'I've become blasé about memorable matches. I've been playing so long.

'When you lose and you play well you often feel content, but if you lose and play badly, you're upset. And if you lose and play badly and are not upset, then you lack a sense of competition.'

His two young sons, unimpressed with their father's fame, came in with Wilma, an attractive brunette. One of them asked if he could buy a game in a London toy store. Grinning at me, Rosewall looked over his shoulder, as the family had sat down in the booth behind us, and said yes.

He only laughed when I asked him to recommend some players who could give interesting comments about him. I noticed he talked more often of his losing matches than winning ones, and when he mentioned the latter he seemed almost surprised.

When he spoke of his two WCT wins, his face lit up and he became excited, but for no other of his victories did he react this way. From the way he spoke I guessed that the memories of the other matches were all bathed in a romantic glow of the past, they were obviously not uppermost in his thoughts.

He mentioned how it was difficult to get playing time on the indoor courts at The Queen's Club on rainy days. It had been raining steadily for two days. Ken's doubles partner was Owen Davidson, a fellow Australian and one of the world's best doubles players. 'Luckily Owen Davidson is a member, but if you are not a member, you can only play in the player's time. When you have only an hour, it goes fast.' He laughed when I remarked that it must be a constant problem finding practice courts in new cities on tour.

Wimbledon now has a somewhat circuslike atmosphere, with heavy crowds milling incessantly under the arches and in the passages of the stadium. Some of the young seemed rowdy. Outside there were discarded papers scattered all over. But on court No. 1 and the centre court the deep green of the grass was glistening. These were like green carpets—rich, uniform green in sunlight, subdued and slightly grey when cloudy. The arrangement of the umpires' and linesman's chairs was like at a medieval tournament. Outside the main building there was the excitement of watching the electronic scoreboard. There were people sitting on chairs beside the outside courts in the late evening, taking their rest after a day's work even when there was no play in the court directly facing. On an exterior court with stands, the crowd, mostly young, handclapped in time against Bob Hewitt, who was playing Dick Crealy.

Ken says of him, 'Bob Hewitt is a Jekyll and Hyde. On the court he has a terrible disposition. I've even seen him during a match tell his wife in the stands to move on or move out. Off the court he is a very nice man and has a perfect disposition. He is a very graceful player with an all-court game and wide, imaginative placements with lots of touch; his serve, as Stan Smith points out, is weaker than the rest of his game. Part of the reason is that he hits the ball softer than a man of his height and strength should. The serve is also affected by his tossing the ball a little too high, and he has a slow back-swing and swing toward the ball giving it time to drop into the hitting area, though his total serve action is fluent and smooth. Both he and Frew McMillan seem to be in a bad mood when they play doubles together, rarely speaking to each other, but it seems to suit them, as they are one of the world's top combinations, winning the WCT doubles in 1974 and Wimbledon earlier than that.'

I said, 'I saw Hewitt leading Dick Crealy at Wimbledon, making beautiful placements. Then he got angry, hit balls out of the stands, the crowd began to clap him, and he blew it.'

Rosewall performed the miracle he had hoped for in his interview a few days earlier with Collins. He was seeded only ninth when the tournament began. In the early rounds he won over Barry Phillips-Moore and Vijay Amritraj, the latter in four sets. He came from behind to eliminate Roscoe Tanner, rapidly emerging as one of the best young players. But he was expected to lose to John Newcombe, the No. 1 seed, fresh from an outstanding season on the WCT circuit, winner of the 1974 finals in Dallas. Rosewall ripped through Newcombe in the first set 6-1, allowing John only 5 points in the first five games. It was a grey, windy day, and play was interrupted by a pigeon flying above the players around the court, prompting the referee to ask the crowd if anyone had a gun. Rosewall lost the second set 1-6, but won the third 6-0, demonstrating his remarkable anticipation. During the last points in the fourth set the crowd rose to its feet, willing Rosewall to win, which he did 7-5. He had won the match. He had defeated Newcombe, the No. 1 seed. He was now in the semi-finals, facing Stan Smith.

And two sets down, 4-5 in the third set on Smith's serve and a few games later match point against him in the tie-breaker, Rosewall came back and beat Smith to the tumultuous cheers of the spectators, reaching the finals in his fortieth year, almost certainly an unprecedented feat in modern times.*

Ken remembers, 'I've only lost to Stan Smith three times. He is not that manoeuvrable, and you try to angle the return of serve low and wide to make him bend over. Also his backhand

---

* The day of the finals the *Daily Telegraph* reported that Rosewall, if he won, would be the second oldest Wimbledon winner in tennis history, the first being Arthur Wentworth Gore, who won Wimbledon for the third time in 1909 at forty-one and was the runner-up in 1910. Allison Danzig, now retired, for years the well-known tennis correspondent for the New York *Times*, wrote me that Gore was again the runner-up at Wimbledon in 1912.

is hit in front of him with a flick of his wrist and, if he can't get
in position, he has difficulty with it. His forehand is very good,
but his ground strokes are not as good as his serve. The way I
beat him at Wimbledon was just that—in the third set at
match point against me I drove those shots wide-angled and
deep.'

The excitment in the tennis world generated by Rosewall's
victory over Smith was typified by a lawyer in New York City,
Steve Schecter, who was inspired to write a poem, *Ken
Rosewall*, an excerpt of which is:

> For three hours he battled the mighty Stan Smith
> He certainly showed his greatness was no myth
> He makes you want to stand up and cheer
> A great player and sportsman year after year.

The next day Rosewall confronted Jimmy Connors, who had
had an easy run in the draw, beating Stockton in the semi-
finals.

Thousands of miles away in Australia Ken's father sat down
in the living room at the home of some friends who had a
colour TV set. Subsequently he told me, 'I watched his
Wimbledon match with some friends on TV here in Australia.
When he came out on the court, I said, 'I don't think it looks
good.' I could see he had tiredness all over his face.' To the
disappointment of the English crowd and his fans throughout
the world, Rosewall lost to Connors in just over an hour 6-1,
6-1, 6-4.

Rosewall and his family returned to Pittsburgh after his
extradinary Wimbledon feat, where he continued coaching
such players as Vitas Gerulaitis and the English player Gerald
Battrick. Rosewall usually played the lead-off men's singles,
while Goolagong played the women's singles. After reaching
the semi-finals of WTT playoffs at the end of the season, Ken,
Wilma and the two boys moved to the New York area, settling
in at the Westchester Country Club in preparation for Forest
Hills. There on the green grass courts of the Westchester club,
despite a day of rain, he was able to practise with John
Alexander, who was staying nearby with friends. The
Rosewalls arrived on a Sunday. Monday he had a 'hit' with
Alexander. Tuesday it rained. Wednesday Forest Hills began.

Forest Hills at Forty

The problem for a tennis player in his fortieth year trying to win Forest Hills is difficult, to say the least. His reflexes have declined steadily since the age of 30. His concentration is not as strong. Rosewall says, 'I feel myself that at this stage of my life I do have lapses in concentration.' His stamina, so essential for five-set matches, sometimes two in two days, has deteriorated. The enemy, the other players, aware of this situation, will try to run the forty-year-old as much as possible, back and forth, up and down, not hitting a winner when it might pay to keep the ball in play and wear the middle-aged opponent down some more.

Because of the age factor there are other hazards. Hot weather can be fatal to one's chances. For Rosewall, singles matches without a full day's rest in between are a danger. Muscles stiffen more at that age, and relax slower. And there is the lurking psychological fear, unlikely but nevertheless there, of serious injury striking. Amateurs die of heart attacks on tennis courts at age 40. Slightly more menacing is the possibility of injury due to tired muscles, even to a man of Rosewall's age and in his superb condition. Though he had played World Team Tennis during the summer, it was Rosewall's third tournament of the year.

Who were some of the other players blocking Rosewall's path to the title? His first-round opponent was Colin Dibley. Despite Dibley's fearsome reputation on the court with his booming serve—summed up in Richey's remark, 'Teach a gorilla how to serve and you've got Dibley'—a quiet, yet frank charm exudes from his tough, wrinkled face. He gives the immediate impression that he is complimented when he is being interviewed, and after first lapsing into a set way of speech which he has presumably decided is right when being quoted, he positively lights up and radiates warmth and enthusiasm when discussing Rosewall.

Dibley said, 'You have to make a very good serve and he'll make a good return, and then you again have to make a good shot, a volley, because his next shot will be very good. His shots are very accurate and his overhead, which most people don't realize, is very accurate. . . . I used to practise with him when he was home for five or six weeks between WCT tours. I'd work from six to two in the Customs House and then I would play him. He likes my serve as it gave him a little trouble. He and Mr. Shaw encouraged me to turn pro. I played him a lot in practice, as I was about the only good player around Sydney. I'd never won a set off him in a match, and only the last one in practice. He makes me double-fault sometimes when he puts so much pressure on my serve. I try to hit out on his serve as sometimes it is a little weaker. I try to hit to his forehand volley, which is not quite as effective as his backhand.'

Rosewall said, 'I was a little worried about not having played in any tournaments, having been in World Team Tennis and Dibley not playing WTT, when we faced each other at Forest Hills in the first round in 1974.

'I had always played men bigger than me, even as a twelve-year-old barely able to see over the net, and my opponents were older, so a big serve like Dibley's never bothered me. I played the first serve about two steps behind the baseline, and then moved in two paces on the second. In fact, the hard fast serve like Dibley's is easier on grass because the bounce is more predictable than a spin serve. Dibley's weakness is his forehand volley, which is too wristy, and his ground strokes have never been emphasized like his serve. He has given me a lot of credit for encouraging his career, but I don't know if that is true.' Rosewall defeated Colin Dibley of the awkward strokes and booming serve, clocked at 148 m.p.h., easily, with a score of 6-4, 7-6, 6-1.

His second-round opponent was Bob Lutz, formerly a top player, now slowed by knee operations. Rod Laver has said, 'Lutz has great talent for the *dolce vita.*' Rosewall told me, 'Bob Lutz can't move very well because of his knees, but I don't know if I'd moved him around more than usual, as I normally try to run my opponents around the court.' Like Dibley, Lutz went down in three sets, 7-6, 6-3, 6-3.

Then came Charley Pasarell. Rosewall said, 'Charley Pasarell has never lived up to his promise. It may be that his family has money, and things have come easier. He hits with power and a big serve but does not vary his game. He will do well against the top player and then lose to people below him in the first or second round. There is a certain quirk of psychology with Pasarell whereby when he confronts a leading player he is loose, and yet against a player inferior to him he feels pressure. When he is expected to win, he lacks confidence in himself.

'I was ahead two sets on Pasarell, winning them 1 and 0. With scores like that you feel he has to improve his game a lot to win the third set. He goes for a lot of winners with big strokes. He had three or four winners in the game he broke my serve, but in the next set I raised my game.' The score was 6-1, 6-0, 4-6, 6-4.

Meanwhile, most of the other stars, with the exception of Borg, who lost to Vijay Amritraj, were advancing through the early rounds. Among the leading players whom Rosewall might have to meet were Stan Smith and Nastase. Nastase had a very nice touch and beautiful reflexes. There was Roscoe Tanner, twenty-two, who with his straight shoulders and back and slightly military gait walked like a West Point second lieutenant. He had a very fast first serve and a second serve with a lot of spin. There was John Alexander, an Australian in his early twenties. His ground strokes left something to be desired, though he, too, had a blindingly quick first serve. In his match against Jimmy Connors, Alexander had several break points in the fourth set, down two sets to one, but he did not drive himself enough and failed to go for the hard-to-get shots. Alexander looked like a tall lean Texas ranger. But Connors' shots were accurate and, a known rebel, he defied the law as represented by Alexander, ran for everything and won. There were Ashe and Newcombe. By the end of the first five days Rosewall had reached the fourth of seven rounds.

It was Monday of the second week. Rosewall was a little tense before his doubles match. He and his partner, Owen Davidson, were to play the two Amritraj brothers, Vijay and Anand, in a best-of-three sets match. The early rounds of the doubles tournament at Forest Hills in 1974 had been shortened to three sets instead of the more usual five. Though it was an unimportant contest and his team was favoured, Rosewall had a tough singles match the next day against Raul Ramirez, and a long doubles the evening before could sap his strength. Rosewall observed to me, 'If I had any brains, I'd stop playing doubles in big championships. Doubles can sharpen your game and some players use it to practise, but at my age it can weaken me for singles.'

Referring again to his impending doubles match, his partner being the left-hander Owen Davidson—one of the world's best and an outstanding player in mixed doubles—against the Amritraj brothers, he remarked, 'It could be a tough match, but we should win. They play well, though Vijay is the better singles player. Our problem is the rough surface of the court, but they don't move that quickly. So we may try to hit at wide angles.'

During the match Maureen O'Keefe, the assistant to Rosewall's business agent, observed, 'Vijay and Ken are trying each other out.' If Rosewall beat Ramirez, he would face Vijay, assuming the latter beat Marty Riessen. At the beginning of the tournament Vijay had triumphed in five sets over Borg, an upset, and at Wimbledon he had taken a set off our hero, an improvement for Vijay, as at Forest Hills a year earlier he had lost to Rosewall in three sets. Rosewall was thinking, 'No sets a year ago, One three months ago. Two days from now two sets or the match?'

Vijay is tall, angry-looking, very dark with exceptionally thin lower legs. His brother, Anand, is less thin with a more placid countenance.

Maureen said of Rosewall during the doubles match after he had lost a point, 'That's his hangdog look.'

I said, 'It's the little man versus insuperable odds.'

We agreed: 'That's part of his appeal.'

A man sitting near us remarked, 'He's a secretive little man.'

Rosewall did not play very well in the doubles. His shots were often loose and he made a number of errors. His serve was much faster than I had thought, and his overhead was deadly, except for one horrendous error in the semi-dark just before the match was called at one set apiece due to darkness and rain. Rosewall, I noticed, squinted a lot, particularly when receiving, blinking frequently. When Davidson served, he leaned away from the serve. Was this to avoid being hit? Rosewall swayed from side to side before receiving, like a cat preparing to jump.

The next morning I met Rosewall at the Westchester

Country Club, where he was staying with his wife and sons in two attractive bedrooms overlooking green lawns and trees. Most of the other players and tennis entrepreneurs were staying in Manhattan, but Rosewall had been invited as a paying guest.

The architecture of the Westchester Country Club is an unbelievable hodgepodge of imitation Tudor, American nineteenth-century summer home and ordinary brick. The row of five grass courts was beautifully verdant and smooth—in better condition than Forest Hills. Rosewall said, 'I practised here before the tournament began last week—once with John Alexander, who is staying nearby with friends. Another day I got a hit with two of the better club players which the club pro arranged. One day a friend of mine, John Mangan, who lives in the area, took me to an indoor court where I was able to play when Forest Hills was washed out by rain, and that was very much appreciated.'

Rosewall ate a substantial breakfast of coffee, toast and boiled eggs, American style. He looked fresh from a night's sleep. There was a certain tension in the air, but he chatted amiably. He was impeccably dressed in blue blazer and blue and white check trousers with a dark bluish sports shirt. It had been raining outside.

'I'll know at ten whether we play when I phone the referee.' The time was 9.40 A.M.

After breakfast he had slight difficulty in finding a number at Forest Hills that would answer.

'Mike,' he said briskly, 'are we playing?' Pause. 'Okay, I'll bring my spikes.'

He drove Wilma, the two sons and me in a rented Impala to Forest Hills. I noticed he was a careful driver. Despite the minutes ticking by he talked amicably.

I mentioned how much driving he must have done in the old touring days and remarked, 'Playing against the same player in a close series of matches and then travelling with him must have been tricky.'

'We usually went together in a couple of station wagons. But Pancho Gonzales would often go separately. He'd leave right after a match and drive with his brother and his dog. It wasn't a bad idea, as you always had to unwind before going to sleep.'

He talked about Pro-Am golf tournaments, the busy country outside of Sydney and the careful community control of the ecology in the suburb where he and Wilma lived.

Rosewall said, 'Young players should not be discouraged by the bad bounces on grass. Some players used to give up playing on grass when they were used to a smooth surface. The California players used to have trouble, and so did the European and South American, but now everyone plays everywhere. One tip for young players on grass is not to be too perfect on the stroke—you may have to mis-hit.'

During the drive his older son, Brett, said, 'Dad, when you've played your match, can we go into town? I want to do some shopping.'

'I may have to play a doubles match. We'll see.'

Rosewall said, 'There are more left-handed players than there used to be, more proportionately, even though the number of professionals has increased. In the old days left-handers used to have weak backhands, like Mervyn Rose and Art Larsen, who had that sad accident.'

As we drove into the manicured, lush suburb of Forest Hills, Rosewall said, 'That house over there is the Stone house. He was a TV star and a friend of his who bought it used to lend it to the Australian Davis Cup team back in '52, '53, '54 and '56. I stayed there. I guess before me Frank Sedgman stayed there, and afterwards other Australians like Ashley Cooper and Mal Anderson.' It was a largish, undistinguished-looking house surrounded by trees and green.

Rosewall parked his car in a driveway, blocking another car's exit. He said, 'Vitas Gerulaitis' sister has a friend whose house this is, who said we could park here.' He went around to the rear, rang the bell and gave the keys to a young housewife wearing curlers, who seemed delighted to accept the keys and to greet him, warning Rosewall protectively in Jewish-mother style, 'Be careful. The steps are slippery from the rain.'

At the gate to Forest Hills Brett guarded his rackets while Rosewall went into the clubhouse to get tickets for the family.

An Emotional Cliff-Hanger

Rosewall did some exercises, almost like a ballet dancer,

standing beside the net before warming up with Vitas Gerulaitis. I thought he looked sharp—obviously a better player than Gerulaitis.

Rosewall's body, when studied on the tennis court, is a strong one, though weighing only 140 pounds. The upper half of the torso is slightly like an inverted cone, tapering wider as it goes up to the shoulders. The calves and thighs are muscled, and as he stands on the grass awaiting the serve, the tendons and muscles stand out in a tanned complex of strength. The only anomaly is the awkward way his left hand holds the front part of the handle of the racket, the wrist bent down at an angle.

Rosewall really comes alive on the tennis court. His face lights up with joy, frustration and activity. His emotions, tightly controlled off the court, show through during a match, and these days he has even become slightly playful on the court. Once during the doubles match the evening before against the Amritraj brothers he had bounced a loose ball with his behind, to the amusement of the centre-court fans. At Wimbledon in June I had seen him twirl his racket like a yo-yo: Previously he had always been the methodical star, a taciturn, polite Australian.

When he came on the grandstand court, the sun had come out, and I wondered how the hot, muggy heat would affect him. As usual he looked small compared to Ramirez, a tallish Mexican young man with a sort of classic profile. While they had warmed up separately, Rosewall had appeared more precise and accurate than the Mexican, who had a touch of Spanish arrogance and pride in his manner.

The first set Ramirez played badly, Rosewall very well. Against Ramirez he made some fantastic backhands down the line—impossible rescue shots—and his volleys were beautiful spin scoops of Ramirez' returns of serve.

But, starting the second set, Ramirez' first serve, a topspin one, hit loosely, began to go in. It was noticeable on one point that Ramirez tried to run Rosewall, hitting a lob and keeping the ball in play rather than going for a winner. Ramirez always returned to the service line quickly, gesticulating impatiently with a flick of his fingers to the ballboy, as if to keep the pace fast and tire his opponent. However, when changing ends

Ramirez was usually last on the court. They reached a tie-breaker. Ramirez committed a double fault and Rosewall began to serve, with the score 1-1. Rosewall double-faulted and hit a screaming backhand just beyond the baseline. Rosewall and Ramirez took a point each, but the score was 2-4, and Ramirez quickly won the set.

Rosewall started to mumble 'golly Moses' in disgust, and once or twice threw his racket to the ground or hit a loose ball. The sun came out again. Ramirez was playing steadily and well, and one began to understand why he was seeded No. 16 and had beaten Smith twice on the WCT tour. The only ground for hope other than Rosewall's immense skill and experience was that as the set progressed Ramirez began to gesticulate a little more, pace in dramatic semi-circles occasionally between points behind the service line or glance in the direction of the crowd, sometimes to a friend. The perspiration showed on both men, and Rosewall paced himself carefully, often looking overwhelmed by immense odds. His first serve was frequently not going in, and he showed a tendency to get ahead on his serve, say 40 or 30-0, and then lost the next three points. Finally he lost his serve on several errors. This meant a service break for Ramirez, who merely had to hold his own serve to win the set. Ramirez would then be ahead two sets to one.

Rosewall broke Ramirez' serve back, and broke it again with a series of forehand drives hit cross-court. The shots were very hard and low, tearing past the feet of the incoming Ramirez. Ramirez, according to Jim Hambuechen, Rosewall's agent, had served to Ken's forehand, supposedly his weakest side, when a more experienced player such as Newcombe would have served at his body, forcing him to hesitate between forehand and backhand. I doubted this, as Rosewall's speed would have enabled him to get into position easily for a shot at his opponent. 'That's a fair comment,' Rosewall said of Hambuechen's remark. 'Ramirez moves quickly, is a good scrambler. His serve's not all that fast.' Ramirez said to me a few months later, 'I should have served to his body, but he had been hitting his backhand well, and I thought I'd try the forehand.' Rosewall held his serve and won the third set.

In the fourth set Ramirez crumbled. His cross swung on his

chain outside his sport shirt, but God did not help him until Rosewall lost three match points in a row, one of them a beautiful backhand drive-chop by Ramirez, which bit into the grass so sharply it dropped almost dead. Rosewall was starting to think, 'I'm getting a little bit tired. If he wins this fourth set . . .' Ramirez said, 'I was hoping he'd tire in the fourth set when I had a couple of break points, one at 5-3 against me, I think, but he ran for everything. I admire him for what he does at his age.' During these match points a group of tough children started to shout and kick cans behind the fence. A lady linesman said, 'Shut up,' but it had no effect. The distance from the kids to Rosewall was no more than thirty feet. One could see Rosewall was straining to end the match as he served each time, and finally he forced Ramirez into an error.

At the press conference in the men's locker room in the clubhouse afterwards Rosewall looked frail beside the en-circling press, who were mainly pudgy men with paunches. The questions from most of the press, about eight reporters crowding around Rosewall as he sat on a bench, a towel around him, proved to be singularly obnoxious and inane, some showing that they had not watched the match, or, if they had, had seen it without comprehension, others implying that perhaps Rosewall should retire soon and wasn't there something grotesque about a man of his age beating the young Ramirez. The latter implication seemed typical of the American habit of overemphasizing youth. Rosewall replied quietly that he intended to go on playing, adding that perhaps some of the older players should take longer rest periods. 'I played about six months this year.'

Rosewall was persistently patient with all questions, and the conference ended after a beaming Bud Collins informed Rosewall, 'Ken, you've lost weight.' This did not appear to be the case. Collins was the author of the book about Laver, Rosewall's great rival, and a constant laudator of Laver on U.S. television. Collins' arrival brought an electricity into the air between him and Rosewall, who initially ignored his presence, but they were soon smiling at each other.

One of his questioners said, 'Does playing in the doubles hurt your chances in the singles?'

Rosewall said, 'You have to make an effort in the doubles.'

Rosewall then took a shower, rested and went out on the centre court in the early evening to play the doubles match which had been suspended after two sets due to rain the night before. His partner, Owen Davidson, fortunately played as badly as the tired Rosewall in the match against the Amritrajs and in fact lost his serve, costing them the set and match. It was now about 6.30 P.M. Back in the clubhouse I congratulated Rosewall on his win over Ramirez, commenting on his brilliant forehand shots.

Rosewall remarked, 'You can't make those forehand drives all the time,' implying it had not been easy to get out of the crisis in the third set. But he looked happy and content. He said to one of the tournament employees, 'I need a massage.'

A middle-aged American with a tanned face, presumably a club tennis player, kept shouting from the top deck of the clubhouse to the crowd below, 'Vijay, do you want to play mixed doubles?' After the fifth such shout, Anand Amritraj looked up, saying, 'I'm not Vijay.'

The next day Rosewall was not scheduled to play. The following morning he confronted Vijay in the first match of the day, starting at 11.30 A.M. on the centre court. There was bright sunshine and cool air. The grass was especially green. The first set renewed fears of Rosewall's age. Amritraj was making some good passing shots and fast, spinning serves. Rosewall, who had looked quick in practice and the better player, was double-faulting, not getting his first serve in, hitting ground and net strokes out. Amritraj tried once to run Rosewall.

Emotion came early in the second set when Rosewall again fell behind on his serve and male voices here and there in the crowd began to shout, 'Come on, Ken, put it together, Ken,' and you could see him almost stiffen and be encouraged; the serve became powerful, the ground strokes deadly. Rosewall kept moving his serve around the court, keeping the somewhat stiff Amritraj off balance. In the first set and the first part of the second set particularly, Amritraj had had more success hitting Rosewall's first serve, perhaps because, as it was aimed at either corner, Amritraj knew where it was going and also because serves to the corner would not cramp as serves to his body would.

I watched Rosewall's face through the binoculars. There was the cool, likeable concentration, the face flying through the air, as he served and ran to the net. I watched Amritraj's black pupils and white eyeballs, looking up and to the left and to the right, peering out of a face of frustration.

It was noticeable that Rosewall hit a lot of balls directly at Amritraj when they were close to each other at net, and Amritraj invariably could not get his body out of the way to make a good return.

Rosewall made a series of beautiful shots—the fantastic backhand hit from high, swooshing past Amritraj, the impossible rallies where Rosewall would stab through a winning shot, the almost endless deep, perfect placements. Amritraj began to make mistakes, to press, and it was all over in two hours. Rosewall had won 2-6, 6-3, 6-3, 6-2.

Afterward, Rosewall said to me, 'I might have been encouraged by the shouts from the crowd. Then Amritraj began to make some mistakes and became frustrated.'

In an interview with me some months later in Philadelphia Vijay Amritraj said, 'He's one of the three best players of all time—the others being Gonzales and Laver—and he is the finest stylist.' He admitted that Rosewall exploited his lack of manoeuvrability. 'I can't move that well because of my height. Every time he'd have a short ball he would hit it at me and I couldn't get it. I prefer it wide. I did better against him at Wimbledon and Forest Hills in 1974 than our first meeting in 1973, when I tried to hit aces. I slowed the ball down and tried to get the first serve in. You've got to serve well against him.' Vijay has a soft, charming manner—boyish—and I noticed he blushed with embarrassment and excitement when a middle-aged woman asked him into a company party sponsoring a new court surface where there were obviously a number of girls; but I admired his refusal after a moment's hesitation. Some of the American press have accused him of lacking the 'killer' instinct.

Rosewall would now meet John Newcombe in the semi-finals. Talking to me in Australia three months later, Ken remembered, 'I'd probably practised my serve before the Newcombe match at the Westchester Country Club.'

Meanwhile, how were the other players doing? Kodes lost to

Connors in four sets. Kodes' serve was like a man trying to chop a branch off a tree with a kitchen knife—laboured, unrhythmic and frustrating—but he showed flashes of amazing speed around mid-court. His strong jaw and brow and stocky body made him look like a worker in a Communist Party ad in Russia, and since he was from Czechoslovakia, this seemed somewhat appropriate.

Watching Stan Smith practise his volley at the net on the grass at Forest Hills, I thought he seemed like a clumsy giant with his big strokes and self-conscious form. A day or so later he lost badly to Tanner, who in the previous round had eliminated Nastase.

In the clubhouse I saw Tanner with his hair cut in a perfect bang in front, trimmed equally trimly along the side above that smiling face. Connors sat playing backgammon with his blue coloured socks exactly the right height. His face wore a suspicious look—open, as if to kill—with a trace of a smile. Connors said of Rosewall, 'The guy's a legend in his own time.'

Rosewall had a day of rest after the Amritraj match. Then, the following day, it rained so heavily that the semi-finals, scheduled for Saturday, had to be postponed to Sunday.

The night before Rosewall's semi-final match against John Newcombe the New York *Post* ran a feature story quoting Tony Roche and Neale Fraser on Newcombe's chances against Rosewall. Roche, Newcombe's doubles partner, is an old friend of John's. The *Post* said, 'Roche and Fraser favour Newcombe for these reasons: Newk's powerful serve, pressure on Rosewall to hold his service, Rosewall's custom of letting the ball bounce on the uneven grass court.'

Anatomy of a Match

On the day of the match the key questions were whether Rosewall's courage and skill could overcome the multiple dangers of Newcombe's power game and genuine ability, the slowly increasing heat of the afternoon and Rosewall's age.

Smith, with a big friendly smile, warmed up Rosewall. Rosewall's choice of Smith as a warm-up partner was a wise one as Smith's game resembled Newcombe's. Smith, occasionally grinning, seemed to relish the task. Having suffered at Newcombe's hands many times in the previous twelve months, notably the loss in the Davis Cup and several defeats on the WCT tour, thus ensuring that Newcombe was ranked higher than him, Smith wanted, one guessed, to see Rosewall win. Rosewall, after the Smith warm-up, walked happily back to the clubhouse, talking animatedly with a photographer, his green shirt wet from sweat.

Sunday afternoon at 1 P.M. the stadium was packed with people. The temperature was about 80° F., rising slightly, as Rosewall and Newcombe walked out on the court together. Ken remembers 'We made polite conversation.'

The first set started off with hard tennis, both men playing their best on every ball, stroking it as powerfully and accurately as possible. Rosewall said, 'The Newcombe match was an important one, and I tried to keep the pressure on all the time. His backhand is slightly weaker. So I would try to hit my backhand deep to his backhand.'

After Rosewall won his serve for 3-2, I thought Newcombe's game looked slightly loose and seedy compared with his championship form earlier in the year when he had won the WCT tour and finals. His long curly hair seemed to add to this impression. I wondered if Newcombe was losing his interest in tennis. In previous years he had stopped playing for extended periods. Newcombe won his serve easily, putting pressure on Rosewall, 3-3.

Then Rosewall committed two double faults, lost his serve and fell behind 3-4. At 4-5 on Newcombe's delivery the younger man now had a chance to win the set. Rosewall made that extra effort. He hit two beautiful backhand drives and a backhand return of serve, chopped delicately, short-angled to the sidelines, forcing the incoming Newcombe to bend down and make an error, the same brilliant dink which Newcombe had used with deadly effectiveness against Smith in the 1973 Davis Cup. Rosewall hit a fantastic backhand passing shot. After Newcombe's double fault, Rosewall had broken him back to 5-5. Newcombe saved set point against himself with a hard overhead and Rosewall fell on his stomach trying to reach it, but the crowd cheered his efforts. However, Newcombe stepped up the pressure and won the tie-breaker on a doubtful ace.

Rosewall broke Newcombe's serve on a hard backhand return of serve which Newcombe netted. Rosewall was going out on the court earlier than Newcombe on the change of ends. Rosewall hit an overhead, and Newcombe 'hammed it up' by swinging the racket like a butterfly net while pursuing it. The crowd laughed. (Rosewall said to me later, 'John Newcombe uses a lot of gamesmanship.') Newcombe double-faulted and Rosewall pretended to be hurt when the ball hit him in the stomach, proving he could joke as well as Newcombe. Rosewall was running for everything. Ken remembers, 'Nowadays, as I have an age problem, Newcombe may not go for the passing shots, preferring to lob me or dink it to me to make me run.' Newcombe was starting to press a little on his first serve. When Rosewall won the second set, 6-4, they had been on the court one hour and twenty-four minutes.

The third set continued the seesaw pattern of the previous ones. Rosewall relaxed too much, falling behind 2-5, tension in the air rising, though in one game he had two break points, but Newcombe, responding to the pressure, served some good hard ones and saved the game. However, in one of his serving games Newcombe made several errors such as driving two volleys into the net and double-faulting, and suddenly they were even again, and went into a tie-breaker. Rosewall forced a series of errors from Newcombe with his hard cross-court drives on the forehand and backhand, compelling Newcombe to hit the ball into the net, and the tie-breaker was his 5-1. The crowd cheered enthusiastically. They had now been playing for two hours and ten minutes.

The nervous strain on the two men showed early in the fourth set when Rosewall first spoke angrily to the net-court judge for failing to call a let on his opponent's serve, and secondly when a call, initially for Rosewall, reversed for Newcombe, promoted a dispute between them. The spectators, glued to their seats, were clapping and cheering every point. Newcombe let the pressure get to him, yelling 'out' on a Rosewall shot which was judged to be in. Newcombe's grunts as he served could be heard throughout the stadium. Rosewall's swing of the arms just before serving was similar to a boxer's drawing an arm back before throwing a punch, or better, a baseball pitcher doing his preliminary swing of the arms before actually going into motion. Finally in that classic tennis phrase Newcombe 'broke,' losing his serve on two double faults and, more importantly, on two powerful Rosewall returns, one of them a forehand, supposedly his less effective stroke. The score now stood at 4-2, and the remainder of the match, four games, consisted of their exchanging serves; but it was enough for Rosewall to win, as he struck a hard forehand volley to gain the match point and hear the roars and cheers of the crowd who were rising to their feet in honour of his great victory, reaching the finals in his fortieth year.

The match had lasted two hours and forty-five minutes. Referring to Rosewall's longevity, some fans said, 'He isn't real.'

Ken told me some months later in Australia, 'Newcombe relaxed too much in the match. He had played better when he won WCT earlier in the year, and after I beat him at Wimbledon he wanted to win against me, but sometimes even when you want to, you find you just can't do it. Newcombe likes to run around his backhand in the ad court and hit it down the line, but he lost his edge after WCT and couldn't do it at Wimbledon and Forest Hills as well. His forehand was very good, though he made some errors on it, too.

'Newcombe will not usually hit his backhand down the line to me when I serve to him, as he did in killing Kodes late in the final in Forest Hills in 1973, because he knows that I will hit a cross-court forehand volley which will pull him way over. He'll stroke the backhand cross-court to my backhand, because he knows I am likely to volley my backhand cross-court to his, and he could then get set for a passing shot, a lob or a cross-court dink.'

Rosewall said at the press conference around his locker in the Forest Hills clubhouse, 'It was only when I turned pro at twenty-two that I really learned how to serve and volley.' This was an afterthought, as someone had just said, 'How would today's Rosewall do against the eighteen-year-old Rosewall?' and he had replied, 'Some days today's me would win.'

'What's it like to be an institution?' a reporter asked.

'Ah, well, I think it's the same for everybody,' said Rosewall, embarrassed. 'We all like to play well. I've just been fortunate to do well in many of the major open events.'

A reporter said, 'Are you the greatest player in tennis?' Rosewall's facial muscles went through a variety of positions. Finally he said, 'I don't know about that. Anybody's entitled to an opinion.'

Rosewall's face had an aura of youthful happiness. The lines and folds showed more that day than after the Ramirez or Amritraj matches. Perhaps the concentration had taken more out of him than one suspected.

Psychologically, the key was that Newcombe played a little too much to the crowd, while Rosewall played very well, but not exceptionally. Rosewall had served better that day than before, and Newcombe had trouble with his first serve after the first set. 'He was serving well in patches after the first few games of the second set,' Rosewall said.

Newcombe's face at his locker room conference was dark with annoyance and disappointment.

Meanwhile, Roscoe Tanner was losing to Jimmy Connors in three sets in the second semi-finals of that Sunday afternoon.

In the round of 16, Tanner had defeated Nastase in five sets. Nastase had won the first two, then had started to make jokes to the crowd and had lost his concentration. However, if one looked at Nastase solely as a performer rather than as a tennis player, one had to admit that his expression of disgust after Tanner had served a powerful ace was marvellous to see. Tanner had then beaten Stan Smith in the quarters. Roscoe Tanner, with an attractive face and light brown hair, has a lot of charm in conversation. He told me some months later in a personal interview while we were watching matches from seats among the crowd at the 1975 Philadelphia indoor tournament, where I had found him, 'I like playing Rosewall, unlike a lot of other players. He hits the ball in the centre of the racket and flat, which is a style I like. I feel I have to serve and volley very well against him.'

I said, 'Ken says he tries to play your volley.'

Tanner's eyes widened with tension, and his face fell slightly. He said, 'He puts a lot of pressure on my volley, which is why I have to serve in a super way so he can't hit a good return, and I can then attack with my volley.

'Just after Nancy and I were married twenty months ago, we saw Ken and Wilma walking hand in hand on the streets of

London or New York—after all those years of marriage. He's a champion I would like to imitate off the court, though not on the court, because my style is very different than his. He is a gentleman, never lets it go to his head and is always the real Ken Rosewall—unlike some other champions. He doesn't talk often, like most Australians who drink a lot of beer and like to talk a lot, but what he says is always intelligent and worth listening to.'

Rosewall gave a charming interview on CBS-TV after the Connors and Tanner match in which an interviewer asked him, 'How do you do it after all these years?' He replied, after a pause, his head slightly bowed, smiling modestly, 'I try to stay in shape, and I try to do my best.' When the interview was over, Rosewall walking away, Rosewall nodded politely to Connors coming on to be interviewed. There was a slightly sad quality to Rosewall—all that control and moderation and clean living and the wonderful wins, and yet one felt the final victory was never there, as if with Rosewall it would never come in this world.

Ken remembers, 'I watched the Connors-Tanner match and then did a TV interview with Tony Trabert. I thought the masseur would be at the Westchester Country Club until a certain time, but when I arrived he'd gone ten minutes before.'

I said, 'So if you hadn't done the interview you'd have been there in time?'

'Yes.'

Ken continued, 'I tried to get a left-hander to practise against, but they had all left. Then I had dinner with some friends and the next morning made two calls tò Australia, one to my wife and the other to my father, packed and went to Forest Hills.'

The final took place on Monday, the day immediately following the semi-finals, which were on Sunday. Connors had been born the week Rosewall had played at Forest Hills for the first time. That was 1952. Dave Anderson, in a column in the New York *Times* on July 7, 1974, had written, 'Other players have called Connors "cocky punk" and a "child." '

The morning of the match Connors looked lean and mean. Nearly a year later Rosewall remarked to Ned Chase and me during an interview, 'He is lean. He's in very good condition.

And he is mean. He has to be at the top. Before Segura replaced Gonzales as Connors' coach, Connors certainly could have taken lessons in being mean from Gonzales.'

Connors used to be a likeable kid, immature, to be sure, but now with success he's become tough. In fairness to Connors, it should be pointed out that his conduct on and off the court was less unattractive at the time of Forest Hills than it had been previously, and during 1975 his deportment might be described as acceptable. Connors started playing—like Rosewall—at the age of three, in Connors' case taught by his mother and to a lesser extent by his grandmother. His mother had been a good tournament player. His father, the manager of a St. Louis, Mo., toll bridge, was not interested in tennis. Connors played often on fast wood surfaces indoors during the winter as a child and teen-ager, which undoubtedly helped his fast reflexes, enabling him to take the ball early, notably on return of serve. Connors' use of two hands on the backhand gives him additional power on that side, though many experts say it reduces mobility in terms of reaching a short ball angled wide to the backhand. The outline of Connors' life story is well known, but Pancho Gonzales aided him with his serve, which has a smooth action similar to the great Pancho's, and Segura has played an important role both as father figure-counsellor and instructor on all-court strategy. Interestingly, Connors tried to play like Gonzales for a while, but he was shorter than Gonzales, and his serve was not strong enough for the big serve–net rush style of play. Then Segura achieved more influence over Connors than Gonzales, teaching him the tactics for an all-court game, refining the strokes originally taught him by his mother.

Connors warmed up for half an hour with Gerulaitis and Segura. I had thought he looked good at first—fine shots, a few errors—but I predicted a close match. Now, at the end of the warm-up, I thought he looked too loose, too many errors, lack of concentration. In fact, Gerulaitis looked as capable if not better. There was a certain nervousness about the trio. Segura was constantly encouraging and criticizing in a soothing voice, sitting on a folding chair on the grass, but his face looked worried. When Connors walked off Court 16, after the practice was over, he looked tough, angry and a bit more hopeful. There was a little of that cocky look, so familiar to him, and yet on TV the day before in the postmatch interview Connors had been respectful of Rosewall, 'the master,' and pleasant, if hard in his replies. 'I'll try to play him the same as I did at Wimbledon. I will try to move quickly around the court. I'll go to bed at the usual hour, eat a light breakfast, practise for an hour, hour and a half, but my programme won't be any different than any other day.'

At lunchtime in the clubhouse restaurant Connors led his mother along by his little finger—a determined American blonde with an innocent expression.

Some months later in Australia Rosewall said to me, 'Do we have to talk about the Connors match?'

Then he continued, 'An official of Forest Hills told me to be there at a certain time, and when I arrived another official said, "You're late. You're on." Maybe the first one had forgotten the doubles final had been shortened to three sets instead of five.' Because of the heavy rains throughout the tournament the men's doubles final had been shortened from best-of-five sets to best-of-three sets. Rosewall continued:

'I was under a psychological handicap, having lost so badly at Wimbledon, and up against someone like Connors, who takes the ball so early and hits it so hard. I had planned to arrive in good time, have a warm-up, take a shower and change my shirt. I had to change my shirt in the referee's booth.

'Maybe it was because Wilma and the children had left three days earlier. They had been with me for four months, though they were with me at Wimbledon when I lost to Connors.'

Rosewall was very late in arriving at Forest Hills. He only warmed up twenty-five minutes, keeping the crowd waiting ten minutes, as Smith and Lutz easily won their doubles final 6-3, 6-3, the match ending earlier than expected. During practice I thought his ground strokes and net game appeared to be as sharp as ever, but his serve was not as accurate as it had been against Newcombe the day before. I predicted a close win for Rosewall.

Before the match he seemed a little hard and brittle. He changed his sweaty green sport shirt for a fresh one before walking off the practice court. I admired how cool he was as the crowd and officials waited for him. He posed patiently by the net as a lone photographer snapped him, and he looked very happy. He then walked with a photographer and a trainer, who was carrying his bags, through the press and officials' marquee, gradually becoming engulfed by the larger crowd around him.

Rosewall served first, winning the first point on a superlative serve and net volley. Then he double-faulted. My heart sank. He had double-faulted on the second point at Wimbledon.

During the first set a man in the crowd yelled, 'Connors, you're a bum.' Jimmy turned around and gave the hidden heckler what appeared to me to be the finger.

The first set might be described as a gentle breeze* for Connors. Rosewall made another early double fault, and Connors drove deep, was quick and made a number of excellent topspin passing shots. Rosewall looked sluggish, as if asleep. Rosewall made one particularly bad forehand easy volley which he struck on the top of his metal racket and hit into the net. The score was 1-6.

The second set was also a breeze. Rosewall's only points came on Connors' errors. Connors only missed those of average difficulty and won all the rough rallies. On a typical point there would be a furious exchange of drives, volleys and lobs, and Connors would end it with a magnificent shot. Rosewall would appear to be tiring gradually during such a point, so that finally he would make a shot which Connors could get on top of. Sometimes, even before Rosewall had tired significantly during a rally, Connors would make a brilliant shot. One example was a heated exchange with Rosewall hitting a shot which pulled Connors, while at net, wide of the deuce court. Connors hit the ball back to Rosewall, who then stroked a good drive to the ad court, but Connors had raced to his left across the court and cut off the drive with a deadly, inspired drop volley that Rosewall had no chance of reaching. Rosewall, for his part, never made any of the brilliant shots that he had displayed in earlier matches during the tournament. When Connors would make a mistake, it would come on a relatively

---

* Connors said afterwards, 'From the moment I took the court and hit the first ball, I felt I was gliding.'

easy return of a Rosewall shot. Connors would hit the net or drive the ball out of the court, as if for a moment during an unimportant point he had let his concentration lapse. The score of the second set was 0-6.

The third set was just like the first two, except that Rosewall made Connors work on a couple of his service games. Though Connors always bounces the ball five times or so before serving, Connors began to stall and bounce the ball a lot more than usual before serving on a key point when he was behind. The score of the third and last set was 1-6.

The only hint of emotion came in the postgame presentation when Connors said, 'It's a thrill for me to play Rosewall, who I think played here before I was born. It is an honour for me to play on the same court with this gentleman.'

As the commercial presentations went on and on, Rosewall slipped away, climbing up the ramp into the darkness of the marquee.

The atmosphere in the locker room was electric with shock. The USLTA press officer, Rosewall and I walked over to the press conference in total silence. Some months later Pret Hadley, the USLTA man, remarked, 'He showed a lot of class in consenting to leave the clubhouse, walk through the crowd and return for the interview.' On the way children stopped him several times for autographs, which he gave each time. One little American boy said, 'You're a great player, Mr. Rosewall. You just didn't try hard enough.'

At the postmatch press conference in the big drab tent used for lunches Rosewall said of Connors, 'He's been advised by some of those around him. He's been told how to play me.'

Segura had been beaten time after time by Rosewall in the old pro touring days. Segura is a little man, like Rosewall—his regular losses to a comparable figure must therefore have been all the more humiliating. I had in fact seen Rosewall in an indoor stadium at Wembley in England in about 1962, when his speed and accuracy were incredible, defeat Segura, flailing bravely but futilely with his two-handed strokes. In fairness to Segura, however, he was slightly past his prime by then, though according to the records of that time winning tournaments.

During the Connors-Rosewall fiasco, Segura had sat in the

special boxes under an awning wearing a bright silk neck scarf. He had looked beautifully turned out for his vicarious triumph.

Many times during the press conference Rosewall looked like he was going to cry, but the control on his face indicated this would not happen.

Before he left for the airport, I suggested, 'I was praying for rain last night. You were very sharp against Newcombe. A day of rest and it would have been a different story.' Sitting on a bench, he replied softly, shaking his head, 'No, it wouldn't have made any difference.'

Some months later Rosewall told me while we were in his home in Australia, 'Jimmy Connors has worked hard at his game, a very good all-court game. He hits the ball fiercely, more consistently hard than Newcombe. If he paces himself and takes sufficient vacations and does not lose interest, as some players do when they reach the top, he could be a leading star for years. I understand he travels everywhere with his mother, and he is in a very difficult position suing all the players in the ATP including me, because he was banned from the French Open. In effect, he is saying, rightly or wrongly, "I'm suing you and I want some of your money." This does not make him popular in the locker room. The strategy I would use is to aim angle shots wide to his volley on either side, as this is not that certain yet, but this is easier said than done as he hits the ball so hard. He's a nervous player, constantly fretting, letting out all his anger on the court, and this rushing around and intensity could wear him down in a five-set match. Everyone's shooting at him now that he is the top player, but it will be interesting to see how he holds up against Newcombe and Nastase . . .'

'. . . or you,' I interjected, 'if you have a day of rest. In my opinion you could beat him then. Newcombe was hitting the ball hard when you beat him in the semi-finals.'

'Nastase and he have played each other evenly in minor tournaments. And Newcombe beat him three out of the four times they played, though they were even in their last two big matches, Newcombe winning over Connors in four sets in the 1975 Australian finals and Connors winning over John in four in the 1975 CBS-sponsored $250,000 Las Vegas match.

Connors had beaten Ashe three times in a row on slower surfaces, but Arthur played him very cleverly, defeating Jimmy in the '75 Wimbledon final by mixing up his shots to Connors and exploiting Connors' volley and usually getting his first serve in to Connors at three-quarters speed, though Jimmy was said to be injured that day. Connors seems to have gained an edge over Kodes in 1974 and Smith starting in 1973.

'Connors hits my serve hard, coming in early on it. He's been well coached by Segura on how to play me.

'Connors can afford to make some errors on easy shots when he wins all the tough points.'

Losing badly to a player is discouraging. Meeting Connors for the second time, starting to be demolished again, Rosewall faced a serious psychological hurdle.

Under normal circumstances, postulating no day of rest and his age, Rosewall should perhaps have lost in the final about 6-3, 6-3, 6-2. But Connors was expertly coached by Segura. And Connors had the one great asset that could neutralize Rosewall's strongest point—equal speed of foot and reaction time. Usually Rosewall, even a tired Rosewall, has the edge over his opponent in this department.

In tight rallies Rosewall's trigger reflexes and determination to run for every ball will help him to win some of them. In my opinion, Rosewall as a young man had been faster than Connors—the quickest player I have ever seen. But at age thirty-nine he had slowed to the point that Connors was just as speedy. Thus an alert, rested Connors, knowing where Rosewall was going to hit the ball, thanks to Segura, got there quickly, and with his superior strength smashed it back for winner after winner.

The loss to Connors was the worst in the ninety-three year history of Forest Hills, matched only by Gottfried Von Cramm's 1, 1, 0 defeat by Perry at Wimbledon in 1936. Von Cramm had been injured. Connors won 82 points, Rosewall 42, of which only 19 were on his serve. At Forest Hills even Richard Sears (1881 and 1882) and Tilden (1921) gave up more games in winning—five in each case.

In England the next day the *Guardian* described Rosewall as looking at Connors 'warily, rather as a man might look at a dog that had bitten him before.' Rosewall said afterwards, 'I never dreamed that I would lose that match worse than I did that Wimbledon final. I was keen and eager.'

The one-sidedness of the match caused an immense amount of talk in tennis circles for days and weeks afterwards. Some said Rosewall hadn't tried hard enough. A still photo in one of the English newspapers showed him kneeling on the court, his racket hanging from his hand, like a swordsman submitting his sword to a new king, presumably Connors. There was something theatrical about the pose. And yet Rosewall had run out every point. Perhaps the effort was only superficial. Possibly deep down the critics were implying, he had said to himself subconsciously, 'If I can't win, I may as well go out with a bang.'

One distinguished tennis observer maintained that Rosewall should have entertained the crowd by some theatrics like Nastase's. 'That's not his style,' I said. A letter writer to the New York *Times* called the match 'almost embarrassing.' Another tennis expert suggested, 'Rosewall comes from a lower middle-class Australian family inhibited by the English class system. He was baffled by the swinging open atmosphere of Connors and the new American young and all their affluence.'

But the wisest opinion was that of a doctor who plays tennis. 'He's got to have a day of rest.'

Rosewall had used up all his nervous energy beating Newcombe the day before. In the sense that Connors plays an all-court game, the same as Rosewall, and similarly has very quick reactions, particularly on the return of serve, Rosewall had met a young version of himself, though of course their styles differ, as regards Connors' two-handed backhand and slightly harder hit ground strokes. But no other tennis athlete in the history of the game since it became a major sport around the First World War* had ever reached the finals at such an

---

* In the early days of tennis when it was a country-club and garden-party sport there may have been some gentlemen of middle-age who played in relaxed tournaments. Allison Danzig, the tennis historian, wrote me recently in a letter, 'So far as I know, Rosewall is the oldest player to reach the final at Forest Hills.' Few would doubt that Rosewall is the oldest player ever to reach the finals of *both* Wimbledon and Forest Hills in the same year.

advanced age. By widening the horizons of human endeavour Rosewall had encouraged millions of middle-aged tennis players.*

* Chase says, 'Many older stars encouraged it more, especially Borotra, Tilden and Mulloy. Gardnar Mulloy won the Wimbledon doubles with Budge Patty in 1957 over Hoad and Fraser 8-10, 6-4, 6-4, 6-4, when Mulloy was 44 and didn't drop his service once!'

9

The Future

At the beginning of December 1974, with Ken's agreement, I flew from New York via Los Angeles, Hawaii and Fiji to Sydney, where the Rosewalls maintain their principal residence, the other being in Phoenix, Arizona. His two sons go to a private day school in Sydney, and Brett and Glenn are of course in Australia almost all of the year, except for four months in 1974 when Ken and Wilma brought them to Pittsburgh, Wimbledon and Forest Hills, when Ken was mainly playing in WTT. Wilma, too, is in Sydney most of the year, though sometimes she accompanies Ken on trips to tournaments around the world or on visits to the John Gardiner tennis ranch in Arizona, where Ken is the visiting pro. When Rosewall is not on tour or teaching in Arizona (or Vermont, where Gardiner has a new tennis camp), he lives at home in Turramurra, a pretty suburb on what is called the North Shore of Sydney. Sydney is divided by a river. The centre of Sydney, which is where the famous opera house is, is on the harbour, where the river runs into the ocean. The northern suburbs are an attractive region of well-kept houses surrounded by gardens and swimming pools, shaded by trees, cut out of the semi-junglelike rolling hills and valleys.

The street where the Rosewall house is located runs between pretty homes, lawns, bushes and flowers, looking like a cross between Southern California and England, with a touch of the Australian wild, manifested by the gum trees everywhere and cries, weird and wonderful, unbelievable, squawky, scratchy and musical, of the birds, the mynah and the kookaburra, whose occasional deep-throated self-mocking call, as strange as an echo in a tunnel, would excite Ken into saying, 'That's a kookaburra.' The less said about the front exterior of their home—resembling a certain type of functional modern architecture, with its deck above the garage—the better, but the interior has ten rooms with lots of wood and trophies. The Rosewalls did not build the house but bought it. The atmosphere is warm and the house is ideal for living, with the back side leading onto a swimming pool and garden with large blue jacaranda bushes.

The appallingly ugly exterior is surprising in view of the good taste in dress of both Ken and Wilma and Ken's natural grace as a player. Yet the inside is warm, and the numerous trophies do not obtrude but are a recognition of the man of the house's internationally known skill and of the fact that he has made it all possible. The rooms are comfortable, the front a dreamy expanse of lawn and high trees. So that the exterior facade, perhaps like the Rosewalls, forbids strangers and those who are not invited, but once you are inside you are surrounded by friendliness, as if taken into their hearts.

Wilma has a manner best described as refined, upper-middle-class English. She also has a girlish way of kicking slightly or waving her left leg when she is about to leave a room. She is a good cook, sympathetic mother and supportive wife. She gardens ('I don't like pulling weeds when Ken's away'), plays bridge, attends a women's 'Stocks and Shares Club' and plays golf. Ken says, 'Wilma has travelled with me a great deal in the last few years and we're very fortunate in having a lady friend who's been able to look after our two boys while we're away, and they seem to get along very well together, apart from other friends who are able to help out with the two boys. They're very busy with their school work.

'Wilma plays more tennis than golf and I think enjoys it more. In Australia there are separate clubs for golf and tennis. In addition, if a husband belongs to a club or the wife belongs, it does not mean the other partner is a member. The wife, for example, has to join herself. Wilma and I are both members of the same golf club and play together sometimes. She's a beginner, but I've been playing golf on and off for years. Like many tennis players I play golf for relaxation.* Wilma and I

* Jack Nicklaus plays tennis for relaxation.

belong to separate tennis clubs, but we often play social tennis together on courts belonging to friends, 'and now we play tennis more with the boys, who are becoming interested in the game, though they have no ambitions to become top players.'

Brett, who is nearly as tall as Ken, has a superb electric train layout in the basement. He looks like his father. Glenn resembles his mother more and has a cute, little boy's smile and some of his father's grace of movement.

The back and side of Ken's neck are heavily tanned from the sun. From the corners of his eyes to his jaw run two curved deep lines, caused, I guessed, by the endless grimaces of pain and determination as he raced for the ball countless times. His eyes are yellowy-green, occasionally showing tiny specks of red. He is always immaculately dressed, usually in sports clothes, and moves as a young, lithe figure, constantly in control yet powerful. His voice is a blend of upper-income English, American and Australian and has a hard, pleasantly resonant quality tinged with boyish enthusiasm.

Family Tennis

The day of my arrival we went over to a park to play some 'social tennis.' Coming up to the tennis court where Ken, Wilma and the two boys, Brett and Glenn, were playing, was a fascinating experience. It was summer in Australia and hot, and there were a lot of flies. I had just arrived from 35° F. winter weather in New York. I had always seen Ken play surrounded by thousands, and here he was on a Laykold court, green coloured, amid the green grass of a well-tended public park in a pretty suburb with nice coloured benches scattered here and there. Mrs. McIver, Wilma's mother, an elderly brunette lady, sat on one. No one else was watching. The children were uncanny, their strokes just like their father's—particularly the thirteen-year-old Glenn—both left-handers. Glenn ran for everything. He seemed like the Ken of thirty years ago—disgusted with a bad shot, secretly joyful on a good one. He aced his older brother by swinging a left-handed serve down the centre line, to the amusement of Ken and Wilma. Brett, who lay down on the court for a minute or two while Ken was chatting with some people on the adjacent one, only seemed to try when serving to his brother.

Mrs. Rosewall said to me, 'You must be tired from the jet-lag. Ken's done it so often, he's used to it.'

'Not really,' Ken said.

But the most eerie sight was Rosewall himself, who had such an extraordinary ability to reach any ball hit as if releasing a hidden force of power—zap, he was there—and some of the family's shots to him were quite good, particularly those from Wilma, an ex junior-tournament player. Rosewall's power of retrieval was like a mythical force which suddenly erupted.

Poor Wilma, who had been laughing and encouraging the boys, sprained an ankle. We drove to my hotel after the accident, talking about the book. Ken said, 'I'd better see about that sprained ankle.'

The next morning, after picking me up to take me to his house, Ken said, 'My wife said I hit two shots too hard to Glenn, but I don't think so.'

I said, 'It didn't seem to bother him.'

Ken said sardonically to Wilma, 'At least I did something right for once.'

Wilma replied sweetly and genuinely, 'You do lots of wonderful things.'

Rosewall remarked later, 'I don't want to push him, but I'd like to see Brett take an interest in tennis. Glenn is thirteen years old and Brett fifteen.'

Talking casually about the Sydney suburbs and tennis courts, he said, 'I'm going to have to practise more. Your timing doesn't come back as quickly at my age.' Rosewall reminds me of Evelyn Waugh's writing style: the punch line comes at the end.

Rosewall Street

On the way back we drove down a lower-middle-income street of newer red-brick homes. I suddenly noticed that it was called Rosewall Street. 'Is that named after you?' I asked excitedly. 'Yes,' he said with a grin. 'Nobody asks permission. They just go ahead and do it. There is a Hoad Street here in Sydney and a Sedgman Street in Melbourne. I don't know if there is a Newcombe.'

'That's really something,' I said, 'usually one has to be dead to have a street named after one.'

'I sometimes drive down my street.'

Later we passed through a rundown section of central Sydney. Rosewall said, 'That's our "inner city." ' I said, 'The "inner city" is an American phrase. Is it also used in Australia to describe the slum conditions of the downtown areas of big cities?' 'No,' replied Rosewall.

Over the years Rosewall has acquired an international education; the office in his Turramurra home is lined with books, including works on tennis, popular novels and non-fiction on a wide variety of subjects, such as Australian life and culture.

While Ken and I were driving through another part of Sydney I noticed a private club. Ken said, 'That's a very posh, exclusive club. I could never join. Your great-grandfather has to have belonged supposedly. His descendants would then be eligible to become members.' He turned a corner.

'If Evonne Goolagong's ever going to beat Margaret Court, 1975 is the year to do it, with Margaret coming off her year out with a pregnancy. But Margaret is a terrific competitor and Goolagong, though she has the game, lacks the one hundred percent concentration.'

After the light had turned green, Rosewall went on, 'In a Sydney tournament the other day around eleven o'clock at night after my match, this man came on the court and stared at me. He kept staring. Finally I said, "How're you doing?" He said, "I'm so and so. You don't remember me. You ought to. I was in school with you twenty years ago. We knew so and so." I said, "I'm sorry. I just don't." He said, "Come and have a drink with me at a party I'm giving for my friends." It was late, I'd had a long match, had to drive home and play the next day. I said, "Thanks, but I've got to get home." He said, "That's the trouble with you guys. You wouldn't have anything if it wasn't for box holders like me." So finally I said, "Okay." I went for five minutes and said hello. I didn't have a drink. In Australia we have "knockers." ' Rosewall subsequently loaned me a book entitled *Knockers,* concerning the Aussies' habit of attacking each other and themselves.

Rosewall left me at my motel and went over to Newcombe's

house, which is in an adjoining suburb about a mile from the Rosewalls', 'for a hit.' Ken told me the next day that Newcombe, arriving from the golf course, had said, 'I may have strained my arm.' So he did not play Ken. 'Newcombe is often late.' So Rosewall had practised his serve. 'His court has a natural brick wall with concrete over it, and I was able to hit volleys against it. Then I played Glenn after dinner for forty-five minutes, as it was still light.'

There was a touching boyish quality about him when, a few days later, he showed me a seemingly endless assortment of photos and newspaper articles and old tennis pro-grammes—something appealing and wistful. Among them was a white card with a photo inside. 'This is this year's All England Club Christmas card,' he said proudly and happily. The All England Club owns the grounds, courts and stadium on which the Wimbledon tournament is played annually. The card showed a delightful, boyish Rosewall smiling while accepting a small medal from an aristocratic, slightly over-weight man who was also smiling graciously. Rosewall was receiving the runner-up award after the 1974 Wimbledon final against Connors.

'Who's the man with you?' I asked. 'Some official at Wimbledon?'

He laughed. 'You don't know who that is? That's the Duke of Kent.'

The card made me think that though Connors won the tournament, Rosewall had scored the significant advance in modern tennis history by reaching the final of this immensely difficult contest when he was older than anyone else who had ever tried it. A top young athlete should win 'Wimbledon, but for a forty-year-old to have played him in the final is medical and sporting glory.

Daily life for Ken often includes a visit to John Newcombe's house. Contrary to reports in the American press, which have proudly announced the Newcombe family move to Texas, Newcombe still lives primarily in the Spanish-style villa with white walls, iron windows and dark tile roof that faces a lush green hillside of trees rising above it, and below a tiny valley or crevasse, where nestles a green-surfaced tennis court immediately beneath a wide stone terrace. The juxtaposition presumably means that Newcombe values home and family above tennis, though not perhaps as obviously as Rosewall, who does not have a court anywhere near his abode.

When Ken and I arrived, on the terrace were John Alexander, Tony Roche and a youngster in white, Tony Parun, 'the brother of Onny Parun,' Ken explained to me. John Alexander came forward to shake my hand, dark chinned and dark eyed, with a soft, shy manner despite his swarthy tanned skin and appearance of virility. 'There's a shortage of steel for razor blades,' joked Ken. Tony Roche, attired in an outrageous, scarlet-maroon sweatsuit, was as friendly and affable as a dachshund, exuding warmth and humour. 'Why don't you ever bring any tennis balls, Muscles?' joked Alexander and Roche as we walked down the steep slope to the court. Neither Roche nor Alexander had any, while Rosewall carried two dozen-each boxes. Rosewall, Roche and Alexander walked onto the court while I sat on the grass behind the wire fence and watched them. Standing beside the net, the three stars selected rackets for their practice session. All the while they were chatting and joking. Tony Roche made a remark, and suddenly there was a burst of laughter. I wondered why. Alexander and Roche went to the other end of the court. Rosewall walked back towards me and said, 'They're talking about a golfer they know who walked over a little bridge and his clubs fell in the water.'

It may have been my imagination, but Rosewall was treated affectionately and enthusiastically with humour as a boyish friend, and yet as he stood by the court, small in height between Roche and Alexander, he was also king of the mountain—the only one of the three with a writer faithfully trailing his footsteps, besides being the best tennis player in the group and a great player in tennis history. He rallied ground shots at Roche and Alexander, the ball moving like a bullet, Rosewall's accuracy and depth far better than Alexander's and somewhat better than Roche's. As I left, I looked down on the trio from the terrace above, Alexander and Roche now at the net, the ball snapping like a cracked whip back and forth.

Later in the day Ken said, 'When I'm on tour I sleep nine hours a night; at home, where I am relaxed, eight. I go to bed at ten-thirty, get up at six-thirty. With all due respect to the new vegetarians, I eat steak on tour six out of seven nights, particularly if I'm in a place like Timbuctoo. I need the strength and a solid meal. When I turned pro, Hopman said I shouldn't as I wouldn't have the stamina because of my size, that I should stay an amateur with him. So as a pro I would force myself to eat a full dinner even if I wasn't hungry. Particularly as I have gotten older, I can't eat for four or five hours before a match. So I'll eat only two meals a day, though I might have a very light snack or cup of tea in the middle of the four- or five-hour wait. Rod Laver, though, can eat a big meal before a match. I've seen him do it within an hour before. He must have food in his stomach when he goes out on court. Maybe with his style of play, hitting the ball hard all the time, he burns it up. Not me, I can't even eat a hamburger.

'On tour I really don't do any physical conditioning, preferring to save my energy for the matches, and there is often not time travelling from one place to another. When I was sixteen, working at Slazenger's, they sent me and Billy Gilmour, who later became Aussie junior champ, to a gym three afternoons a week for a year to lift weights, do exercises to develop my reflexes and run. At home—especially when during pro days I wouldn't play for six weeks or so, or even in 1961, when I was home for seven months—I would run in the oval in the park; and I play tennis now at home between tournaments to keep my game sharp, and I'm away as much as I ever used to be.' On other occasions Ken has said that he is playing less. 'The problem is to maintain one's match competitiveness while I have to rest longer between tours due to my age. Also because of my personal feelings for my family I want to be home more often.

'Relieving boredom when waiting for matches is difficult. I chat with the other players, watch TV, read. It's better when my family is with me, as in London we can look around. The most difficult is when rain interrupts a match. Locker rooms are not very attractive places. You are there with your opponent. There's a lot of noise with guys talking. This can be a help to get your mind off it, but usually I prefer to be quiet and find a room other than the locker room. In 1974 the tournaments I played in had more rain than I can ever remember—four days at Wimbledon, two days at Forest Hills, two each in Tucson and Tokyo, three in Hong Kong and two in Johannesburg.

'I don't seem to perspire as much as most players. It may have been because my father taught me not to drink much during playing. Why he did this, I don't know. Liquid is heavy. Gonzales sweated a lot and drank a lot of liquid when changing ends, and it didn't affect him. Perhaps my father noticed I didn't perspire much and so did not want me to be burdened with too much water. I suppose it discourages some of my opponents when they see how cool I look, although I don't feel that way inside.

'I never read most of the stories about me. I skip through them. Some of the press you have to be careful with. The press has been pretty good to me over the years.'

Barry Lorge had written in *Tennis*, November 1974, 'Legendary, too, is the way Rosewall downplays his feats in soft-spoken clichés.' Actually, Rosewall's wit is a good deal sharper than Lorge's, but a key to Rosewall is that the fantastic self-control so essential to a precision game such as tennis appears in this other way.

'Among my best tennis friends are Tony Roche, Mal Anderson, Fred Stolle. Rod Laver and I are friends and longtime competitors. Our paths have gone in different directions, as he has an American wife and lives in the U.S. I'd play him on tour and then we'd room together and sit down and have dinner together and a couple of beers. Lew [Hoad] and I were friends, though in the pro days we would stay in single rooms if possible, and he now lives in Spain. Roy Emerson is a very good friend of mine. All the Australian players are very good friends of each other. Roy and I met as juniors. He's only two years younger than me. He was on the Queensland public schools team, and I was on the New South Wales public schools team when we met in 1948. Roy's sister was on the girls' public schools team and Wilma was, too, and Roy's sister married Mal Anderson. Of course Roy and I were together on the Australian Davis Cup teams. Nowadays I don't see him so often, as Roy lives in America and has his business interests there.

'Outside of those friends who are currently playing, John

Barrett and Arthur Huxley of Slazenger's and Dinny Pails and his wife are among our best friends. It often seems one sees less of one's friends. Maybe that's why they stay close friends.

'Years ago I played mixed doubles with. Margaret Dupont and an Australian Championship winner, Beryl Penrose, now Mrs. Collier, whose son is in school with Brett.

'I never see any of my old public school friends. I travelled so much, but we are in touch with old junior tennis friends of mine and Wilma's.

'Wilma and I thought of moving to America when Rod and Roy did, and as Fred Stolle is now doing. But Fred's children are young, whereas ours are teen-agers in school. Also when we considered it, I was touring a lot and it would have meant Wilma and the children would have been alone in a foreign country, though we have a number of good friends around Phoenix, where we would have gone.'

Near Phoenix, the Rosewalls have built an attractive ranch-style house, cut into the slope of Camelback Mountain and overlooking Paradise Valley, which they rent out most of the year. It has a tennis court on the roof, lots of curves and a gracious feel about it.

In recent years when Rosewall stays in the house at the Gardiner Tennis Ranch, where he is visiting pro, he runs everywhere. An assistant teacher at the resort who told me of this said, 'It's one of the ways he stays in such good condition,' but I suspect Ken's main reason is that, while passing by them, he can avoid having to talk to the dozens of guests.

Ken continued, 'We don't want to keep up with the Joneses. I don't want a larger house or yacht, but I do want to build a tennis court soon as the boys are playing more, and though it may be too late for them to become pros, they would like a court. And I like playing social tennis just for fun. Frank Sedgman and his wife have four daughters and when they put in a court the girls wouldn't play, but when it was too late for them to be really good the girls started using it a lot.'

The Future of Tennis

One day I asked Ken a lot of questions about the state of the game in various countries and his opinion on the future of tennis. He said, 'It could be that the reason there are so many feuds in tennis, and bannings and squabbles between one group and another, is that tennis is a one-on-one contest, a psychological warfare, and yet non-violent, and the only way to release the anger is off court. Another reason is that these feuds are the growing pains of a developing sport.

'Australian tennis declined due to the introduction of TV in '56, whereas before TV playing tennis at night was a favourite pastime. Lots of courts had lights in all economic sections of Sydney, and it was a beautiful sight to fly over Sydney at night and see all the courts lit up. There are still some, but not as many. Rising land values eliminated a number of Australian courts. Many older people turned to lawn bowls, others to golf, squash and sailing. But sales of tennis equipment are rising again, and interest is reviving due to the televising of well-run professional tournaments.

'I don't know why tennis hasn't grown in England. Some of the profits from Wimbledon were used to build one or two indoor courts in various parts of England, but they looked like brick compounds and were badly built—it was a pity as they could have been well done economically and practically. Even though there are not enough indoor courts, there are sufficient around England for the top juniors to play as much as they need. Is it lack of incentive? It couldn't be these days. I think it's lack of drive.'

One of the reasons British tennis appears to be weak may be emotional difficulties. Rosewall himself pointed to the problems of Sangster and Cox on the court. The English have always had the reputation of being cool under fire and of not showing their emotions. On the surface it might be thought these qualities were ideal for a game requiring precise control such as tennis. However, these characteristics, when carried to an extreme, are not so important as to outweigh imagination, hard work and an open response to new challenges, areas in which—witness Britain's declining economy—the English are clearly lacking.

Ken continued his remarks on tennis. 'Twenty-three million people watched Laver and me in our 1972 WCT match, and this was one of the impetuses for the growth of the game's popularity in America. When I first arrived in the U.S., in

1952, there were seven million players, but a lot of these, I think, called themselves tennis players but played only once a month or every three months. Now there are more than thirteen million who play one, two, three times a week. A 1974 Nielsen survey showed that there are thirty-four million players in all in the U.S. Open tennis on TV helped a great deal. Tennis with its one-on-one format in a court is ideal for the TV screen. Most of the growth in the States is due to adults liking it for the exercise, but the Americans should borrow from the Australian system of teaching children. Australian pros make their living from tennis classes, some of which are held in the public schools, and some in tennis schools or private schools. Parents of children of low-income families can afford, due to the minimal fees, to send their youngsters to tennis classes at tennis schools run by such people as Vic Edwards, who coaches Evonne Goolagong.

'I think we will see the development of the all-court game, which is what I've always played since turning pro, and which Jimmy Connors plays now, rather than the smash serve and volley. This is much more exciting and fun for the amateur player, who wants exercise.

'In 1974 NCB lost some of its audience when Smith and Newcombe played in four or five WCT finals, as they had the same game, slamming big serves at each other and no rallies.'

I said to Rosewall, 'It was so boring, I turned it off after one set and flicked it on only for the end. Normally I watch seven out of eight WCT tournaments on TV.'

Ken said, 'It would be a good idea to use more often in America the slower, heavier European ball rather than the light, fast American one. The Australian and European ball is better for all-court tennis and lasts longer. I recommend the slower indoor surfaces like the rubberized materials or clay.

'Technically, I don't think a one-bounce rule or putting the serve three feet back or limiting the server will come into the game in the future. These have all been tried in the past. Jimmy Van Alen* had the server three feet behind the baseline at his Newport Casino. We used the one-bounce rule on one of

---

* 'Of all the players of the current era,' said James Van Alen, 'Rosewall is the nicest.'

the pro tours. The server had to let the ball bounce once on return before going to the net, and the receiver had to let the server's return of his return of service bounce before going to net, and the result was the server usually charged the net after hitting the return.

'What we will see are changes resulting from the metal racket—greater speed and spin—and more double-handed backhands like Connors' and Borg's, though Borg lets go of the racket with his left hand and hits it free at the end of the backhand stroke. We will see more of Borg's forehand hit with tremendous twist of the body, resulting top spin and from every position of his body—close to him, far out, one foot forward, then the other and open stance. But I would urge new players to learn the regular forehand instead. There must be thousands of youngsters imitating Chrissie Evert and Jimmy Connors.

'It's likely that WCT, with Hunt's money behind it, will survive the war with Riordan and ATP.'

A current feud in tennis exists between Bill Riordan, Jimmy Connors' manager, and the ATP, led by its director, Jack Kramer. Riordan is suing the ATP, claiming $41 million in damages because Connors was banned from playing in the 1974 French Open, while Kramer is suing Riordan and Connors, accusing them of making 'defamatory' statements.* As a general rule, the ATP and WCT cooperate with each other, while Riordan has successfully urged Connors to stay out of WCT and play instead on Riordan's winter circuit. Hunt, of course, is Lamar Hunt, whose fortune has backed WCT in its growth in the seventies.

'There's so much money around these days that half of these new players shouldn't even be playing compared to some of the older pros who played before the big money came in,' Ken said. 'Many of today's players could not make their Davis Cup teams or become national champions, but they can make a very good living with all the money available now just by playing in the first round of forty-five or fifty tournaments.'

---

* By late 1975 the lawsuits had been settled out of court, and Connors had announced that Riordan was no longer his manager. Perhaps a new era of peace was developing in the tennis world.

Having watched some of the lesser-known players practise at the Philadelphia indoor tournament, I can confirm the accuracy of this remark.

Selecting only those who Rosewall played when they were at their best, thus eliminating 'one of the very greatest of all,' Jack Kramer, who was almost retired and suffering from a back injury when Ken first played him, and Segura, and also excluding Santana because he never played him and Roche because of his many injuries, Rosewall a few years ago listed 'the ten greatest opponents I have ever played: (1) Laver, (2) Gonzales, (3) Sedgman, (4) Hoad, (5) Newcombe, (6) Emerson, (7) Trabert, (8) Ashe and (9) jointly, Smith and Nastase.' Recently Rosewall told Ned Chase and me, 'If you look at films of the old stars, their level of play was not up to today's standards, but in their time they were the best under those conditions, and if they played today they would be on top with today's equipment, physical conditioning and competition. There was less competition in the old days, as there was little money available, and players then did not have the incentive to work as hard, except in the major events, as today's young players. Often they would travel by boat, rather than go by plane, and play in some second- or third-rate tournament in order to have a holiday.'

Ken said, 'There's not much difference in talent among the top players. The qualities that define the differences which exist are slight variations in physical conditioning, talent, temperament and practice, but I would say talent and temperament were the more important of these factors.

'The game has become faster over the past twenty-five years. There is more net rushing. The ball is hit earlier and harder, and serves are better.

'I agree with David Gray's* statement that "tennis is not an exact science but a great emotional drama. Ultimately it is a game of reduction—one player makes the other surrender." I do make the other players surrender—by making less errors and hitting more winners. Gray is a fine writer. The English tennis writers are the best because they devote full time to it.

'It's a great feeling when you play tennis well for two, two

* David Gray is the tennis correspondent of the *Guardian*.

and a half hours. Every stroke, or almost every one, has to be good. I prefer playing outdoors for the sun and the air.

'I don't think women should receive the same prize money. They only play three sets, and their field is half that of the men's 128 at Forest Hills and Wimbledon, and twenty or thirty of them are just not up to the calibre of the other women.

'Umpires should be allowed to remove a player from a match if he misbehaves or penalize him by taking away a game or a point, but the umpires must be good ones so that this power is not abused.'

A few days later during my visit to Australia the importance of temperament was illustrated by two incidents concerning Ray Ruffels, a twenty-eight-year-old redheaded Australian with a stocky build and a history of ankle trouble, which after fruitless visits to doctors he cured by going to a faith healer in the Philippines. I watched Ray play Ken in a long practice match on a hot afternoon on the dry grass of the White City Club court. It was fun to observe, as the tennis was beautiful, almost lyrical, and there was nothing at stake. Crossing ends, they chatted amiably and joked briefly. Other players nearby such as Phil Dent stopped and watched and threw quips. They played three sets with a tie-breaker, splitting the first two, Ruffels winning the tie-breaker in the third. Ruffels walked back to the clubhouse jauntily and happily, and Ken, who had played well, seemed unperturbed. Ruffels is not ranked within the top 20, nor possibly the first 30 or 40—one of those relatively unknown players who always wins a few rounds, maybe one or two, and then loses, never winning a tournament. I said to Rosewall, 'He's not that good in a real match, is he?'

'Ah, well,' replied Rosewall, characteristically not wanting to cast aspersions on a fellow player and friend.

Sure enough, while waiting to see Rosewall play a centre-court match in the New South Wales tournament about a week later, I observed Ruffels lose to John Alexander. Alexander was ranked 25th in the world for 1974 by the ATP and Rino Tommasi, the Italian tennis statistician, but 1974 was a poor year for Alexander, while in 1975 he has been playing well, one of the eight WCT '75 finalists. Ruffels was not ranked within the first 50 for 1974, but this may have been due to his injury.

He was on the Australian Davis Cup team from 1968 to 1970 and was 14th on the WCT circuit for 1972.

Ruffels had lost the first set badly and was down a service break, and they held service until Alexander served for the match in the second set. On match point, Alexander, forced into a weak defensive position rear of the baseline by Ruffels, who had advanced to the net, threw up a short easy lob slightly to Ruffels' backhand. With all the time in the world as the ball floated down to him, Ruffels got into position, tightened, cocked his arm and smashed it into the net. The match was over. A great crisis player like Rosewall would never have done that.

Rosewall pointed out to me Ruffels' house—a brick bungalow in a below-middle-income area; although Ruffels was not so far behind Rosewall in talent, he could not win when the chips were down, and the difference in their living standards was wide.

Several days before the same New South Wales tournament, Wilma said in a steely voice to Ken in their living room, 'You'd better start practising for the tournament.'

At the tournament, in the clubhouse and locker rooms there was a lot of tension, as there usually is at such events, for there were numbers of psychological prize fighters, i.e., the players, wandering around between matches.

The weather was hot. Rosewall won his first-round match easily 6-1, 6-2, over a young Australian, who was placed in the draw because he had qualified in the preliminary qualifying tournament. 'I was playing okay,' Rosewall said to me in the car afterwards. I agreed. The following day the weather was as warm, if not warmer—a typical Australian summer day with the sun high overhead, relatively heavy humidity and the temperature, I estimated, in the mid-90's. As Australia now uses the centigrade system, I never knew what the day's heat was unless I asked, since my knowledge was limited to the Fahrenheit system.

Rosewall's second-round opponent was Raz Reid, a young American. That morning Wilma had said to me at their house while Ken was getting his rackets, looking up at the sun, 'Raz is a young American. He played WTT last summer. He runs a lot. . . . All I want for Ken is to be happy these days . . . just as long as he gets one or two wins under his belt.' Reid's youth and the heat were both sources of possible trouble for Rosewall. The longer Reid kept Rosewall out under the sun, the more likely it seemed that Rosewall would melt before Reid. Before the match, Ken and I had an hour-long frustrating drive through heavy traffic to reach the house of Peter Whitchurch, where we looked at the 1953 Davis Cup film projected on Peter's movie screen. Ken had arranged this showing for me at my request. Then we drove to the White City stadium for his match against Reid, who in 1975 was to play on the WCT circuit, and who was to take a set off Jimmy Connors a few weeks later in the 1975 Australian Championship.

From the first shot it was obvious that Reid, a relatively unknown player, was playing very well. I was reminded immediately of Ken's earlier remarks about young players who are loose and have nothing to lose when challenging an established star. The challenge of Rosewall had presumably inspired Reid to raise his game to heights he had never reached before. Clean-cut and attractive, Reid is a boyish-looking tall man—a typical young American athlete with his easy manner and tan. In the first set Reid built up a lead of 6-1 in the tie-breaker. One more point—one more Rosewall error or Reid winner—and the first set was his. In the press box two smarmy, smirking members of the press cheered for Raz—'Come on, Raz'—hoping for an upset, which would make a better story for them.

And yet mysteriously, in a way that was almost magical, *Rosewall won the next seven points in a row.* Reid did not make bad errors, and yet Rosewall slashed back Reid's hardest serves, outran and outshot him in the rallies and served himself with precision and depth.

In the second set, Rosewall relaxed, threw several break points and lost 4-6, to his own disgust.

In the third set a singularly insensitive middle-aged waitress began to parade herself back and forth in the boxes just behind Rosewall as Reid was serving. She was supposedly taking orders, but, wearing black mini-skirt and red halter, she was more intent on waggling her hips and protruding her breasts as she minced along on ridiculous high heels. Reid stopped playing for several seconds, often as long as a minute, and the umpire called, 'Please stop moving in the stand.' But the bulky goddess would stop and then perambulate on. Then Reid would stop. Finally, Rosewall shouted, in a refreshing outburst of anger for him, 'Come on and play—or what?'

Rosewall was a master of surprises. In a tight rally against Reid, Reid hit a deep cross-court forehand to Rosewall, who raced over as Reid came carefully to net. Instead of whipping it cross-court as one expected, Rosewall lifted a high slow delicate lob which landed on the baseline—exactly. Reid, to hand it to him, got back and hit a slow backhand over his shoulder and relatively deep to Rosewall's backhand. Instead of pounding the ball anywhere in the court as one would have expected, Rosewall hit a soft backhand cross-court that floated gently down near the alley halfway between the base and service lines, completely befuddling Reid, who stood on the baseline watching it go by. The change of pace had caught him completely by surprise.

A few minutes later Reid fell over himself while running furiously in a wild rally, Rosewall racing for a forehand which he hit out down the line, and twisted his ankle. Delight in his voice, Rosewall yelled with relief, happiness and mockery, 'You're not hurt, are you?' Reid got up and played on, seemingly unhurt. But his game was not the same, either because the ankle genuinely hurt him, distracting him, or because his spirit was broken. And Rosewall won 6-2. The irony was that youth had been outrun by age, that middle-age had proved tougher and uninjurable on the court, and that guts, persistence and sheer magic in the tie-breaker had broken a young American who had played well, free and easy, with nothing to lose, against the world's greatest player.

The following day on hearing a radio report, later proved false, that Borg had been banned for a year for saying, 'I was not trying' in this same Australian tournament, I said, 'I have thought ever since I saw Borg that he lacked the drive of you and Connors.'

Rosewall snorted and laughed. 'Well, when you can make $300,000 in one year, he doesn't have to try. When I was eighteen, I didn't have a pot to piss in.'

The day I left Australia, just before Christmas 1974, Wilma

said, 'We were at a dinner last night in Sydney for seventeen
given by Jack Kramer and Gloria, and John Newcombe leaned
down the table and said, "Look at that little fellow. I'm
overweight and there he is forty without a pinch of fat on
him." When we married, we thought it would be a year or two
of touring, but it has gone on year after year and he keeps
playing better and better. We've had our ups and downs, but I
wouldn't have changed a bit of it.'

Rosewall is said to be a shrewd investor, buying land around
Brisbane. Fred Stolle says, 'When you hear Muscles has
invested in something, you can invest in it, too, without
question.' His other friends agree on this, too.

One of Bud Collins' mildly funny jokes about Rosewall is that
he has made a fortune from tennis and buried it beside a gum
tree guarded by a wombat. This crude bit of humour does not
seem to me to be entirely accurate and, though Rosewall has
undoubtedly made considerable sums in recent years, his
expenses must be high with the travel for him and Wilma and
the boys, and the comfortable life with three cars. He once
referred to an 'unfortunate' investment in a bowling alley in
the area where he was born and raised, and his sale of a piece of
land in what is now a very valuable residential area of Sydney.
Ken says, 'I invested some money in a bowling alley, built in
conjunction with a shopping centre in Rockdale, almost in the
area where I grew up. It's been a long battle, but gradually it
seems to be making money. Ten-pin bowling hit Australia with
a boom, but it was a short-lived boom, and after a while there
were a lot of poor investors. Another firm in the bowling
business I'm associated with is a public company, and it's
done reasonably well.' This, plus his losses on the market, led
me to think that the Rosewalls' fortune, though they are
comfortably off, lies in Bud Collins' imagination. As Ken
wistfully said, 'When you're travelling as a tennis player, you
depend on the advice of others, and it's hard to catch up on
what's happened while you're away.

'I have my jobs with Slazenger's in Australia, Seamco in the
rest of the world, John Gardiner's tennis ranch and Cathay-
Pacific, the airlines. In 1975, I'll play nine or ten tournaments,
including Wimbledon and Forest Hills.'

There is a bittersweet quality to Rosewall's career. When he was the best, he wasn't recognized. When he was recognized as one of the best players of all time, he was past his peak.

Though some of their techniques differ, it can be said that Connors' style is a direct outgrowth of Rosewall's—an all-court game—and an answer to the advocates of the big serve with its emphasis on blasting the ball off the court after a brief rally. Of course, Rosewall is a counter-puncher, while Connors is a slugger on his ground strokes, but, similar to Ken a slightly harder-hitting counter-puncher when returning the big serve.

The key to Rosewall's character over the decades is that he learned how to come out of himself, to be himself.

Rosewall says, 'Probably the biggest reason I've lasted so long is that I learned the game the right way.

'I like to see what the other fellow is going to do first. I'm a counter-puncher.'

I had said, 'Why do you enjoy tennis?'

'I guess like other children you try to do well in sports whether its cricket, rugby or tennis, etc., when your parents are watching, though I started travelling so much that mine saw less of me.'

As he drove down the Sydney Freeway ahead of me in his new Holden Caprice on the way to the airport when I was leaving, Rosewall still looked the small hero against the vast machine, surrounded by the other cars, the white concrete freeway and the large skyscrapers towering above him and all around. But on further reflection I knew that the key to Ken is not on the highway or at home but on the court—at least for those of us who are tennis lovers—though for his family and friends the real Ken is undoubtedly the man in his house and on his lawn, watching the children play with the swing while the kookaburra and other birds sing, or cleaning the swimming pool surface with a vacuum pump or kissing Wilma good-bye as he leaves to play in Sydney or maybe Singapore.

A Lesson for Life

For the rest of us, who are not privileged to see him in the privacy of his 'castle,' the significance of Rosewall is Rosewall the tennis player, the man on the court, on the grass, on the clay, on the green indoor surface: the figure dancing into action. What is it that is so fascinating about him? Why did he become a hero of mine and of many others? Obviously there is something about him which relates to our lives, as his little drama on the court is a paradigm of the bigger dramas we all go through, and yet his 'little drama' is a big, real-life drama for him and his opponent, for only one can win and one has to lose, and much, all of life in fact, is tied up with what he does out there. What does he do out there? It is the effortless grace combined with the powerful visceral force of his play which is so intriguing. It is softness and skill, delicacy and deception, mystery and flight intermingled with murderous speed, anger, fight, fury, power and drive, the sheer irresistibleness of his will overcoming like a sledgehammer or a bulldozer his hapless opponent. It is strength and grace, combined with his very small stature, winning, saying in effect, no matter how hard the odds, how formidable the opponent or the mountain, 'You, or I, can do it, too,' as he both lashes and strikes that backhand in a perfect, graceful arc, the ball flying to the end of the court within the lines, touching, taking off—for a winner, for victory.

Epilogue

Ken Rosewall began 1975 and his forty-first year by playing Davis Cup for Australia against New Zealand, defeating Onny Parun, a tall, young New Zealander who had been one of eight finalists in the 1974 Grand Prix series, in four sets, and then Brian Fairlie, another well-known New Zealand star, also in four sets in a match lasting four hours and fifteen minutes. Australia of course won the match, 4-0, Newcombe defeating Fairlie, Newcombe and Geoff Masters winning the doubles, the fifth contest of Masters versus Parun not completed because of lack of time.

Undaunted by these drains on his energy, Rosewall immediately flew to the United States, where he proceeded to play for Australia on the winning team which defeated the U.S. in the World Cup, 4-3, though he lost to Stan Smith when his team was already ahead 2-0. Then Rosewall won a tournament in Mississippi, conquering Butch Buchholz in the final, who had beaten Newcombe in the semi-finals.

Then in the $150,000 American Airlines tournament in Tucson, Arizona, Rosewall beat Cliff Richey 6-0, 6-1, in forty minutes, reaching the quarter-finals. He was to play Vijay Amritraj, who was once again a good illustration of the problem an older star faces against a young opponent who has nothing to lose, and is determined to avenge earlier defeats. Never have I seen Vijay play better, hitting successful first serves, crowding Rosewall on his second serve, running for everything. Rosewall lost the first-set tie-breaker, making the score 7-6. But in the second set Rosewall tightened his game, made almost no errors, unreeling a series of beautiful all-court shots, and won 6-0.

In the third set Vijay started to limp, but he fought back, and Rosewall, having trouble with his first serve, entered the tie-breaker, which he won 7-5, winning the match and sending him into the semi-finals. Amritraj had been a brave, respectful opponent, applauding Rosewall's shots on occasion, and Rosewall patted him warmly and comfortingly on the back at the net after the last point.

The next day in the semis Rosewall faced Ilie Nastase, who had beaten Rod Laver in the previous round. Rosewall's lifetime record against Nastase was 3-0. In the other half of the draw were John Alexander and Newcombe. Due to Nastase's conduct there then occurred a deplorable spectacle. Rosewall began to play considerably better than he had against Amritraj. He employed all the techniques against the Rumanian he had told me about, rushing the net to take advantage of Ilie's high topspin shots, driving cross-court Nastase's short second serve, hitting down the middle to him, while Nastase tried to play Rosewall's forehand. Rosewall's serve was almost brilliant, hard and deep on the first, almost invariably deep on the second. His superb net shots, the whistling sharply angled cross-court backhands brought Rosewall to 6-3, 5-4, 0-15 on Rosewall's serve in the second set. It was a best-of-three set tournament. Nastase by then had already tried distracting Ken by standing on the wrong side of the court when receiving serve, arguing with linesmen, mimicking Rosewall when he occasionally made a bad shot. Rosewall served an ace, which appeared to be clearly in, making the score 15-all.

Nastase protested the ace, marched off the court, declared 'I quit,' and sat down, acting like the petulant child he often is. Amazingly, the umpire, instead of defaulting him on the spot, persuaded him to return, and Rosewall lost his concentration, seethed with anger inwardly, and only started to protest Nastase's tactics when it was too late, after Nastase had won the second set and was leading 5-0 in the third. Ken fought off a series of match points and won two games in a row but nevertheless lost the set, 6-2, and the match. Nastase's unsportsmanlike tactics provoked dozens of protesting phone calls to the tournament officials, as the match was being broadcast on nationwide TV.

The next day Alexander, who had defeated Newcombe, supported by the crowd, won the finals in two quick sets over Nastase. Nastase was fined by the Association of Tennis Players, and the rules were changed by the ATP to prevent this sort of behaviour, but justice and better tennis should have awarded the match to Rosewall, confirming Ken's observation to me months earlier that qualified umpires should be given stronger powers. That Rosewall would probably have won the tournament was indicated by subsequent events.

Rosewall two weeks later won two qualifying matches to enter a WCT tournament in Houston, Texas. Then he beat Barry Phillips-Moore 7-5, 6-1. He beat Cliff Richey 1-6, 6-4, 6-2. He beat the No. 1 seed John Alexander, who had already won enough points for the Dallas finals of WCT, in the quarter-finals. That was on a Friday. On Saturday Rosewall beat another Dallas finalist, Harold Solomon, 6-4, 6-7, 6-4. On Sunday, though Rosewall was fatigued by the qualifying and regular matches during the week, he won the tournament, beating Cliff Drysdale 6-3, 3-6, 6-1, earning $12,000.

Ned Chase, who was present at Wimbledon 1975, wrote:

'In his forty-first year, Rosewall was the No. 2 seed in Wimbledon, a truly extraordinary accomplishment, but altogether fitting in the light of his superb record and the fact that he had been the 1974 runner-up at both Wimbledon and Forest Hills. He won his opening rounds with characteristic ease. But in the quarter-finals he met a rehabilitated, razor-sharp Tony Roche, a great Australian lefty who only a few years before had been tapped as the next pro champ with his wins over Laver, only to have his career temporarily blighted by tennis elbow. The match on the Centre Court was a delight to watch, Rosewall effortlessly counter-punching against Roche's powerful all-court attack. Rosewall started slowly, then implacably raised the level of his game inch by inch, losing the first set but relentlessly taking the long second set. In the beautifully fought third set, with both players absolutely evenly deadlocked, suddenly there was a crisis—a bad call against Roche, a long delay after his protest, finally a reversal of the decision *against* Rosewall, all further complicated by the umpire's miscalling the score. This further prolonged the delay. Finally, after both players had become cold, Rosewall, a figure of dejection over the reversed call and delay, proceeded to lose this key set to a reanimated Roche playing perhaps the best tennis of his life. This ended Rosewall's 1975 Wimbledon.

'Significantly, with his unmatched talent and unwavering morale, he immediately won a tough post-Wimbledon tournament in Europe, making quite clear that, still, in his forty-first year, he was close to the very top, still a master world-class star when all his peers, who had started out with him over two decades back, were now sidelined or only playing in the special tournaments for the junior vets and seniors. An incomparable record.'

Appendix A

Advice for Good Club Players

Rosewall's instructions on how to play tennis are both simple and intelligent. His every stroke is natural, marked by an easy swing and perfect position of the body. The advanced club player will know most of the basic tenets for a good forehand, backhand, net shot, lob, serve and overhead, but watching Rosewall is an illustration of how synchronization of mind and body with years of practice can bring these elementary rules to the level of an art. Rosewall adds some sophisticated distinctions to a primer on the game.

Ken says, 'I like to use an eastern forehand grip which is slightly to the left of the hold taught by many American pros. Similarly, my backhand is slightly to the right of the position often urged by teaching pros. This way I can get every kind of shot.

'From the serve the ball should be tossed up so that it would fall, if not hit, about six inches in front of the left foot.

'The major change I've noticed in the game in recent years has been the introduction of the metal racket, which makes it possible to hit every shot a little faster. All over the world except in Australia I use a Seamco. I believe there'll always be a greater supply of wooden rackets than metal and it's always advisable to use the best of the metal rackets. The other ones can cause possibly more problems than what they're worth, as far as breaking of strings or bending or splitting in some of the weaker parts of the metal frame. Certainly the cheaper type of the wooden rackets, depending on how much the individual plays, can be very suitable to a player who's not in competition and plays just for fun every now and then.

'A player who hits the ball hard should have it strung with gut tighter than average. One who depends more on accuracy and placement should string it with regular pressure, say 55 pounds. All strings of gut vary. Most of them nowadays are beef instead of lamb, which seems to be more popular. The gauge of the beef gut I use is known in Australia as Light 17, and the name of it is Clipspringer, distributed by both Seamco and Slazenger. Most leading players have several rackets strung at different pressures, depending on the resiliency of the gut, some of which can be more fiery than others, depending on the machine on which the rackets are strung, which also vary, and depending on the conditions of play. The racket under very heavy hot, humid conditions on a slow court where the ball gets fluffier would be softer-strung. On a very fast court with fast balls in a hot, dry atmosphere like in Tucson, Arizona, where the ATP tournament is played, the racket would be strung tigher, producing less of a trampoline effect than a soft racket. My most recent Seamco rackets were strung by Dick Bosworth in Hartford, Conn., on a machine at 61-pound pressure, and some of my wooden Slazengers strung in Australia would be at a similar pressure.'

Rosewall uses an exceptionally heavy racket—14 ounces and $4\frac{7}{8}$ inches round the handle. This may be one of the reasons he hits the ball harder than generally supposed, and in fact his backhand ball has a reputation of being fast, and his forehand ball 'heavy.' The explanation for this is that he whips the backhand around with perfect form with slight underspin, while the forehand, slightly less smoothly hit, is met a fraction of a second late and hit hard to make it catch up with the steady follow-through, holding the ball on the racket longer, and the ball is struck flat; though occasionally when the opportunity for a forehand cross-court return of serve develops Rosewall will hit with a little topspin, so that it careens down and past the feet of the net rusher.

Rosewall said, 'Spikes are used rarely today, though on a wet gras court, such as Forest Hills two or three years ago, they were helpful to me and grip the court very well with their quarter-inch spikes distributed around the sole. Regular tennis shoes, coming in all sizes and costs with leather, nylon or canvas upper soles, have either a herringbone surface, best suited for grass and slippery clay, or a flat sole with no tread, good for synthetic surfaces where there is no sliding on the court.

'I have to be careful what I say about wood and steel rackets.' Rosewall uses a Slazenger wood in Australia and a Seamco aluminium in the rest of the world. 'If I play well, I like a metal. Though it weighs and balances the same as the wood, it feels lighter and has less wind resistance, and the ball seems to come off faster like a trampoline. But I've played with wood all my life. I'm part of the Slazenger family. I enjoy playing with wood.

'I would advise club players to approach the problem of the differences between grass and clay the same as tournament competitors. With grass you'll get much more spin, lower shots, better for the drop. You must bend your knees and lean over more to watch the ball. With a fast serve, receiving, it sometimes pays to shorten the backswing to play a defensive return unless you are going to go for a winner. Indoors, when first playing Gonzales, I shortened my forehand from a loop swing to straight back. Clay courts are all pretty much the same whether their composition is en-tout-cas or the pure clay like the red European clay. But grass can differ. Here at White City in Sydney the surface is tough and hard and produces a fast bounce, while at Brisbane the grass is softer and springier on the foot. Where the white line is spread on the grass to mark the lines, the ground becomes hard and the ball will take off when it hits it.

'In Sydney there are only two kinds of surface—the sandy clay and grass, but in the New York City area and suburbs there are a variety of indoor and outdoor surfaces, including concrete, asphalt, en-tout-cas, sandy-coloured clay, red clay, wood, grass and various synthetic surfaces. The differences between surfaces are obvious. For example, the rubberized surface gives a higher jump to the topspin and a lower jump to the underspin than the carpet, which is now rarely used, having recently ceased to be popular. Why the difference between carpet and rubber, I don't know.

'Compared to tournament tennis, club players often should not follow their serve to the net. The biggest weakness in club tennis is the serve and volley. Another error I noticed in local tennis is the tendency to hit the ball too hard and with too much wrist, instead of following the racket through with a firm arm and wrist so that the player can develop a fluent swing whether the ball is three feet high or three inches high. No ball ever bounces exactly the same. Paradoxically, the club enthusiast might be wiser to practise his ground strokes first, for if he only has a big serve he won't get much exercise. One trouble with striking the ball with too much effort is that the amateur club player often hits it off balance, and this can lead to elbow, wrist and shoulder injuries.

'As regards improving one's game I would recommend both practice on whatever shot is the weakest and singles play for a set. Two-on-one is good training for sharpening the volley and passing the net man, but some may prefer one-on-one as they might only have an hour and want more play.'

I said, 'I think your serve has been underrated. Even Rod Laver when he turned pro in '63 said your serve was much faster than he thought.'

'My father and I could have worked more on my serve to develop a smooth motion.'

'You've said, "I'm a counter-puncher." So maybe there is a connection, as with the serve you are starting the punch.'

'Could be.'

'You also had the necessity of being "economical" in your action in order to get the ball over the net due to your height, and so as you worked hard on your serve, particularly as a young pro, maybe it was better to work on being economical. But then you are saying that you might have worked more, too, on a fluent motion!'

'Yeah.'

'Which style do you recommend for club players—the economical one or the one with the natural motion?'

'I would advise players depending on whether they have a natural serve motion or not. Some do and some don't. With those that are free and easy on a serve, I would advise them to develop the smooth action, but with those who are not natural, to work on an "economical" swing for accuracy.'

'What is not recognized on your serve is how deep you place it,' I said.

'That's true, when I am serving well.

'The toss is important to get it the right height so you can hit with a fully extended arm. This is a problem I work on

when I am throwing the ball too low. Recently I've been
throwing it a little too much to the right. But Tom Okker's
only an inch taller than me, and he hits a fast serve.'

'I don't want to argue, forgive me, but I think he's five foot
nine inches, or ten inches, to your five foot seven inches.'

'I guess that is right.'

Rosewall prefers to play his backhanded drop-shot to his
opponent's forehand rather than cross-court, as do many pros.
This cuts down the time the ball is in the air and reduces the
opponent's time of reaching it.

Rosewall gives some interesting advice when playing in the
wind: 'Shorten your backswing and follow through when the
wind is behind you, and be careful about staying within the
lines and over the net.'Playing into the wind, lengthen the
backswing and follow through and use spin-shots which are
exaggerated by the wind. When rushing the net with wind
behind, use topspin, which the force of the air will push down
onto the court. Approaching the net against the wind, I employ
slice, which aided by the wind makes the ball tend to die. Lobs,
floating about in the turbulence, are very effective.

'In doubles it's always advisable at tournament level to
come to net, even on clay, though I have seen a few European
players play quite a bit from the backcourt; and in women's
professional tennis, though net play is standard, backcourt
position is slightly more frequent. In fact, the summer of 1974
in WTT our women's team at Pittsburgh of Evonne Goolagong
and Peggy Michel played Bartkowicz–Gunter, and Peaches
Bartkowicz stayed back throughout the set. Gunter and
Bartkowicz had good ground strokes and lobs. They surprised
our women and won. This was very unusual.

'In club doubles one should only go to net if one is confident
of a serve and volley. Club players could try a couple of trick
positions sometimes used by the pros, but they should be
careful not to take the game too seriously and be accused of
gamesmanship, if by doing so they annoy their friends on the
other side of the net. These should only be performed if there is
a happy acceptance of the idea that anything goes within
limits.

'One is the doubles switch whereby the net player gives a
signal to his partner, the server, as to whether he is going to

cross over. This can be done by opening the palm behind his back to indicate, say, that he will not cross, or closing his fist to say that he will. Another method of signalling is by one and two fingers. This tactic would only work if the net man or woman is a good volleyer with quick reflexes, as the receiver may often mis-hit the ball, necessitating a speedy reaction by the net man.

'Another technique is for the net player to stand in the middle of the service box on the service side. This is useful if the receiver is grooving his returns and causing the server difficulties as he comes to net. This is sometimes done against me in the ad court, as I have a fairly good backhand return of serve.* The net man also, still in the box on the service side, can stand just by the centre service line, though he must not have his foot on it. However, he must crouch down, as the server will knock his head off with the ball. The advantage of this is that the man can run to either side quickly, out-foxing the opponents.

'I notice in amateur tennis that the lob is not used enough. When it is hit, it is often done with a jerky motion, when it should be hit with a high follow-through in the direction of the ball. Top players are much better at concealing the lob, but amateurs can do it, too, by making the same backswing on either forehand or backhand, starting to swing toward the ball and then gradually curving the racket higher than the normal rise it takes on a ground stroke. Thus the parabola of the curve of the lob-hitting stroke becomes higher.

'I rarely have leg cramps, which I avoid by taking salt tablets in hot weather and drinking enough water after a match. If I do, I straighten the muscle.' Rosewall demonstrated by pushing down the muscle in the rear of the lower leg with the heel of his palm. 'This may not be what the doctor recommends. Tony Roche told me his thumb cramped in the Indian open. He'd say, 'It's okay' to his opponent. Then he'd straighten it.' Rosewall demonstrated how Roche yanked the thumb. 'It would snap on his racket. He'd serve, straighten it again. It happened in the second round in the Indian heat and he still got to the finals.

* Editor's note: The best in the world.

'I guess the married men are better equipped to handle extraneous noises like babies screaming, shouts from the crowd and the sounds of trains and planes because they are used to it at home. But planes, which are frequent at Forest Hills, are a special problem. Some players depend on the sound of the racket meeting the ball to judge it. If I hear "pow," I know it is harder hit than "ping." ' Rosewall's imitation of these two sounds reminded me of his long dormant interest in music and that comparison once made between him and Bach.

'In key points like 30-30, 15-30, ad-in, ad-out, I play naturally, the best I can. I don't try to do something I haven't done before. Some players tend to be overanxious. It depends on the situation. If there's an opportunity to go for a winner, I'll take it. Otherwise I'll play it safely.'

I said, 'When Connors starts bouncing the ball a lot before serving in the third set when you have him deuce or ad, using what I would call "delaying tactics," what do you do?'

'One can always turn one's back if one thinks the opponent is going to serve after the fifth bounce, but then he may start doing it again. If a man like Connors or Andres Gimeno, who was a very nice fellow and bounced seven or eight times, does it to get his rhythm and calm his nerves, I just wait. If it is for gamesmanship, I might do something else. Then I try to guess where my opponent is going to serve. I have some knowledge of his past habits, because I have studied his serve during earlier matches when I've played him or when he has been playing another opponent.'

Appendix B
Rosewall's Records*

Australian Championship (grass):
1953
1955
1971
1972

U.S. Championship (grass):
1956
1970

French Professional
                Championship:
1958 (clay)
1960 ,,
1961 ,,
1962 ,,
1963 (indoors)
1964 ,,
1965 ,,
1966 ,,

French Championship (clay):
1953
1968

World Championship of Tennis
                (indoors):
1971
1972

British Professional
                Championship (indoors):
1957
1960
1961
1962
1963

U.S. Professional Championship
                (grass):
1963
1965

* Rosewall's wins in the Wembley 1969 and U.S. 1971 Professional
  Championships are not included, as these tournaments diminished
  in importance after the beginning of open tennis in 1968.

Index